SPORT IN CAPITALIST SOCIETY

- Why are the Olympic Games the driving force beh.   .own on civil liberties?
- What makes sport an unwavering ally of nationalism and militarism?
- Is sport the new opiate of the masses?

These and many other questions are answered in this new radical history of sport by leading historian of sport and society, Professor Tony Collins.

Tracing the history of modern sport from its origins in the burgeoning capitalist economy of mid-eighteenth-century England to the globalised corporate sport of today, the book argues that, far from the purity of sport being 'corrupted' by capitalism, modern sport is as much a product of capitalism as the factory, the stock exchange and the unemployment line.

Based on original sources, the book explains how sport has been shaped and moulded by the major political and economic events of the past three centuries, such as the French Revolution, the rise of modern nationalism and imperialism, the Russian Revolution, the Cold War and the imposition of the neo-liberal agenda in the last decades of the twentieth century. It highlights the symbiotic relationship between the media and sport, from the simultaneous emergence of print capitalism and modern sport in Georgian England to the rise of Murdoch's global satellite television empire in the twenty-first century, and it explores, for the first time, the alternative, revolutionary models of sport in the early twentieth century.

Sport in Capitalist Society is the first sustained attempt to explain the emergence of modern sport around the world as an integral part of the globalisation of capitalism. It is essential reading for anyone with an interest in the history or sociology of sport, or the social and cultural history of the modern world.

Tony Collins is Professor of History and Director of the International Centre for Sports History and Culture at De Montfort University in Leicester, UK. He is the author of several books, including *Rugby's Great Split* and *A Social History of English Rugby Union*, and was a lead consultant for the 2012 BBC Radio 4 series *Sport and the British*.

SPORT IN CAPITALIST SOCIETY

A short history

Tony Collins

Routledge
Taylor & Francis Group

LONDON AND NEW YORK

First published 2013
by Routledge
2 Park Square, Milton Park, Abingdon, Oxon OX14 4RN

Simultaneously published in the USA and Canada
by Routledge
711 Third Avenue, New York, NY 10017

Routledge is an imprint of the Taylor & Francis Group, an informa business

British Library Cataloguing in Publication Data
A catalogue record for this book is available from the British Library

Library of Congress Cataloging in Publication Data
Collins, Tony, 1961-
Sport in capitalist society : a short history / by Tony Collins.
p. cm.
1. Sports–Political aspects. 2. Sports–Economic aspects. 3. Sports and state.
4. Capitalism. I. Title.
GV706.35.C645 2013
796.06'9–dc23
2012039888

ISBN: 978-0-415-81355-6 (hbk)
ISBN: 978-0-415-81356-3 (pbk)
ISBN: 978-0-203-06811-3 (ebk)

Typeset in Bembo
by Taylor & Francis Books

Printed and bound by CPI Group (UK) Ltd, Croydon, CR0 4YY

CONTENTS

INTRODUCTION

Why did modern sport emerge first in Britain? What forces propelled it around the world? Why has it become a vehicle for nationalism? What made sport such a bastion of masculinity? How did the spirit of amateurism rise and eventually fall? Why have major sporting events in the twenty-first century become synonymous with authoritarian control and corporate excess?

Sport in Capitalist Society seeks to answer these and other questions by examining the history of sport over the last 300 years. It argues that modern sport is as much a product of capitalism as the factory, the stock exchange or the unemployment line. Modern sport emerged in eighteenth-century Britain as part of the growth of a commercial entertainment industry, and sport's binary world of winners and losers matched perfectly the cultural dynamic of capitalism.

The emergence of amateurism in the mid-nineteenth century provided sport with a moral mission that would allow it to spread across the globe as an ideological underpinning of imperialist expansion. At the same time, the emergence of an industrial working class in the towns and cities of Europe and North America powered the development of professional mass spectator sport, most notably soccer and baseball.

Spurred by its symbiotic relationship with the media, commercialised sport extended its appeal around the world as a vital cultural component of modern capitalism. Yet despite the gradual extinction of the amateur ethos, by the start of the twenty-first century sport combined its eighteenth-century commercial imperative with the disciplinary impulse of its nineteenth-century amateurism, a perfect simulacrum of the reality of the capitalist 'New World Order'.

This book aims to investigate these broad historical trends which have shaped modern sport from the eighteenth century to the present day. Its focus is on Britain, Europe, North America and Japan, the regions in which sport acquired huge cultural and commercial significance in the early years of the twentieth century and which, as the major capitalist powers, have dominated the rest of the globe ever since. It does not seek to be exhaustive in its coverage of countries, sports or tournaments, but to explore the underlying dynamics that have driven the expansion of sport. As well as being a work of synthesis it also includes new and original research on the eighteenth and nineteenth centuries.

Sport in Capitalist Society rejects the idea that sport's development can be explained by the teleological concept of 'modernisation' – after all, one generation's modernity is another's antiquity – or by reference to an equally vague 'civilising process', which carries with it the assumption that the modern era is more 'civilised' than the past. Instead, the book takes a historical materialist approach, which sees modern sport as a product of capitalism, shaped and moulded by class society and its consequent oppression of women and non-white peoples.

It neither dismisses sport as a perversion of play nor believes that all would be well if it were not for club owners or administrators. Men and women play sport but not under circumstances of their own choosing, one might say – and it is that relationship between sport and the social, economic and political circumstances under which it is played that this book seeks to explore. To borrow from Spinoza, the goal of *Sport in Capitalist Society* is neither to cheer nor to jeer sport, but to understand it.

1

CAPITALISM AND THE BIRTH OF MODERN SPORT

> The whole human species may be fairly considered and treated as jockeys, each running his race to the best advantage.
>
> Anon., 1793.[1]

Men and women have always played games. The impulse to play is as vital to human culture as the desire to sing, the urge to draw or the need to tell stories. As a form of physical exhilaration, group solidarity or downright sheer pleasure, games are common to almost all societies in almost all periods of history. Few things in everyday life have been taken quite so seriously as play.[2]

Games developed from humanity's efforts to master nature and sustain life. Throwing contests emerged from the hunting of animals or the need to repel enemies. Running races evolved from tracking animals or maintaining communications between settlements. Combat games were derived from military skills. Often the dividing line between work and leisure was unclear and sometimes non-existent. For most people throughout most of human history, life was work and work was life. Games happened when this relationship was temporarily suspended, for example, after the completion of a harvest, and enjoyment could fleetingly take precedence over necessity.[3]

This pattern was replicated around the world and across all pre-industrial societies. Early games were sometimes non-competitive, occasionally non-physical and often intertwined with ritual activities. With rare exceptions, such as the games of the ancient Greek Olympics, it would be anachronistic to use the modern term 'sport' to describe them. The methods of play and meanings ascribed to these games were very different from today. They may have had a ceremonial, religious or ritual purpose. The idea of specialist players would almost certainly have been unknown. And winning was often not the purpose of play.[4]

For the great mass of the people, games and their role in society changed little over the centuries. But by the sixteenth century, three general categories of games had emerged. Some were adjuncts to military training, as can be seen in combat or equestrian sports such as archery or jousting. Others were linked to religious or other ritual events, for example, the community feasts and games known in Britain as Church Ales or the football matches staged on religious holidays such as Christmas or Shrove Tuesday. And there were games played at fairs or festivals, such as Maypole dancing or smock racing, as women's running races were known.[5] Of course, there were also many games that were played when people simply had spare time on their hands, some more spontaneous and ad hoc than others.

These categories were not mutually exclusive. They overlapped and sometimes merged into each other. Medieval elites often used their extensive leisure time to develop sophisticated contests, and the richest could afford to employ professional practitioners and coaches of fencing, real tennis, horsemanship and other games.[6] But all of these activities differed from the modern sports in that they were not generally codified, organised on a commercial basis nor seen as separate from everyday life. Gambling would sometimes take place and pub landlords, on whose land sports were often staged, could capitalise on the opportunities for increased drink and food sales. Yet before the eighteenth century these were largely incidental factors and did not provide the impetus nor the structure for the development of games as a separate and distinct sphere of cultural life.

But from the start of the 1700s, the nature of the most prominent games in Britain began to change. By the 1750s a fundamental and qualitative shift in the nature of the three most prominent British sports – horse racing, boxing and cricket – was taking place. Although they had their roots in the rural sports of the past, these games began to differ markedly from their predecessors. What now distinguished them from their rural antecedents was the emergence of generalised rules of play and their ability to systematically and regularly generate revenue. In short, these sports were becoming commodities, which one might pay to watch, be paid to play or upon which one could gamble significantly large amounts of money. Modern sport as we know it today was beginning to emerge.

How therefore do we explain the fact that modern sport developed first in what George Orwell described as 'a cold and unimportant little island' on the north-west coast of Europe?[7] And why at this moment in history?

It was not because the British were more sports-loving than their European neighbours. Other European nations had similar strong traditions of games. Local sporting customs can be found in almost every region of early modern Europe, from *Calcio*, the elaborate Italian football game of Florence, to simple running and jumping games found across the continent. Bull-fighting in Spain reflected the popularity of blood sports across the western world, which in Britain was highlighted by cock-fighting and bull-baiting. France in particular had a strong tradition of games similar to that of Britain. *Soule*, a ball game played between parishes and other local communities, was common in northern France. *Savate* was a popular form of combat not unlike modern kick-boxing. *Jeu de paume* was a medieval forerunner of tennis.[8] *Jeu de mail* used a mallet to propel a ball in a similar way to croquet.[9] Moreover, like the British nobility, the French aristocracy were keen and conspicuous gamblers. An observer in the early seventeenth century would have noticed little difference between sporting habits on either side of the English Channel.

Yet neither France nor any other nation would see their traditional games provide the basis for the sporting revolution that swept Europe and the rest of the world in the late nineteenth and twentieth centuries. Only those sports that originated in their modern form in Britain, or that were based on the British model, played this role. Even those American games that were to become major sports of the twentieth century – the rugby-derived American football, the traditional English game of baseball and the Muscular Christian-invented basketball – had their roots in Britain.[10] In contrast to Europe, American sport was chronically underdeveloped and anaemic until the middle decades of the nineteenth century, if played at all.[11] Britain's centrality to the birth of modern sport can be seen in the way that previously rural traditional games were transformed by the economic and social changes that were taking place in the British Isles in the eighteenth century.

In the eighteenth century Britain was an emerging capitalist, but not yet industrial, economy.[12] The last vestiges of feudalism in the countryside were being extinguished. Over the previous two centuries, the nature of the economy and society had changed dramatically. In contrast to the rest of Europe, agriculture was in the main no longer organised according to the fixed hierarchic traditions of feudalism but run on a profit-driven capitalist basis by its aristocratic landowners. The English revolution of the mid-seventeenth century had disposed of the remaining economic detritus of feudalism. Competition for leases, land and work became the norm. Unlike their European cousins, English aristocrats now measured themselves not by the size of their retinue but by their wealth. This was an economy organised to generate profit, whether in town or countryside, at home or abroad, or in leisure and recreation.

Due to the different trajectory that the economic development of agriculture had taken in Britain, and especially in England, the aristocracy's attitude to money differed sharply from that of the European nobility. The British had much more of it, not only from agriculture but also from war profits, government contracts, stock market speculation and overseas investments in the newly acquired British Empire. Moreover, the long and deep-rooted tradition of extravagant aristocratic gambling dating back at least to Elizabethan times dovetailed with the new mania for financial speculation. As Lawrence Stone highlighted, for the aristocracy there was 'no psychological difference between placing £100 on the throw of the dice and investing it in a risky voyage of exploration, between buying a share in the Virginia Company and backing a horse'.[13] Aristocratic status in Britain was demonstrated not only by conspicuous consumption but also by flamboyant disposal, especially by the younger scions of the aristocracy for whom gambling was a symbol of inexhaustible wealth, masculine excess and endless leisure time. In 1750 the Duke of Cumberland lost £10,000 on the disputed fight between Jack Broughton and

Jack Slack.[14] This was by no means unusual nor, by a long way, the largest sum to be lost on a sporting wager.

In contrast to Europe, where the aristocracy still stood firmly on its feudal, pre-capitalist foundations and did not share the monetary imperative found across the Channel – the French aristocracy's love of gambling had been severely tempered by the shocking collapse of John Law's speculative Mississippi Company in 1720 – British aristocratic patronage of sport grew enormously in the eighteenth century.[15] Until the end of the Napoleonic wars much of sport was effectively controlled by 'The Fancy', an informal network of aristocrats, gentry and their hangers-on. By 1751 Henry Fielding was noting that 'to the upper part of mankind, time is an enemy, and ... their chief labour is to kill it'.[16] The aristocracy's abandonment of militaristic feudal recreations such as archery, jousting and the tournament sports so beloved by Henry VIII was not because the aristocracy had become peace-loving. With the exception of the 1730s, eighteenth-century Britain rarely had a year without an overseas war, and some sporting aristocrats combined both military and sporting interests, most notably the Duke of Cumberland, known as the Butcher of Culloden for his bloody retribution on the Scots in 1746. Rather, feudal militarist sports no longer reflected the culture of the aristocracy. To compete, to win, to profit. As in business, these were now the goals of the sport-loving British aristocracy.

This transformation of Britain into a capitalist economy was reflected by the emergence of ideas of self-interest and competition in political and cultural life. During the late seventeenth century the idea that human nature was inherently selfish and competitive came to dominate philosophical and economic discussion. Its greatest advocate was Thomas Hobbes, who argued in *Leviathan* (1651) that the natural state of humanity was a 'war of all against all'.[17] This belief broke sharply with older conceptions of human nature based on Christian ideas of unchanging hierarchy, duty and obligation. Indeed, the term 'human nature' itself did not enter common usage until the eighteenth century. By 1700 economic theory was squarely based on the assumption that individuals acted in their own self-interest.[18]

This became the dominant view of social life in the eighteenth century. It was perhaps most elegantly conveyed by Alexander Pope in his 1733 *Essay on Man*: 'Self-love, the spring of motion, acts the soul/Reason's comparing balance rules the whole'.[19] Its rawest exposition could be found in the work of Bernard Mandeville, who in his *The Fable of the Bees* and other works outlined a vision of society governed only by the self-interest of individuals. Without the guiding principle of self-interest, 'society must be spoiled, if not totally dissolved,' he wrote in his 1723 'Search into the Nature of Society'.[20] Daniel Defoe's *Robinson Crusoe* (1719) and Jonathan Swift's *Gulliver's Travels* (1726) owed much of their popularity to the timeliness of their discussions of this changing relationship between the individual and society. Defoe's *Moll Flanders* (1722) offered a rather more rambunctious exploration of the same issue as Moll seeks to profit from her body. By 1776, Adam Smith's assertion in *The Wealth of Nations* that 'it is not from the benevolence of the butcher, the brewer, or the baker that we expect our dinner, but from their regard to their own interest,' would have appeared to be completely uncontentious to the majority of his readers.[21]

Sport, an activity that was by its very nature a competitive win–lose binary, therefore underwent a social amplification of its importance. Man against man (women were rarely considered), whether in the prize-fighting ring, on the race-course or in the cricket team, was no longer merely a recreational pleasure. It was now also a metaphor for, and a reflection of, everyday life in capitalist society.[22]

The novel idea that sport was analogous to life itself – unthinkable in any previous age when games were merely diversions from life's cares – was summed up by an anonymous author of doggerel in the early nineteenth century:

Now, life to me, has always seem'd a game –
Not a game of chance, but one where skill,
Will often throw the chances in our way ... [23]

Drawing this analogy between sport and life became increasingly common for writers and journalists. The very first sporting monthly, the *Sporting Magazine* (1792), proclaimed itself to be the journal for 'the Man of Pleasure and Enterprize [sic]' on its masthead. 'The whole human species may be fairly considered and treated as jockeys, each running his race to the best advantage,' wrote the author of *The Jockey Club, or A Sketch of the Manners of the Age* in 1793.[24] Pierce Egan, the Regency journalist whose talent for penmanship and self-promotion reshaped sports writing into something more than a mere narrative of events, argued in *Pancratia*, his 1812 outline of boxing history, that explorers had discovered that 'those in continuous hostility, cherished with ardour every gymnastic sport'.[25] And the 1824 version of *Boxiana*, his grandiloquent chronicle of prize-fighting, even began with a quotation from *The Wealth of Nations*.[26]

Sport was merely one example of the way in which leisure in general was being commercialised in the eighteenth century. For the first time, leisure activities offered extensive and regular opportunities to make money – a nascent entertainment industry was emerging.[27] Spending power and leisure time expanded for the middle as well as the upper classes. The theatre, music and the arts all expanded greatly throughout the century. In the reign of Charles II not a single theatre existed outside of London, yet by 1775 every major town in England had one. Similar points can be made about libraries, music venues and art galleries. Shops and consumer goods became an important part of the urban economy. One of the most prominent signs of this rapid expansion of commercial leisure was the growth of the press. The repeal of restrictions on publishing at the end of the seventeenth century stimulated the development of national and provincial newspapers and magazines. The first daily newspaper, the *Daily Courant*, was established in 1702, followed by many others. Over thirty provincial newspapers were founded between 1695 and 1730. Periodicals were also established; the *Tatler* in 1709 and the *Gentleman's Magazine* in 1730 being the most well-known examples.[28]

Print capitalism and sport therefore developed a symbiotic, mutually interdependent relationship from the early eighteenth century. Indeed, sport would not and could not have been commercialised or codified without the simultaneous development of newspapers and magazines. This would become an iron law of sport. As we shall see, in eighteenth-century Britain, nineteenth-century USA and twentieth-century France and Japan, the press was both the driver of commercial sport and also its beneficiary – as would be the case for radio and television in the twentieth century. Even in the first half of the eighteenth century newspapers raised revenue from sport through advertising, but also generated significant column inches from reporting on sport. Conversely, sport received publicity for events but also, just as importantly, became part of everyday discourse. The *Weekly Journal* advertised prize-fights as early as 1715 and by the late 1720s advertisements for sporting events were commonplace.[29] Moreover, the reporting of sport in the press both reflected and shaped its relationship with the wider culture of society. This can be seen in the challenges issued by boxers and the announcements of forthcoming fights. In 1727 John Whitacre described himself as the 'famous Lincolnshire Drover' who was 'as brave and hardy a man whoever mounted a stage to box'. His opponent, John Gretton, responded that he would 'hit this impudent spark such knocks that will make him forever hereafter not even think of a challenge of the like kind on me, the champion of the universe'.[30] This narrative of challenge, contest and competition – so central to the development of a capitalist society – thus became embedded in this newly emerging sporting world of the eighteenth century.

The development of sport as part of this wider commercial entertainment industry was neither uniform nor evenly distributed around Britain. It was focused largely in and around the dynamic capitalist economy of eighteenth-century London and its south-eastern hinterland. By 1700 London was the biggest city in the world, having grown from 200,000 inhabitants in 1600 to well over half a million. It dominated the trade and industry of Britain and its embryonic empire, handling 80 per cent of England's imports and almost 70 per cent of its exports. In 1750 London was home to 11 per cent of the English population and it has been estimated that one in six Englishmen and women lived there at some point in their lives.[31] The wealth of the city underpinned its rich cultural life, the growth of commercial leisure and the nascent consumer culture. As Dr Johnson famously remarked, 'when a man is tired of London, he is tired of life; for there is in London all that life can afford'.[32] London and the south-east was the crucible in which modern sport emerged from rural, unorganised recreation. Just as the theatre, music, literature and many other leisure industries were revolutionised by the development of capitalism, so too was sport. These economic changes not only made sport a commercial enterprise, they also led to fundamental changes in the ways that sport was played, organised and regulated. This process can be seen in the development of the three most important sports of the period: horse racing, boxing and cricket.

Before the commercialisation of sport in the eighteenth century, the idea of commonly agreed, national, written laws governing the playing of sport did not exist. Although occasionally some games did have written rules, these were neither generally accepted by all players nor vested with any regulatory authority.[33] The introduction of codes of rules that were accepted by all players and for all major contests were a direct consequence of the commercial development of sport. This itself was an extension of the way in which the law in the eighteenth century was itself acquiring a new significance. Britain was a society that was moving away from religious and monarchical authority and asserting the centrality of an impersonal and 'objective' rule of law based on property rights.[34] Transparency and formal equality before the law were essential for the smooth transaction of business, just as they were for the regulation of gambling and the playing of games. This was reflected in the fact that these rules were often drawn up as part of the 'articles of agreement' for a match, which also laid down the amount of money to be won and other conditions of the contest. It is therefore not coincidental that this period of the evolution of the law also saw horse racing evolve its first general code of rules, as well as the first rules of boxing, drawn up in 1743, and the first generally accepted rules of cricket, formulated in 1744.

Horse racing occupied a symbolically important role in the cultural life of the British monarchy and aristocracy. The centrality of breeding and bloodlines to horse racing reflected the genealogical obsessions of ruling-class families. As Karl Marx pointed out:

> we find in the aristocracy such pride in blood and descent, in short, in the life history of their body. It is this zoological point of view which has its corresponding science in heraldry. The secret of aristocracy is zoology.[35]

Until the end of the seventeenth century, an average horse race was literally a two-horse race, in which two horse owners would ride against each other for a wager. Race meetings were primarily social events – so much so that Newmarket sought to discourage lower-class spectators from attending its races – and irregularly organised. But from the 1680s, professional jockeys began to be employed and the first professional trainer, Tregonwell Frampton, was engaged at Newmarket. Over a hundred towns in England staged races by the mid-1720s. Racing, because of its links with royalty and the highest echelons of the aristocracy, was both more organised than other sports and more bound by convention than other commercial sports, and so retained many of its more traditional aspects. For example, it was unusual for a race-course to charge all race-goers for admission to the ground, as opposed to the grandstand, until 1840.[36]

Yet the publication of what was to become the *Racing Calendar* by John Cheyney in 1727 – with its lists of runners, races and jockeys – signalled for the first time the embryonic organisation of a sport on a national basis. The *Racing Calendar* also carried a set of rules for horse racing which, due to its wide circulation, helped to standardise the conduct of meetings. By 1751 these appear to have become largely accepted and a set of formal 'Rules Concerning Horse-Racing in General' were being published in the *Racing Calendar*. Cheyney's *Racing Calendar* also recorded the winners of the previous seasons' races, making comparisons easier and therefore ensuring fair competition between horses. Cheyney was explicit in the reasons for publishing the *Calendar*: 'there was no regular account kept how the horses etc, came in; but as I have taken pains to inform myself, in the best manner I could, I hope that what is published may be depended upon'.[37] The *Racing Calendar* could also be said to mark the beginnings of what would become known as sports statistics. Again, this was propelled by the growing commercial needs of sport. Like the economy itself, transparent competition required clear and verifiable information, especially for the purposes of gambling. Indeed, this same impulse was behind the emergence of record-keeping in other sports. Baseball, perhaps the most anally retentive sport of all when it comes to statistics, developed its arcane categories of measurement in the 1860s and 1870s when irregular fixtures and huge travelling distances meant that objective means of evaluating players were developed in order to facilitate their transfer between clubs.[38]

The formation of the Jockey Club in 1751–2 (its actual date of foundation is unclear, as perhaps might be expected from what was essentially a semi-secret society) took this process a step further through the establishment for the first time of a governing body for a sport, albeit self-proclaimed and unelected. Underpinning these developments was the quickening economic development of horse racing. The emergence of sweepstake gambling in races meant that the returns on betting increased (because bets were no longer restricted to wagers between individuals), thus reducing the financial risks for owners, who could potentially win more money for a lower stake. Returns on bloodstock investment were raised by racing horses at a younger age. Races became shorter, jockeys lighter and handicapping brought a measure of equilibrium to contests, thus offering greater possibilities for owners to win races and punters to beat the odds. As the century progressed, horse racing therefore became increasingly organised and, consequently, increasingly profitable. The creation of what became known as the 'Classic' flat races – the St Leger (1776), the Oaks (1779) and the Derby at Epsom (1780) effectively established the framework of the sport which lasts to this day.

The clearest example of this relationship between commercialism and codification of sporting rules was boxing.[39] Although combat sports are probably as old as humankind, such contests in Britain up until the early eighteenth century involved a combination of hand-to-hand fighting, wrestling and weapons such as swords and wooden clubs known as 'cudgels'. In 1710, James Figg, a well-known swordsman and 'cudgel-player' declared himself the British champion and opened an 'academy of arms' in London's Tottenham Court Road, which both staged fights and offered instruction to students wishing to master the 'noble science of self-defence'. The inspiration for Figg's 'amphitheatre' was probably the 'Bear Garden', an arena for bear-baiting and other blood sports that had existed in London for a hundred years or so from the late sixteenth century. Figg had earned his reputation fighting in booths at fairgrounds but his establishment of a permanent base for the sport reflected the increasing financial viability of London's sporting culture. In 1725 Ben Whittaker fought an Italian, known in the press as 'the Gondolier' at the amphitheatre in Oxford Road for prize money of 20 guineas. This was not an inconsiderable amount, yet the *Daily Post* confidently assured its readers that wagers on the fight totalled 'many hundreds of pounds'.[40]

Figg died in 1734 and his mantle both as champion fighter and boxing's leading businessman was assumed by his former pupil and self-proclaimed 'professor of athletics', Jack Broughton. He felt that boxing had suffered because it did not have a suitably prestigious venue that offered both reasonable admission charges and segregation of the classes. Current venues, he thought, did not differentiate between 'persons of the first rank and condition, and those of the meaner and lower class'. In 1743 he opened his own amphitheatre in central London – 'contrived as entirely to prevent the gentry's being incommoded by the populace' – at a cost of £400, the capital for which came from aristocratic backers. He also insisted that boxers who wanted to fight there had to pay him to stage their fights.[41] Thus the twin pillars of British sport for the next century were established: rigid class differentiation and a drive for profit.

Just as importantly, Broughton understood that sport could not be commercially successful without a commonly accepted code of rules that facilitated an uncertainty of outcome in contests. 'The public may not be imposed on by any fictitious or unequal battles,' he pointed out. Only fighters who have 'signalised themselves to the satisfaction of the spectators' were therefore allowed to appear at his venue.[42] This desire for transparency led him to draw up a code of rules for all boxing matches staged at the amphitheatre. These outlawed hitting a man when he was on the floor or grabbing him below the waist. Crucially, they clearly defined when a fight had been won or lost and appointed umpires for the settling of disputes. Broughton's rule five even insisted that money won in contests had to be distributed in view of the public at the end of a fight to demonstrate the integrity of the contest. As with horse racing, Broughton designed his rules to ensure open and clear competition, not least to enable gambling to take place free from ambiguity.

The same concern for competitive transparency and the requirements of gambling shaped the development of the third major commercial sport of the eighteenth century, cricket. Bat and ball games known as cricket, creckett and other similar names had been recorded since the sixteenth century, but in the absence of detailed descriptions, we have no way of knowing how far these games resembled anything that could be regarded as modern cricket. But it is clear that from the early eighteenth century cricket had acquired a prominence and status that far outstripped other bat and ball games. The social tenor of those leading cricket is attested to by the names of the aristocrats involved: the Duke of Cumberland, the Duke of Dorset, Lord Mountfort and, perhaps most importantly, the Duke of Richmond. The game's elite nature can be seen in a report in the *Daily Journal* about a match that took place at Berry Hill in July 1725:

> between a set of gamesters of the West of this county headed by his Grace the Duke of Richmond on the one side, and a set from the east of the county, headed by Sir William Gage, Bart. and Knight of the Bath, on the other side … His Grace the Duke of Norfolk gave a splendid ball and entertainment that night at the Castle.[43]

Central to this interest was gambling. In the early part of the century, stake money for cricket matches – the amount wagered by the participants – reported in the press varied between 50 and 100 guineas. By the 1790s, stakes or wagers of 1,000 guineas per match were frequent.[44] Given the amount of money involved, disputes were not unknown and sometimes ended in the courts. In 1719 the Men of Kent took the Men of London to court over a disputed wager of £60.[45] And it was this increasingly commercial nature of the sport led to the development of codified and commonly accepted rules for cricket. The first recognised set of written rules was that of 1727, drawn up as part of the Articles of Agreement for two twelve-a-side matches to be played by teams selected by the Duke of Richmond and the future Viscount Middleton.[46]

By the 1740s, cricket could attract sizeable crowds – the Artillery Ground in London, the primary venue for matches, charged between between twopence and two shillings and sixpence to watch a game. This too meant an increased pressure for uniformity of competition and transparency of results, not only to aid gambling but also to standardise the format of matches for all clubs. In 1744 'Noblemen and Gentlemen' of the London Cricket Club, which was based at the Artillery Ground, drew up a set of rules that appears to have had the agreement of other clubs in London. These were superseded in 1774 by a code drawn up by twelve representatives of clubs in Kent, Hampshire, Surrey, Sussex, Middlesex, and London, led by the Duke of Dorset and Earl Tankerville. The importance of gambling to the development of cricket can be seen by the fact that these rules included a section titled 'Bets', setting out how wagers on batsmen in particular and matches in general were to be decided.[47]

The interplay between commercialism, gambling and aristocratic patronage in cricket reached its apogee with the formation of the Marylebone Cricket Club (MCC) in 1787. The club was essentially a continuation of the elite White Conduit Club, led by the Earl of Winchilsea and the Duke of Richmond. When one of the club's professional bowlers, Thomas Lord, opened an enclosed cricket ground in Dorset Square, at which admission could be charged on all sides of the arena, the White Conduit Club decamped from its Islington base and the MCC was born. Like the Jockey Club, the MCC exercised an unelected authority over its sport based solely on its elevated social status. The year after its formation it consolidated its authority by issuing an updated version of the 1744 cricket laws, which like its predecessor included rules for deciding bets. Even its rules for single-wicket matches contained rules for gambling.[48] If the MCC's governance of the sport was unchallenged, so too was the appeal of the new ground, commonly known as Lord's. In the summer of 1793, it staged fourteen matches for stake money totalling 11,000 guineas (a guinea being one pound and one shilling), with no stake being less than 500 guineas. The same amount of stake money was competed for in 1800 when the ground staged thirteen contests.[49]

As can be seen in the examples of the Jockey Club, the MCC and other cricket clubs, the creation of sports clubs was a consequence of the commercialisation, organisation and growth of sport, rather than its cause. Stefan Szymanski's argument that 'modern sport developed out of new forms of associativity created during the European enlightenment', primarily gentlemen's clubs, puts the cart before the horse.[50] Sporting clubs emerged mainly after the commercialisation of sport in the eighteenth century. This can be most clearly seen in Peter Clark's monumental *British Clubs and Societies 1580–1800*, in which sport is almost entirely absent from the interests of the huge number of clubs and associations formed before the nineteenth century. It was only in the mid-nineteenth century that sports clubs became ubiquitous, as part of a new wave of urban middle-class male social and recreational networks.[51] The example of the USA is also instructive. With the exception of horse racing, there was little organised sport played in America before the explosion of commercial entertainment in the nineteenth century, despite the existence of a widespread middle-class associational culture.[52]

The one exception to this general rule was the growth of golf clubs in eighteenth-century Scotland, where the game had become part of the social networks of the Scottish middle classes. Although gambling played some role in golf, it was subordinate to the social appeal of the game, and this meant that, lacking the unifying force of commercialism, the rules developed on a piecemeal, club-by-club basis, beginning in 1744 with those of the Gentlemen Golfers of Leith. It was not until 1888 that the rules of the Royal & Ancient Golf Club of St Andrews in Scotland became widely accepted as regulations governing golf wherever it was played, a period when the sport had both become an important part of middle-class social and recreational culture in the English-speaking world and begun to commercialise itself.[53]

Other sports went down the path of commercialisation but failed to develop into modern codified sports. Pedestrianism, a term that covered running and walking contests, acquired great significance and attracted large amounts of money in the late eighteenth and early nineteenth centuries. These contests were usually challenges to cover a specific distance within a specified time. For example, in 1790, Foster Powell apparently walked from York to London and back again in less than 138 hours for a bet of 20 guineas. Most famously in 1809 Captain Robert Barclay walked 1,000 miles in 1,000 hours for 1,000 guineas on Newmarket Heath, an achievement that attracted bets exceeding £100,000.[54] Such was the intensity of training that many running pedestrianists achieved times that were comparable to those set in the late nineteenth century.[55]

But the esoteric nature of pedestrianism's challenges meant that it was too fragmented to coalesce into a codified and uniform sport. Moreover, it retained many of the characteristics of pre-commercial sport. Its major contests were task-based and rarely featured more than two contestants. More often than not, just one athlete competed against a specific target or time. In this, most pedestrian contests had more in common with the patterns of an earlier agricultural based economy, in which once a task such as sowing or harvesting was completed, work stopped, in contrast to the clock-based discipline and regimented rhythm of the emerging capitalist industrial economy, in which as much work was done as possible in a given period of time, such as a fourteen-hour working day. The measurable and universal competitive human element, displayed most viscerally in the prize-fight and most subtly in cricket, was lacking in pedestrianism.[56]

Like boxing, cock-fighting also attracted considerable aristocratic patronage, large-scale popular support and huge amounts in betting and stake money. For the more prestigious contests 1,000 guineas was not an unusual prize. In 1830, the sport's twilight period shortly before it was banned, birds belonging to the Earl of Derby and Joseph Gilliver fought for 1,000 guineas a battle, and 5,000 guineas for the 'main', the overall winner. But despite being a common sight at race meetings and in the pubs of many towns and villages, cock-fighting was not able to survive the onslaught of moral opprobrium that outlawed most animal sports in the first half of the nineteenth century. Moreover, it offered little opportunity for long-term, continuous commercial exploitation on the model of horse racing. The deadly nature of its contests and the consequent sheer number of cocks that were used made it difficult to calculate odds. A defeated bird was invariably a dead one.[57]

Savate, a French variant of boxing that allowed kicking as well as punching, was never able to challenge British boxing precisely because it lacked a commercial focus. *Savate* was widely viewed in France as a form of duel, rather than an opportunity to gamble or win prize money.[58] Its contests were short and the winner often difficult to determine, making commercial development difficult, in contrast to the clarity of Broughton's rules or the Marquess of Queensberry rules of 1867, which introduced gloves, three-minute rounds and the regulations of modern boxing. When French sports promoters attempted to commercialise the sport at the end of the nineteenth century, it was unable to match the commercial appeal or celebrity culture of British and American boxing, even in France itself.[59] Such counter-examples of sports that failed to develop underline the extent to which it was capitalist commercialism that gave order and structure to modern sport, rather than the nebulous Weberian concept of 'modernisation'.[60]

It is worth noting at this stage that despite its domination of the global sporting landscape in the the twentieth and twenty-first centuries, football played no role in the early development of modern sport. Football games were played in many different ways and in many different locations, yet there were usually no common rules that meant it could be played regularly between teams from different villages, towns or regions. Unlike boxing, cricket and horse racing, it did not have prominent aristocratic patrons who could propel it into national sporting consciousness. Perhaps because of its association with the labouring classes and reputation for violence, often undeserved, the game was viewed with suspicion by the upper classes. It was explicitly banned in Ireland in 1719 by the British authorities as a 'pretence' for 'tumultuous and numerous meetings'.[61] Such suspicions were not unfounded. Football matches were used as cover for a protests against enclosure, for example, at White Roding, Essex, in 1724, while at Kettering in 1740 a match served as a pretext for the attempted destruction of a local mill.[62]

The use of the word 'football' before the twentieth century should not be assumed to be a synonym for Association football or soccer. Although soccer antiquarians and heritage-minded administrators have sought to claim the pre-history of football as their own, there is little in common between modern soccer and earlier forms of football. It is quite obvious from contemporary written accounts, and from observing those games such as the Ashbourne Shrove Tuesday or Calcio Fiorentino games, which survive today as fossilised rituals, that all pre-modern forms of football allowed some combination of handling, throwing and kicking the ball, in contrast with soccer's unique ban on handling by outfield players.[63] As Montague Shearman noted in his 1887 *Athletics and Football* 'there is no trace in the original form of [football] to suggest that nothing but kicking is allowed'.[64] While it is possible to find occasional examples of games that had a set of formalised rules, for example, specifying eleven players per side, these codes were entirely parochial, short-lived, or both. They had no life beyond their immediate origins. In fact, until the 1850s, football was less than marginal to the development of modern sport. But after that point, it would become the driving force behind sport's nineteenth century revolution.

So while football remained a marginal activity, sport was emerging in its embryonic modern form as a form of commercial entertainment, part of a leisure industry that was emerging primarily in London and south-east England in the eighteenth century. The very commercialism of sport, most particularly gambling, stimulated the growth of a market for sport. As would be the case later with local civic pride and nationalist fervour, gambling allowed spectators to participate personally in the event. They now literally had a stake in the outcome of the contest, a level of personal involvement that was unavailable to the theatre- or concert-goer. This made modern sport a uniquely compelling form of entertainment – the equivalent of going to the theatre, placing a bet that Othello and Desdemona would live happily ever after and seeing it unexpectedly happen. Sport was an unscripted melodrama that allowed anyone to have an stake – emotional or monetary – in its outcome.

And because this melodrama revolved around the binary poles of winning and losing, sport's inherently competitive nature – more than any other form of leisure or entertainment – dovetailed perfectly with the newly dominant conceptions of the competitiveness of human nature. Sport was not merely co-terminous with the expansion of capitalism but an integral part of that expansion, not only in economic organisation but also in ideological meaning. At the level of everyday discourse and seemingly empirical 'common sense' – what might be termed 'deep politics' – modern sport was capitalism at play.

2

CLASS CONFLICT AND THE DECLINE OF TRADITIONAL GAMES

It is all disappointment, no sports and no football. This is the way they always treat poor folks.

Derby worker, 1845.[1]

For over 700 years, or so was claimed by local custom, the men of Stamford in Lincolnshire would assemble every 13 November to chase a bull through the streets of the town.[2] Shops in the market town were shut, streets were closed and business ground to a halt. It was if, a commentator in 1829 recorded, the town's populace had 'licence to cast off all appearance of decency and order, and plunge into every excess of riot, without shame or restraint'.[3] But in the new capitalist society where time was money and money was time, this could not be tolerated. The first attempt to ban the bull run was made in 1788 and met with stiff popular resistance. The battle raged for the next fifty years, even after the 1835 Cruelty to Animals Act outlawed it. It was only in 1839, due to the presence of a regiment of dragoons and hundreds of special constables that had been sent to Stamford to ensure its suppression, that the bull run finally ended, demonstrating both the depth of popular support for traditional recreation and the lengths to which the authorities would now go to stop them.

The Stamford bull run was one of hundreds of traditional recreations that were often portrayed as part of the bucolic paradise of 'Merrie England' in which feudal England was seen as rural idyll of deferential social harmony – allegedly the field from which the bull run began was originally provided to the town by the Fifth Earl of Surrey.[4] These traditional games included animal-baiting of various kinds, stick and ball games (with the partial exception of golf) and football. They were rarely played for commercial gain despite their undoubted popularity, had little in the way of rules – still less governing bodies – and were staged usually during festivals or holidays.[5]

But the encroachment of capitalism into every aspect of economic and social life was also undermining the basis of these traditional pastimes. It is perhaps anachronistic to speak of traditional games as independent or self-sufficient activities. The majority of games were closely intertwined with fairs and festivals and were rarely staged with any degree of regularity outside of the context of May games, Whitsuntide celebrations or other religious or popular holidays or fairs. These games did not die overnight, there was no 'leisure vacuum' or sharp break between the sports of rural and industrial society.[6] Rather, the relationship between old and new was one of combined and uneven development, in which examples of continuity coexisted alongside instances of rapid change. Some traditional sports, such as the northern stick and ball game of knur and spell, did survive and retained their popularity until the early part of the twentieth century, especially in those areas where the economy remained predominantly agricultural or was based on small-scale village-based industries.[7] Others, such as bowls, or pigeon shooting until the First World War, owed much of their survival to close links to pubs and publicans' commercial needs to attract customers. Regional variations were often stubbornly resistant to change. A handful were radically transformed by modern technology, such as the re-invention of rabbit coursing as greyhound racing in the 1920s.[8]

But the decline and gradual disappearance of many traditional games cannot be disputed. This was not due to their intrinsic qualities as games but to changes in the world which provided their context. As communications and travel improved from the late seventeenth century, the importance of large-scale annual fairs began to fade. Local markets could be served by merchants on a regular basis and the opportunity for elaborate games evaporated.[9] Feast days, when work in the countryside would stop and labourers and their families would enjoy some of the fruits of their exertions through eating, drinking, dancing, conviviality and sport, began to decline due to the intensification of agricultural work and changes in the social structure of the village brought about by the ever-increasing demands for efficiency. The capitalist rationalisation of rural life accelerated with devastating consequences as the remaining common lands were enclosed. Between 1750 and 1830 in excess of six million acres (around one-quarter of all cultivated land) was turned from common land into private fields through over 4,000 parliamentary Enclosure Acts.[10]

Those who worked on the land in England were not peasants (subsistence farmers bound by feudal ties and tenures to the landowning nobility) but were labourers who toiled in the fields for wages or smallholders whose subsistence also depended on their ability to work for others. By the late eighteenth century, smallholders found it increasingly difficult to meet their daily needs solely by working their own plots of land. Instead, the demands of large-scale capitalist farming meant that they were forced to sell their labour power as agricultural wage-labourers. Village labourers who had been transformed into agricultural proletarians moving from farm to farm in search of work found themselves itinerant and pauperised during times of slump or unemployment.[11] One result of these changes was the collapse of football, cricket and other sports that needed large outdoor spaces. As one Suffolk clergymen reported in 1844, local people:

> have no village green or common for active sports. Some thirty years ago,
> I am told, they had a right to a playground in a particular field, at certain
> seasons of the year, and were then celebrated for their football; but somehow
> or other this right has been lost and the field is now under the plough. ...
> Of late they have introduced a little cricketing and two or three of the
> farmers have very kindly allowed them to play in their fields.[12]

By the time this was written, Britain was well on its way to becoming an urban,
industrial nation. As the factory became the hub of city-based industrial capitalism
the demands for work discipline and efficiency led to concerted attempts to enforce
not only new ways of working but also new attitudes to work itself, based on
sobriety, order, thrift and hard work.[13] The working practices of rural life were
viewed as a hindrance to effective labour. William Windham, Pitt's Secretary at
War, highlighted the issue in his defence of 'traditional' pastimes such as boxing
and bull-baiting, regretting that:

> so many gentlemen should be anxious to deprive the lower order of their
> amusements, from a seeming apprehension that, if they are suffered to enjoy
> these recreations, they will no longer labour sufficiently, and may become,
> from their improvidence, a burden, to which the rich must contribute.[14]

Whereas the agricultural economy demanded labour when necessary and allowed
long periods of leisure, factory work was continuous, intensive and, up until the
factory reforms which started with the 1847 Ten Hours Act, almost ceaseless, as
workers often toiled twelve hours a day, six days a week. Public and communal
holidays, so central to rural life, almost disappeared. There were forty-seven Bank
of England holidays in 1761, but just four in 1834. Eight years later, Cornish
miners had just two holidays from work: Christmas Day and Good Friday.[15]

Practices such as 'Saint Monday', whereby workers would not go into work on
a Monday, or at least worked at a much more leisurely pace than during the rest of
the week, were also viewed as undermining productivity.[16] In order to impose a
new set of values which stressed the importance of hard work, numerous campaigns
to bring 'morality' to the working classes began. These took the form of increased
discipline inside and outside of work, the outlawing of sports that were seen as
immoral or wasteful, and, especially from the mid-1800s, attempts to bring
'rational' recreations to the lower orders which would prepare them for work by
excising immorality and licentiousness from working-class leisure and replacing them
with educative and morally improving pastimes. These measures were underpinned by
the development of a police force, beginning with the 1829 Metropolitan Police
Act, which acted, in the words of Robert Storch, as 'domestic missionaries' with
the aim of suppressing 'immoral' games and recreations.[17]

Thus the involvement of large numbers of people playing and watching games,
taking place over large areas and for long hours was now no longer tolerated. As an
opponent of Derby's traditional football game complained in 1832, 'it is not a

trifling consideration that a suspension of business for nearly two days should be created to the inhabitants for the mere gratification of a sport at once so useless and barbarous'.[18] In 1835 the Highways Act outlawed the playing of football on roads. Moreover, the physical geography of towns changed to reflect the more systematic and rational use of space demanded by a capitalist economy that sought to maximise profit. Writing in 1831, Horatio Smith described the way in which the urbanisation of London had squeezed out the spaces available for popular recreation:

> Every vacant and green spot has been converted into a street; field after field has been absorbed by the builder; all scenes of popular resort have been smothered with piles of brick; football and cricket grounds, bowling greens, and the enclosures or open places set apart for archery and other pastimes have been successfully parceled out in squares, lanes or alleys.[19]

The first half of the nineteenth century witnessed class conflict sharper and more bitter than ever before. The 1810s saw the emergence of the Luddite machine-breaking movement, an armed insurrection by workers in Derbyshire and, most notoriously, the Peterloo Massacre of unarmed demonstrators in 1819. Relations between the classes became fiercely antagonistic, with class conflict and industrial strife commonplace. Under such changed circumstances, opportunities for sporting activity declined precipitously. As E.P. Thompson argued:

> it is clear that between 1780 and 1830 important changes took place. The 'average' English working man became more disciplined, more subject to the productive tempo of 'the clock', more reserved and methodical, less violent and less spontaneous. Traditional sports were displaced by more sedentary hobbies.[20]

This forced disappearance of traditional leisure activities did not occur without resistance from sections of the working class, for whom such attacks were viewed as part of the general assault on their right to employment and a modicum of control over their own lives. It is worth noting that, although time and space for organised sport diminished rapidly, it remained deeply embedded within the culture of the working classes. 'It is all disappointment, no sports and no football,' remarked one supporter of the traditional Derby football match in response to the local council's attempts to ban it in 1845. 'This is the way they always treat poor folks.'[21]

Attempts to suppress sports were sometimes met with determined opposition. Despite troops being called out regularly to enforce a ban on bull-running in Stamford, popular opposition meant that it was more than fifty years before it was finally abolished in 1839.[22] Numerous attempts to stop Shrovetide football being played in Derby were foiled by the working population before the game was finally extinguished in the 1850s. Cock-fighting and dog-fighting did not completely disappear but were driven underground after being outlawed.[23] Despite the Betting Act of 1853 banning street betting and effectively making working-class gambling illegal, the appetite for a wager remained undiminished.[24] In places such as Sheffield and Birmingham, where highly skilled artisans had significant economic power, the tradition of Saint Monday continued well into the later nineteenth century. And attempts by the church, temperance movement and middle-class apostles of 'self-improvement' to impose rational recreation on working-class people were often ignored or subverted. The transformation of the working men's club movement in a few short years from a bastion of teetotalism to a national network of cut-price drinking clubs was perhaps the most spectacular failure of the rational recreationists.[25]

Likewise, the Sabbatarian attempts to make Sunday a day free of any recreation or non-religious activity met with strident opposition. In 1855 around 200,000 people demonstrated in London against the Sunday Trading Bill, a measure directed solely against the working class, for whom the payment of wages on a Saturday left only Sunday free for shopping. This was one more example, noted Marx, of:

> a conspiracy of the Church with the monopoly of capital, but in both cases religious penal laws are to be imposed on the lower classes to set the consciences of the privileged classes at rest. ... The English aristocracy says in the nineteenth century: for us, sanctimonious phrases; for the people, Christian practice.[26]

The Christian sabbath was by then one of the major battlegrounds of leisure. The eighteenth century saw evangelical Christian denominations such as Methodism emerge as vigorous campaigners against sport because, in their eyes, it encouraged licentiousness and vice.[27] A Sunday Observance Act had been passed in 1625, although this had remained a dead letter outside of the Cromwellian era, but the zealous were reinvigorated by the first decades of the nineteenth century. In 1802 William Wilberforce established the Society for the Suppression of Vice, formerly the Proclamation Society, which spent considerable energy pursuing those who broke the sabbath. Its true target was captured by Sydney Smith, who dubbed it 'Society for the Suppression of Vice among persons with less than £500 a year'.[28] In 1831 the Lord's Day Observance Society was formed to campaign against all sports, amusements or recreations held on a Sunday, initiating legal actions and public campaigns that resulted in an almost complete absence of sporting activity on Sundays in Britain between the mid-nineteenth century and the latter decades of the twentieth.[29]

Much of the drive behind these campaigns came from the urban middle classes. Order and control – described at the personal level as 'respectability' – were vital for the smooth running of the burgeoning capitalist economy, and those traditions brought into the towns from the countryside were often seen as undisciplined, licentious and riotous. The campaigns for Sabbatarianism and against animal sports were organised and led by the businessmen, traders and professionals of the rapidly growing towns and cities, led by but not confined to Christian evangelicals. To some extent this had been motivated not only by opposition to what were seen as the morally degrading pastimes of the working classes but also to the dissolute and immoral behaviour of the aristocracy.[30] In 1824 the Royal Society for the Prevention of Cruelty to Animals (RSPCA) had been founded and the momentum of the movement led to the 1835 Cruelty to Animals Act, which outlawed forms of animal-baiting, and eventually to the banning of cock-fighting in 1849 and the legal end of all cruel animal sports. This was the first intervention of the middle class into sport and its role as the moral arbiter of sport would grow to extraordinary levels by the end of the nineteenth century.[31]

Of all the changes that had taken place in sport over the previous century, the outlawing of blood sports would have perhaps been most surprising to the sportsman or woman of the eighteenth century. Although some subsequent accounts have seen the ban on blood sports as being due to the unseen hand of a 'civilising process' at work in British society, it was in reality part and parcel of the tightening noose of restrictions on working-class leisure that sought to create a new moral framework suited to the needs of an urban industrial capitalist economy.[32] Despite some of the reformers' suspicion of the aristocracy, hunting with dogs was left untouched, as was horse racing, a sport that the founder of Methodism John Wesley was not alone in believing to be as cruel as other animal sports.[33] To emphasise the class bias of the legislation, many of the RSPCA's most prominent supporters were huntsmen, and the organisation spent most of its time disciplining urban, working-class cock-fighters and animal-baiters. As Keith Thomas has noted, 'much of the pressure to eliminate the cruel sports stemmed from a desire to discipline the new working class into higher standards of public order and more industrious habits'.[34]

The importance of the middle classes to the campaign against animal sports can be seen when we contrast the experience of Britain with that of France, where the urban middle class was smaller and the economy still predominantly rural until the twentieth century. This meant that sports such as cock-fighting and, more famously, bull-fighting survived and became commercialised, despite campaigns against them by the French urban middle classes. Rural culture in France was never extinguished in the same way as it was in Britain.[35] A similar point can be made about bull-fighting in predominantly rural Spain, where the sport already had a commercial history stretching back into the mid-eighteenth century, but developed into a fully commercialised, mass spectator entertainment at the end of the nineteenth century.[36] In both cases, the weakness of the urban middle class meant that decisive opposition to blood sports was slow to emerge.

There were two other reasons for the relatively rapid eclipse of blood sports. Throughout the eighteenth century, the importance of fair and equal competition in games had been elevated by the centrality of stake money and gambling to sport. With the exception of horse racing, most animal sports did not lend themselves to long-term, commercial gambling. Bloodlines could be difficult to ascertain, records of matches were unclear and they were generally unsuited to be mass spectator events. As we have seen, even cock-fighting, the most sophisticated of animal sports involving anything other than horses, suffered from these problems. For most animal sports, measured and meaningful competition was almost an impossibility, and the interests of gamblers and bookmakers eventually turned elsewhere.

But notions of fairness were also changing. Many Enlightenment thinkers such as Rousseau had insisted that there was no fundamental distinction between humans and animals and, in contrast to Christian thought, that man and beast were part of the same natural world.[37] William Blake expressed similar sentiments most movingly in his *Auguries of Innocence*: 'A dog starv'd at his master's gate/Predicts the ruin of the state'.[38] The fact that animals were tethered in most blood sports was increasingly seen as being unfair. Animals, wrote the anti-blood sports campaigner Samuel Bradley in 1805, 'like man … were formed to feel and to enjoy'.[39] The animal had no way to escape nor, in activities such as bull-baiting, to effectively fight back. This went against the grain of the new ideas about competition and self-interest. Most importantly, animal sports violated the centrality that human competition now had in society. The contest between men for profit or survival was now the essence of society – and in the unequal struggle between man and beast the outcome was a foregone conclusion.

By the end of the eighteenth century, this stance had become more than a philosophical debating point. The impact of the French Revolution and especially Britain's wars against revolutionary France created a national narrative that portrayed Britain as the home of liberty, freedom and fairness, an ideological riposte to the revolution's '*liberté, egalité et fraternité*'.[40] This, alongside global strategic considerations, was most obviously reflected in the abolition of the slave trade, although not slavery itself, by the British government in 1807. Fair play was not just about sport. As Pierce Egan highlighted in his *Book of Sports*: 'fair play is the Briton's motto: she would extend it to the extremities of the earth. No consequence what country, religion or colour.'[41] Homilies drawn from the lexicon of boxing, such as 'never hit a man when he's down' or strictures against 'hitting below the belt', entered everyday language. 'Fairness' in society, in trade, and in sport was becoming a key component of how the British saw themselves and their role in the world.

3

SPORT, NATIONALISM AND THE FRENCH REVOLUTION

An Englishman will take his part, with courage prime and noble heart ... No sword or dagger – nor deadly list – And rise or fall but by his fist!

Pierce Egan, 1824.[1]

In June 1814, the most illustrious prize-fighters in Britain assembled at the London house of Lord Lowther, the Tory politician and future Earl of Lonsdale, whose name still adorns the belts won by British boxing champions. Over the course of the evening, Tom Cribb, John Jackson, Tom Belcher, Bill Richmond and others gave possibly the most star-studded exhibition of sparring ever staged. Their audience included Tsar Alexander I, General Platov and Marshal Blucher, Frederick William III of Prussia and British royal princes, who were en route to the Congress of Vienna, at which they would divide Europe following the defeat of Napoleonic France. The exhibition had been arranged to celebrate the victory of the great powers. A week earlier, Cribb had been presented to the Prussian Field Marshal Blucher. On hearing that he was the champion of England, Blucher replied: 'Then Cribb must be a brother Marshal!'[2] For the first time, sport, nationalism and militarism had been publicly linked in the most overtly political fashion.

Britain's wars with revolutionary France and Napoleon consolidated and made permanent the emerging relationship between sport and British nationalism, a link that was symbolically sealed by Lowther's sparring exhibition. The placing of concepts of fairness at the heart of British ideas about games was not the only consequence that the French Revolution and its aftershocks would have on sport. Indeed, the revolution and its impact formed a fundamental turning point for the subsequent development of sport and its cultural meanings. From this point, sport and nationalism became inextricably linked.

This intertwining of nationalism and physical culture was not confined to British sports.[3] In Germany, the humiliation of occupation by Napoleon's army led German nationalists to found what would become the Turnverein, an overtly nationalist gymnastics movement. Gymnastics had been part of German education from the late eighteenth century, and its major proponent, J.C.F. GutsMuths had published *Gymnastics for Youth* in 1793. In 1811 the Berlin school teacher Friedrich Ludwig Jahn founded an open-air gymnasium that combined physical exercise with nationalist politics. Fired by Jahn's example, the movement spread and similar *Turner* institutes opened across Germany. Many participants also took part in the fight against the French, as Jahn himself did in the Lützowsches Freikorps.[4]

A supporter of German unification and a democratic constitution, Jahn was no radical: 'Poles, French, priests, aristocrats and Jews are Germany's misfortune,' he wrote in 1810.[5] In 1817 German nationalist students inspired in part by Jahn organised the Wartburg Festival in protest at the Congress of Vienna's failure to sanction German unity, at which anti-German books and symbols of the French occupation were burned. Just as the British were to take their sports with them around the globe, German nationalists would also take gymnastics and their *Turner* associations wherever they went in the world.[6]

Nothing stimulated the rise of gymnastics quite like national humiliation. A very similar experience led to the creation of what became known as the Swedish school of gymnastics. Following the Treaty of Tilsit between Napoleon and Russia's Tsar Alexander I, the Russians attacked Sweden in 1808 and seized Finland from it. As in Germany, a nationalist movement arose determined to restore national pride and reassert Swedish culture. Folklorist and poet, Per Henrik Ling, essentially Jahn's Swedish equivalent, developed a system of exercises for educational and military purposes and in 1813 was appointed the first head of the Royal Central Institute of Gymnastics.[7] Partly because Sweden ceased to be a military threat in Europe after the Treaty of Kiel in 1814, its style of gymnastics lost its militaristic tenor and acquired significant popularity among English-speaking physical educationalists in the later nineteenth century.[8]

The defeat of national independence movements in the wake of the failed revolutions of 1848 also led to the rise of the Czech-based Sokol (Falcon) gymnastic movement. Founded by Miroslav Tyrš in 1862 and inspired by the Turnverein, Sokol was overtly nationalistic, seeking Czech independence from the Austro-Hungarian Empire.[9] It was also deeply militaristic, with members wearing uniforms and engaging in military training. The historic Slavophile nature of Czech nationalism led to Sokol evolving into something of a pan-Slavic movement and associations were founded in Slovenia (1868), Croatia (1874) and Serbia (1891). It also became popular in Tsarist Russia, especially after the Russians' ignominious defeat at the hands of the Japanese in 1905, once more demonstrating the connection between military ignominy and the rise of gymnastics.[10]

In Britain, patriotic rhetoric had never been entirely absent from sport during the first half of the eighteenth century. 'Experience convinces us that foreigners tremble less at the firelock than the fist of a Briton,' wrote Jack Broughton, somewhat speculatively, in 1744.[11] Yet the relative unimportance of sport to British cultural life at that time meant that such notions were little more than the rhetorical flourishes of an astute salesman. But by the last two decades of the century sport became more closely associated with the British national character. War made the two of them inextricable. Linda Colley has noted that during the Napoleonic Wars hunt clubs started to wear uniforms that 'mimicked military uniform'.[12] In 1805 William Cobbett linked the importance of sport to victory over France:

> not only boxing, but wrestling, quarter-staff, single-stick, bull-baiting, every exercise of the common people that supposes the possible risk of life or limb, and, of course, prepares them for deeds of bravery of a higher order, and, by means of those deeds and of the character and consequence naturally growing out of them, [helps] to preserve the liberty and independence of their country.[13]

Boxing especially was thought to highlight the differences between British and French national characteristics.[14] 'An Englishman will take his part, with courage prime and noble heart … No sword or dagger – nor deadly list – And rise or fall but by his fist!' explained Pierce Egan, contrasting the supposed continental preference for settling disputes by knife-fighting and duelling.[15] Writing shortly after Bill Richmond had defeated George Maddox over 52 rounds in 1809, William Windham, who in his time as Pitt's Secretary at War had supported the counter-revolutionary rising in the Vendée and the restoration of the Bourbon monarchy, defended boxing as essential to British fighting spirit:

> Why are we to boast so much of the native valour of our troops, as shewn [sic] at Talavera, at Vimera and at Maida, yet to discourage all the practices and habits which tend to keep alive the same sentiments and feelings? The sentiments that filled the minds of the three thousand spectators who attended the two pugilists were just the same in kind as those which inspired the higher combatants on the occasions before enumerated. … Will it make no difference in the mass of a people, whether their amusements are all of a pacific, pleasurable, and effeminate nature, or whether they are of a sort that calls forth a continued admiration of prowess and hardihood?[16]

The same link between boxing and the war against France could be seen in the drinking songs of the Fancy, the informal aristocratic club that provided money and social kudos to the London sporting world. For example, Tom Cribb's victory over Tom Molineaux in 1811 was greeted with a twelve-verse song that ended:

> Now fill your glasses to the brim,
> And honour well my toast, sirs,
> May we be found in fighting trim,
> When Boney treads our coasts, sirs,

The gallant Barclay [the pedestrian who had trained Cribb] shall lead on,
The Fancy lads adore him,
And Devil or Napoleon,
Leave us alone to floor him.[17]

The war with France was conducted not only by means of arms, it was also an ideological war, conducted against the principles of the French Revolution, regardless of the extent to which Napoleon did or did not uphold them. The fear that, as in France, the poor would rise against their masters haunted the ruling classes of Europe. As such, the enemy was not only abroad, it was also potentially at home, in the form of the common people in Britain. 'If men are restrained from fighting occasionally for prizes and honorary distinctions', wrote the radical Whig MP Richard Payne Knight in defence of boxing in 1806, 'the lower order will become a base rabble of cowards and assassins, ready at any time to sacrifice the higher to the avarice and ambition of a foreign tyrant.'[18]

Sport, argued the *Sporting Magazine* in 1804, offered an alternative to 'the captivating fallacies of revolutionary doctrines'.[19] Praising the 1819 Peterloo Massacre of fifteen unarmed demonstrators at Manchester's St Peter's Field, 'One of the Fancy' wrote in a review of Pierce Egan's *Boxiana* in *Blackwood's* magazine that:

the Manchester Magistrates did their duty on the 16th August – but may Pugilism flourish and radicalism decay. … Nothing could be more good-humoured than an assemblage of Englishmen at a fight. No seditious banners – no orators – no occasion afterwards for the grand inquest of the nation to interfere – everything is left to the umpire.[20]

There was therefore nothing original in G.M. Trevelyan's claim in his *English Social History* (1942) that 'if the French noblesse had been capable of playing cricket with their peasants, their chateaux would never have been burnt'.[21] A practical knowledge of sporting technique could also assist Britons who felt personally threatened by those whom Edmund Burke described as the 'swinish multitude'. 'The insolence of the manners of the lower order of people of this country has long been a subject of regret', wailed *The Art of Manual Defence*, a handbook of boxing technique published in 1799. 'The only means of checking the evil is by personal chastisement,' before proceeding to offer easy instruction on how to deliver a fistic rebuke to such impertinence.[22]

This ideological amplification of sport went much further than the exigencies of everyday politics. Its growing identification with the British national identity and character led sport's advocates to claim a deeper and more fundamental relationship between Britain and sport. 'Let us,' suggested the anonymous author of *The Complete Art of Boxing* entirely without evidence in 1788, 'observe the truly heroic discipline of the great Alfred, the British King, when it is clearly demonstrated that boxing and wrestling were part of the manual exercise of the soldiery of those times'.[23] The conflict with France gave further impetus to the myth that the playing of games was uniquely British, and this intersected with a growing nostalgia for a semi-mythical rural England (the landscape was always English, the character British). Perhaps the clearest, and certainly the most eloquent, example of this tendency was Wordsworth's 'Composed in the Valley near Dover, on the Day of Landing' (1802), in which he describes his relief in returning from Europe:

Here, on our native soil, we breathe once more.
The cock that crows, the smoke that curls, that sound
Of bells; those boys who in yon meadow-ground
In white-sleeved shirts are playing … [24]

Cricket, represented by the boys in white shirts, stands for a rural, timeless nation that contrasts with the tumult and conflict of Europe. Wordsworth's vision is a variation of the 'Merrie England' myth in which feudal England was viewed as bucolic idyll of deferential social harmony. As economic and social change gathered pace in the last years of the 1700s nostalgia and a yearning for a neverland of the rural past became very fashionable. One example was the revival of archery, marked by the formation of the Toxophilite Society in 1781 by Sir Ashton Lever, which owed much of its popularity among the upper classes to its adoption of the symbols and customs of the medieval past.[25] The same fashionable impulse lay behind the popularity of books such as Joseph Strutt's *The Sports and Pastimes of the People of England*, first published in 1801, that claimed to trace the lineage of sports back into the mists of British history, although cricket is barely mentioned and boxing not at all. Much of the success of Pierce Egan was due not only to his verdant prose but also to his ability to situate sport within a historical narrative. *Boxiana* (1813), his most famous work, was both a detailed account of his version of boxing history and a meditation on the essential Britishness of the sport.[26] More generally, the idea that fair play was a uniquely British concept that stretched back into the mists of time permeated literature in the 1820s. The phrase 'Fair Play and Old England Forever!' can be found in Sir Walter Scott's historical romance *Ivanhoe* (1820) and his *The Fortunes of Nigel* (1822), as well as in Hazlitt's 1825 essay 'Merry England', which ascribes the victory at Waterloo to 'English pluck and manhood' learnt through boxing.[27]

This use of sport as a palimpsest upon which to invent and re-invent traditions was something that would occur time and time again. This was particularly the case when either sport or the nation felt itself to be under threat. Perhaps the most egregious examples were the later mythologies of rugby's William Webb Ellis and baseball's Abner Doubleday, men who were posthumously anointed founders of games they hardly knew at times when both sports sought to legitimise their role as national institutions.[28] Pierre de Coubertin's reinvention of the Olympic Games in the 1890s also depended on the creation of a mythical amateurism that supposedly inspired the ancient Greek Olympics.[29] In the 1830s cricket began to refashion its history when faced with the rising power of professional players and the decline of its rural traditions. John Nyren's *The Cricketers of My Time* (1832) told the story of

Hambledon cricket club, the powerhouse of English cricket in the 1770s and 1780s, as a bucolic tale of aristocratic *noblesse oblige* and deferential yet proud artisans, united as one by the love of cricket.[30] Thus was established the basic theme of almost all subsequent writing about cricket and, to a large extent, most other sports.

So while the threat of invasion by France and the prospect of revolutionary uprising at home passed, the cultural meaning of sport that had emerged between 1790 and 1820 remained. Sport, because of its ubiquity and apparent longevity, seemed to represent a 'common sense', everyday view of the world. It was nationalist and conservative, without initial capital letters. It was a microcosm of a society that saw itself as a marketplace, in which everyone had the opportunity to be a winner or a loser. It was also, as we shall see, a very male world. The discourse of sport had become a form of 'deep politics', in which political ideas were expressed in a seemingly non-political way, where the unspoken assumptions were inevitably conventional and uncritical of society. Far from being outside of the concerns of political life, sport was so tightly woven into the political culture of the commonplace that its politics appeared to be invisible.

4

THE MIDDLE-CLASS INVENTION OF AMATEURISM

The troubles of the [Rugby Football] Union commenced with the advent of the working man. If he cannot afford the leisure to play the game he must do without it.

Arthur Budd, 1899.[1]

The 1820s and 1830s saw the decline of the eighteenth-century model of sport. It no longer commanded the same intense interest from its aristocratic patrons. The Fancy ebbed away, the conspicuously extravagant wagers of the cricketing nobility dried up and the boxing halls were emptied of their titled spectators. Later commentators and some historians have ascribed the decline in the fortunes of sport to increasing corruption in sport. But there is no evidence that corruption was significantly worse in the post-Napoleonic era than it had been before it.[2] Horse racing was never free of sharp practice in the late eighteenth century – in 1791 Sam Chiffney, the Prince of Wales's jockey had been barred from Newmarket under suspicion of fixing races. Jack Broughton's original boxing amphitheatre had closed following accusations that he had thrown a fight in which his patron, the Duke of Cumberland, had lost £10,000. Cricketers regularly bet on themselves and against each other, leaving room for considerable doubt about the transparency of the contest, especially in single-wicket matches. 'Cheating, in every kind of "sport", is as completely in the common order of things in England amongst the highest classes as the lowest,' wrote a German visitor to England in the 1820s.[3]

In fact, the aristocracy had gradually disengaged from most sports because the eighteenth-century hierarchies of deference and control were breaking down. Peter Burke's belief that the 'the clergy, the nobility, the merchants, the professional men' had abandoned popular culture by 1800 was both premature and too sweeping to apply to Britain.[4] The British aristocracy continued to engage in popular sports until the end of the Napoleonic wars. But within a decade of the Battle of Waterloo, the titled no longer commanded unquestioned authority, whether it was in politics, culture or games, and started to withdraw from sport. This could be seen most obviously in boxing. In 1814 the first attempt had been made by various aristocrats to create a boxing equivalent of the MCC or the Jockey Club but neither it nor a second attempt in the 1820s lasted more than a decade.[5] The failure was due both to the decline of the Fancy – slumming at sporting events lost much of its thrill when it no longer buttressed a sense of social self-confidence – and the rise of urban sporting entrepreneurs, especially pub landlords.[6] The cost of entry into the boxing market was minimal, especially in comparison to cricket and horse racing, and without their previous cultural hegemony aristocrats found it difficult to assert their authority. One of the reasons that Pierce Egan's books, such as *Boxiana*, and journalism were so successful in the 1820s was that they evoked a romantic vision of the recent past, a world of Regency 'bucks and bruisers' in which both the Fancy and the fighters clearly understood and accepted their role in the hierarchy – a romantic nostalgia that bore little, if any, relation to contemporary events.

Although less pronounced, this waning of unquestioned aristocratic influence and the involvement of less socially exalted members of society could also be seen in horse racing. Indeed, this was pointed to as a reason for corruption in the sport: 'I have seen with great regret gentlemen associating themselves with persons much below their station,' tut-tutted Baron Alderson in 1844. 'If gentlemen would associate with gentlemen, we should have no such practices.'[7] One of the given reasons for the launch of the *New Sporting Magazine* in 1831 was the desire, especially on the part of its star writer, Nimrod, to distance itself from plebian sport, so much so that it refused to report on boxing.[8] On the cricket field, the eclipse of the aristocracy was even more apparent. Of the twenty-two annual Gentlemen versus Players matches played between 1819 and 1840, the Gentleman came out on top on just six occasions, whereas the professional Players won fourteen times. The dominance of the professional undermined the authority of the MCC and eventually led to the creation in the 1840s of the All England XI, a professional cricket team that toured the country playing local sides, organised and led by William Clarke, an archetypal pub landlord sportsman-entrepreneur.[9] Its success led to the formation of similar professional teams that dominated cricket throughout the middle decades of the nineteenth century. Unlike the professionals who played as retainers for their aristocratic patrons in the eighteenth century, these nineteenth-century cricket professionals were not beholden to their social superiors. They were often artisans – Clarke himself was originally a bricklayer – and many later became publicans due to their cricketing prowess, giving them a degree of independence beyond the reach of their predecessors.[10]

These changes were directly connected to the shifting relationships between the classes in British society. Rapid industrialisation and urbanisation led to an increase in the size and influence of the middle and working classes. By 1851 the majority of the population lived in cities. The industrial bourgeoisie and the growing army of lawyers, accountants and civil servants that the administration of industrial capitalism required had begun to chafe under the archaic structure of a corrupt parliamentary system. Moreover, they saw themselves as representing the new moral core of the British nation, against what they saw as a dissolute aristocracy and an uncivilised working class. Pressure for reform resulted in the 1832 Reform Act, which brought the vote to the middle classes. At the same time, the working class had also changed. Increasingly radicalised and determined to fight for their political and economic rights, by the 1830s this self-confidence led to the creation of the Chartist movement, which in parts of industrial Wales and Yorkshire had become an openly insurrectionary movement. As Eric Hobsbawm has argued:

> no period of British history has been as tense, as politically and socially disturbed, as the 1830s and early 1840s, when both the working class and the middle class, separately or in conjunction, demanded what they regarded as fundamental changes.[11]

By the mid-nineteenth century sport in Britain had lost much of its social cachet but was still an important component of the commercial entertainment industry. The class polarisation of society had undermined the aristocracy's dominance of sport, with the exception of horse racing, and created a vacuum of control that left sport temporarily in the hands of a fringe of small capitalists such as William Clarke – a petty bourgeoisie of bat, ball and boxing – who saw themselves as part of a new mass entertainment industry of music halls, penny dreadfuls and titillating Sunday newspapers.

This was not to last. The national and cultural significance that sport had acquired in the Napoleonic era meant that it was too important to be left in the hands of marginal profiteers or the lower classes. The growing self-confidence of the middle classes, spurred on by the triumph of the 1832 Reform Act, led to their growing cultural assertion across British society. The formation of the Football Association (1863) and London's Amateur Athletic Club (1866) was part of the same process that saw the creation of the British Medical Association (1856) and the Royal Institution of Chartered Surveyors (1868).[12] In particular, a new conception of the nature and meaning of sport was beginning to be articulated in Britain's private schools, or 'public schools' as they were known in the doublethink of the British upper and middle classes. The education of the British elite, largely ignored by previous generations of aristocrats for whom ancestral lineage mattered above all, had begun to change to meet the needs of an industrialising nation and its expanding empire. As the upper middle classes expanded, so too did the need for the education of an administrative, business and military cadre.[13]

The model for this new educational system was found in a previously obscure school in the heart of the English midlands. In 1828 Thomas Arnold had been appointed headmaster of Rugby School and set about reforming the curriculum and culture of the school with the aim of producing Christian gentlemen. 'What we must look for here is, first, religious and moral principle; secondly, gentlemanly conduct; thirdly, intellectual ability', he argued. Indolence and corruption, code words for the aristocracy, were in his view 'the ruin of us all alike, individuals, schools, and nations'.[14] In the words of one pupil, Rugby School under Arnold became:

> the image of that most powerful element in modern English society, the Middle Class … [it] may even claim kindred and fellowship of spirit with Railway Kings and Cotton Lords, being equally with them the creation of modern, burning, life-like energy. In a late stage of civilisation, like the present, the idea of trade comes prominently and almost exclusively into notice, being able at length to connect itself with that from which it has long been kept apart, education and enlightenment.[15]

By the nineteenth century all public schools played competitive sports – the first Eton versus Harrow cricket match was held in 1805 – but, although he was not personally interested in them, Arnold's educational philosophy provided justification for games to occupy a central place in the school curriculum. As well as teaching teamwork, leadership and physical courage (the key tenets of what became known as Muscular Christianity), it also taught pupils the importance of competition. The wealth of the British upper classes was based on competition in economics and empire and, more fundamentally, in the very nature of capitalist society itself. Just as a new culture of labour discipline, hard work and thrift had to be imposed on the working class, so too did the future ruling and administrative classes have to be educated in the competitive spirit that underpinned Britain's global domination. In some ways this reflected British capitalism's transformation from a mercantile to an industrial economy – the swashbuckling boxers and cricketers of the eighteenth century who played for cash bounties were replaced by team sports that promoted organisation and self-discipline.

This interlocking of educational principle, sporting enthusiasm and moral self-righteousness could be seen at its most smugly didactic in Thomas Hughes' 1857 bestselling novel *Tom Brown's Schooldays*. A former pupil of Rugby School who, like many of its alumni, worshipped Arnold, Hughes set out to write a fictionalised account of life at the school. But the popularity of the book was such that it rapidly became a handbook of public and grammar school education.[16] It also played a crucial role in popularising the idea that sport was not merely a form of recreation but that it also had a moral purpose. Sport and British nationalism were fused together in the heat of the Napoleonic wars, but the Muscular Christians elevated games to a new level. For them, sport was a means to build character, to create 'manly' gentlemen and to promote the virtues of the Church of England, the ideological mortar of the British Empire.

In the worldview of the Muscular Christians, sport had an intrinsic meaning and message that transcended mere play.[17] It was credited with attributes and qualities that set it above other cultural pursuits, giving it a self-conscious superiority over different types of recreation and entertainment. Of course, playing sport was no more nor less invigorating, fulfilling or transcendent than singing, acting or, for that matter, making love, yet its mid-Victorian ideologues would infuse it with a self-righteousness that continues to the present day. Nor were these ideas the self-evident unchanging truths that their advocates proclaimed them to be. They were as much a product of their times as railway mania or the novels of Dickens.

Amateurism, the idea that one did not receive payment for playing sport, was at the heart of this moral universe. But in the early decades of the nineteenth century, the word 'amateur' had a different meaning, being used to describe an aristocratic patron of sport rather than an unpaid participant. Egan's *Pancratia* and *Boxiana* both emphasise the fact that London society 'amateurs' were the arbiters of most issues in boxing. Indeed, the word was almost interchangeable with the 'Fancy'.[18] Aristocrats who played sport, such as cricketers or the occasional pedestrian such as Captain Barclay, were not called amateurs but 'gentlemen', a term which denoted social status rather than whether they were paid for their endeavours. The idea that an amateur was a sportsman who did not receive money for playing was unknown until the mid-1800s.

This new conception of amateurism had two core components: a belief that sport should not be played for material reward and the idea that 'fair play' should govern the conduct of games.[19] These were essentially non-contentious reiterations of common sense. The vast majority of games of any type were played as unremunerated recreation. Sport could not be played without a mutual recognition by its participants of the underlying and unwritten laws of on-field behaviour. But the repackaging of these ideas under the rubric of 'amateurism' meant that they could also be used as an ideology of control and exclusion, dressed up as a moral imperative for sport. Viewed from a broader perspective, amateurism reflected the attitudes of the British middle classes, who wanted capitalist economic competition but also a hierarchical, ordered social structure – in other words, a contest that guaranteed their victory.

A glance at the chronology of amateurism is enough to demonstrate that it emerged in direct response to working-class influence in sport. Initially it was expressed as unadorned social snobbery: the 1861 *Rowing Almanack* defined an amateur by listing the educational establishments and other institutions attended by acceptable rowers and excluded absolutely 'tradesmen, labourers, artisans or working mechanics'. The Amateur Athletic Club, the forerunner of the Amateur Athletic Association, also explicitly excluded anyone who was 'a mechanic, artisan or labourer' from its definition of an amateur.[20] Both rowing and athletics had considerable working-class participation, rowing due to its importance to dockers before the development of modern stevedoring techniques, and athletics because of the persistent popularity of pedestrianism, which by that time had itself become a term indistinguishable from professionalism.

In cricket, the rigid distinction between the classes that had been established in the eighteenth century was reinforced as the MCC sought to curb the influence of the touring professional sides in the 1860s and 1870s. There was an increase in the number of county cricket matches played under the auspices of the MCC and the beginnings of a county championship structure for the game. This helped to undermine the professional teams by offering regular employment to professional players, provided that they met the qualifying criteria.[21] The subordination of the professional to the amateur was rigidly enforced. Professionals travelled separately, used different dressing rooms and entered the field through their own gates. Even their names were referred to in separate ways. Amateurs were referred to using their title, initials and surname; professionals were surnames first, initials last. This convention lasted until 1962. Most county sides refused to allow professionals to captain the team until the mid-twentieth century and no professional player captained the England national side until 1952.[22]

The question of social segregation became especially acute with the unprecedented explosion in the popularity of soccer and rugby in the 1880s. In little over a decade the two football codes went from being social recreations for middle-class boys and young men to become mass working-class participation and spectator sports. The fear that the working class would 'swamp' football and wrest control of it, either consciously or through sheer weight of numbers, was palpable among the leaders of the two games: 'why should we hand [rugby] over without a struggle to the hordes of working men players who would quickly engulf all others?' asked the dual cricket and rugby international Frank Mitchell.[23] Moreover, working-class culture continued to treat sport as a form of entertainment rather than a moral force. Payment for play was an expected outcome of sporting success. In many ways these attitudes were similar to those of eighteenth-century sport. Confronted by a growing number of clubs in the English north and midlands who paid their leading players, the Football Association (FA) had a brief but vigorous debate over the question of payments to players. In 1885 it decided to adopt the MCC model and allow professionalism under tightly controlled circumstances: no professional player could be involved in the running of a club or the administration of the sport.[24]

Yet, though the professionals were to be strictly subordinated to football's middle-class leadership, it was a different matter on the field of play. Until 1882, only teams comprising former public schoolboys – such as the Old Etonians or the Old Carthusians – had appeared in the final of the FA Cup since it started in 1872. Blackburn Rovers dented this record by reaching the 1882 final before losing to the Old Etonians. The following year their local rivals Blackburn Olympic defeated the Old Etonians to win the cup. After the legalisation of professionalism in 1885, no middle-class club ever again appeared in the FA Cup final. The amateurs could no longer consistently compete against the professionals. Despite claims to the contrary, winning was as vital to the middle classes as it was to the working class, and their failure to compete successfully against those they viewed as their social inferiors was a powerful impetus to the growth of amateur ideology.

It was the fear that rugby would also succumb to working-class domination which animated the leadership of the Rugby Football Union (RFU). In the 1870s rugby had outstripped soccer in popularity and in much of the north of England had become the dominant mass spectator sport. The huge influx of working-class players and spectators appeared to threaten the control of the middle-class leadership of the RFU. As future president of the RFU Arthur Budd argued, the experience of soccer was a warning to the middle classes:

Only six months after the legitimisation of the bastard [of professionalism] we see two professional teams left to fight out the final [FA] cup tie. To what does this all end? Why this – gentlemen who play football once a week as a pastime will find themselves no match for men who give up their whole time and abilities to it. How should they? One by one, as they find themselves outclassed, they will desert the game and leave the field to professionals …

The Rugby Union committee finding themselves face to face with the hydra have determined to throttle it before he is big enough to throttle them. … No mercy but iron rigour will be dealt out.[25]

Although it has been argued that RFU's attitude to professionalism was due to its leadership being less confident about its social status in comparison to the supposedly more aristocratic FA leadership, this is not the case.[26] Both opposition to and support for professionalism within soccer could be found in all of the social strata that led the FA and its clubs in the early 1880s. In reality, the difference in attitude was due to timing. The FA by and large adopted the only model of professionalism available to them, that of cricket and the MCC's tight control of the professional players. The only alternative was rowing and athletics' outright exclusion of working-class players, which would have led to football splitting in two. But cricket was an old sport with deeply rooted traditions of hierarchy and deference that even William Clarke's touring professional sides had been unable to break. Soccer and rugby were new sports that were expanding quickly and had no commonly accepted traditions to which their leaderships could appeal. The aggressiveness of the RFU's reaction to professionalism was based on the widespread belief that the FA's approach had failed to stop the advance of professionalism. Rugby therefore needed a different strategy to stop it following soccer's fate.[27] The differences in approach reflected what was essentially a debate among the middle-class leaders of sport about how best to deal with working-class sportsmen. Indeed, the contingency of the different attitudes can be seen in the stance of N.L. 'Pa' Jackson, the sports journalist and leader of the Corinthians, the supposedly pristine-pure representatives of amateur soccer. Although he became known as a vehement opponent of professionalism in both football codes, he had actually seconded the motion that led to the FA's legalisation of payments to players in 1885.

The vehemence of its desire to protect its position led to the RFU introducing strict amateur regulations in 1886, the signal for a cold civil war to break out in the sport. Faced with incessant attacks over their 'veiled professionalism' the strong northern clubs were eventually forced out of the RFU in August 1895. The break led to them founding a new rugby code, rugby league, which legalised professionalism and changed the rules to make the sport more attractive to players and spectators. Following the split, the RFU forbade all contact with rugby league, whether professional or amateur. It became an offence to sign a rugby league form, play with or against a rugby league player or 'advocate or take steps to promote' rugby league, regardless of whether any money was received. The punishment in all cases was expulsion from rugby union for life, either as a player or member of a club. Such sanctions against players were unique in the history of world sport. Every player had to be on his guard against inadvertently dealing with the league 'devil'. 'Ignorance of the rules is no defence' warned a poster distributed to all clubs by the RFU in the 1920s. Ironically, in 1933 a player named Tom Brown, the then England international full-back, was expelled from the sport for life merely for meeting with representatives of a rugby league club. He was only one of the most prominent of hundreds who would suffer the same fate. This 'police state of play' lasted until rugby union ditched its amateur principles in pursuit of satellite television riches in 1995.[28]

This debate over professional sport in the late nineteenth century reflected the wider debate in bourgeois society about the rising power and self-confidence of the working class. From the mid-1880s Britain was wracked by rising class conflict that led to the creation of a new wave of trade unions for unskilled workers and the formation of socialist organisations. The RFU's alarm about the direction rugby was taking was a microcosm of the widespread fear of the working class. Amateurism was their solution to this fearfulness. Indeed, for certain sections of the middle classes throughout the British Empire, the emphasis of the amateur ethos on obedience to authority and authority's ability to regulate who could and could not play were positive and attractive features.[29] Further afield, for the French nobleman Pierre de Coubertin or the American journalist Casper Whitney, amateurism provided a universal value system that could unite the middle classes of the West in common moral self-confidence. As in England, amateurism could be used to impose strict social segregation between the classes or to control and discipline working-class players when it was felt to be expedient. And in South Africa, the social restrictions of amateurism dovetailed with racial segregation based on white supremacy – Springbok rugby union administrator Danie Craven neatly captured the link between the two when he described rugby union's attitude to the league code as being 'the strictest form of apartheid'.[30]

Amateurism's structures of control and discipline also shaped the adoption of British sports in France. It was not only the impact of defeat in the Franco-Prussian war that caused anglophiles like Coubertin to promote sport as a means of national renewal, it was also the scars left by the working-class uprising that created the Paris Commune of 1871.[31] Both of these events were crucial in shaping the mentality of the French upper classes in the latter decades of the nineteenth century, in which the drive to re-establish national prestige and the need to police a rebellious working class dominated the politics of the Third Republic. The appeal of amateur British sport to Frenchmen like Coubertin – who not only founded the modern Olympics on amateur principles but also refereed the first French rugby championship final in 1892 – was two-fold. It provided the rhetoric of a national mission for the middle and upper classes, together with a structure to control and regulate the working class. Amateurism was the perfect expression of Coubertin's broader social attitudes, summed up in his phrase, 'inequality is more than a law, it is a fact; and patronage is more than a virtue, it is a duty'.[32] The strength of the British idea of amateurism can be seen in French rugby union. Long after it had shed any traces of the anglophilia of its original French supporters and links with the British expatriate community, it remained committed to the rhetoric and structures of amateurism, if not its content.[33] They reached their apogee in the Second World War under Marshall Petain's Vichy regime that collaborated with the Nazis in administering the south and eastern regions not under occupation. Vichy declared its support for amateur sports and sought to suppress those it designated as professional, resulting in the banning of the rugby league game in France and the confiscation of its assets.[34]

Amateurism also became a powerful force in the United States. Partly this was because of the strong cultural ties between Britain and America. 'Injuries incurred on the playing field are part of the price which the English-speaking race has paid for being world conquerors,' declared Henry Cabot Lodge in 1896.[35] *Tom Brown's Schooldays* had been published in America in 1857 and was almost as influential there as on the other side of the Atlantic. Teddy Roosevelt, whose boundless physical energy embodied the spirit of America's imperialist appetites, thought that it was one of two books that everyone should read.[36] 'Where is the football man from the field, side line, or stand who does not feel that he is an inheritor in the glories of Old Bigside at Rugby?' wrote the first chronicler of American football, Parke H. Davis.[37] Muscular Christianity therefore found fertile ground across the Atlantic, albeit with a specifically American accent, best exemplified by the Young Men's Christian Association. Amos Alonzo Stagg, one of the most influential figures in the formative period of American football, embodied the tight interlocking of the Christian ideal and sport, being a graduate of divinity school and a seminal coach with the University of Chicago. America also took as its model the British mid-Victorian belief in the centrality of the educational system to the sporting structure, with Ivy League universities modelling themselves on Oxford and Cambridge universities. Today's college and high school sport industry is an exaggerated refraction of the importance of university and public school sport in nineteenth-century Britain.[38]

As in Britain, the impulse towards amateurism was a direct result of a perceived threat to middle-class control of sport. In baseball, it was only after professional sides like the Cincinnati Red Stockings began to dominate the sport in the late 1860s that calls for pure amateurism began to emerge, most notably from elite New York clubs who sought to curb their more successful professional rivals.[39] A similar process occurred in Canadian lacrosse, where the success of the working-class Montreal Shamrocks team led to the leaders of the sport declaring it exclusively amateur.[40] And despite the meritocratic mythology of American exceptionalism, strict social and racial segregation was fundamental to the USA's WASP (white, Anglo-Saxon, Protestant) ruling class. This was especially true in college sport. Caspar Whitney, America's leading sportswriter of the late nineteenth-century and a close associate of Walter Camp, was quite explicit about the reasons for his embrace of the English system of amateurism:

> Why there should be such constant strife to bring together in sport the two divergent elements of society that never by any chance meet elsewhere on even terms is quite incomprehensible, and it is altogether the sole cause of all

our athletic woe. Unlike the quality of mercy, which blesses him that gives and him that receives, this athletic philanthropy embarrasses both.[41]

Although there were many sincere adherents of the rhetoric of amateurism – after all, it seemed to offer a way to avoid the worst aspects of competition in sport – ultimately it was impossible to escape the fact that at bottom it was a justification for social exclusion. The high-born or socially well-connected were by definition amateurs, regardless of the financial gains they made from sport. In cricket, the most notorious example was W.G. Grace, who earned far more as an amateur than any professional player of the late Victorian era.[42] In rugby union, zealous vigilance against those who had played rugby league was combined with diplomatic blindness about 'boot money' payments to players in Wales and South Africa. Few in France beyond the Vichy regime and its propagandists adhered to the spirit or letter of amateurism: indeed, most French sportsmen believed that 'the white flag of amateurism has a silver lining'.[43] Amateurism, wherever it took root, was either ultimately rejected or allowed to calcify into a system of institutionalised cynicism. The only partial exception to this pattern was in Ireland, where the essentially rural nature of the Gaelic Athletic Association (GAA), the general poverty that afflicted Ireland for most of the twentieth century and the fact that hurling and Gaelic football had no rivals for its players, meant that neither the GAA nor its players felt the need for monetary compensation. And despite this economically enforced amateurism, the GAA had none of the machinery of punishment or exclusion that amateur bodies abroad cultivated.[44]

Amateurism at the elite level uniquely thrived into the twenty-first century in the United States, paradoxically home to the most commercialised sports culture in the world. Sport had emerged in American universities in the nineteenth century on the British model of middle-class amateurism. By 1900 gridiron football had become the major winter spectator sport in America, emerging rapidly from its origins in the Ivy League institutions of the north-east.[45] Yet despite the huge crowds it attracted football remained resolutely amateur. This was due to two reasons. First, the students who played the game were invariably from the upper and middle classes and, like their counterparts at Oxford and Cambridge universities in England, had no desire to become, or to be perceived as, professionals. Second, the attendances at college football matches generated very substantial amounts of revenue for university administrations. For example, in 1904 Harvard made a profit of $50,000 from football, in contrast to its arts and science faculties that made a combined loss of $30,000. In 1909–10, Harvard football's total match receipts were $78,583 and Yale's $72,960.[46] For Harvard, Yale and many other institutions, football was a cash faucet that they had no desire to turn off, nor to reduce the flow by disbursing their windfall to athletes. Protection of profit dovetailed perfectly with preservation of social position.[47]

As college football, and later basketball, increased in popularity, profitability gradually began to take precedence over social status. As with all commercial sporting activity the quest for victory meant that leading colleges sought to recruit the best players – or at least until the 1960s the best white players – regardless of social background. Amateurism acquired a new importance, not only as a means of avoiding paying wages to the young players whom the crowds came to see, but also as a way of using moral authority to control those players.

But, like amateurism everywhere else, the system was deeply hypocritical. Not only were high school students offered covert and occasionally overt inducements to join a college, but the educational responsibilities of the university were often disregarded. Black athletes in particular found themselves lauded on the field and treated with disdain or patronised in the classroom.[48] Indeed, amateurism allowed college athletic programmes to abjure any duty towards their players. Amateurs had no employment rights, unlike professionals, and therefore universities had no legal responsibility to compensate players injured while playing sport.[49] Amateurism in US college sports carried with it all the hypocrisy of the British model while also providing a moral and legal rationale for one of the world's most lucrative entertainment industries to forbid its athletes to receive a penny for their efforts – an economic imperative that made it even harder to dislodge than its British progenitor.

5

WOMEN AND THE MASCULINE KINGDOM OF SPORT

> Women are deprived of their rights by the claim that their mental and physical faculties are inferior to those of men because nature designed women to be mother, wife and housekeeper. Thus, in all our laws and in all our institutions, women are considered as inferior to men, as being servants of men.
>
> Leo Frankel, 1871.[1]

At the height of rugby's war over amateurism in the 1890s, an investigating committee of the Rugby Football Union was offered evidence that a star player in Yorkshire had accepted money from a club in a flagrant violation of rugby's amateur regulations. It was the smoking gun that would demonstrate the justice of the RFU's belief that money had a corrupting influence on sport. But the witness was not allowed to testify. The reason was simple: she was a woman. As the chairman of the investigating committee, the Reverend Frank Marshall, stated, 'we have no dealings with women here'.[2]

This was one example of how the Victorians' amateur sporting ideals were underpinned by concerns about masculinity and its importance to capitalist society. As an ideology, amateurism sought to provide a complete philosophy of sport. Alongside a rejection of payments and an espousal of fair play, it also offered a definition of maleness that was squarely based on Muscular Christian ideals. A gentleman amateur – the phrase itself was something of a tautology – was physically courageous, strong-willed, prepared to give and take orders, and, above all, not feminine.[3] True sport could only be a masculine kingdom.

As with the imposition of amateur ideas about payments in sport, this nineteenth-century view of the essential maleness of sport contrasted somewhat with the reality of sport in the 1700s.[4] Although always seen as secondary to men, women were active participants in games until the early decades of the 1800s. Rural fairs regularly staged 'smock races' (running contests) for women, so-called because the prize would be a smock or dress.[5] Women's cricket matches were certainly not unknown in cricket's south-east heartland. In East Sussex during the summer of 1768 women of Harting played those of Rogate three times. In 1811 Hampshire women played those of Surrey, a game on which local aristocrats had staked 500 guineas.[6] As early as 1726 a six-a-side version of football was played by two teams of women on the Bowling Green at Bath. The archery revival of the late eighteenth century also saw a number of upper-class women taking an active part in the sport. As late as 1829 women took part in Stamford's annual bull run.[7]

Perhaps surprisingly to those who view sport through the lens of Victorian morality, women were also involved in combat sports. In 1723 the *London Journal* reported that boxing matches between women were becoming a weekly occurrence.[8] The extraordinary Mary Anne Talbot, who disguised herself as a male sailor and served in both the British and French navies during the 1790s, is reputed to have boxed and defeated male opponents.[9] Adrian Harvey has found at least eighteen female boxing contests that took place during the time of the Napoleonic wars.[10] Many of these fights were organised as part of the commercial entertainment available in London, but they were not staged simply for their novelty value. Women were clearly serious participants in combat sports. In the north-east of England, the popularity of wrestling among both sexes was such that when the local rules were revised in 1793 they explicitly forbade women from competing. 'It would much hurt the sport were that they admitted into the ring', argued a correspondent to the *Sporting Magazine*.[11]

Such opinions were increasingly heard at this time. The campaign against women's sports was part of the general offensive that sought to impose a new morality on the working class. As with the campaigns against working-class 'licentiousness' and animal sports, evangelical Christians were at the forefront of the drive to exclude women from sport. Smock racing raised their ire because women competed in flimsy clothing or occasionally topless. It was, argued a campaigner who took out a court case against an organiser of such a race in 1810, 'the last of amusements for any man to recommend to the females of his household, if he at all regarded their morals'.[12] More fundamentally, the reformers were animated by the well-known connection between popular recreations and sexual promiscuity, especially that of women. Fairs, festivals and sports events were places were young people, and the not-so-young, met to have sex.[13] The evangelicals based their campaigns to end women's sporting activity on the Christian belief that women were the 'weaker sex'. This was not an assessment of their physical strength but of their character: women were morally weak and fickle, and therefore had to be controlled.

This belief dovetailed with the way in which the nature of the family was changing under industrial capitalism. In a rural economy of self-sufficient small-holders or artisans, the family functioned as a unit of direct economic production, each member playing a role in its agricultural or mechanical work. Although this was still a patriarchal environment, the nature of work allowed relatively large amounts of leisure time for both sexes. But the increasingly competitive nature of the agricultural economy meant that new habits and customs had to be learnt. And as workers and their families moved into the industrial cities, old working and lei-sure practices had to be abandoned. The family became an institution that per-formed socially necessary but unpaid labour that subsidised the capitalist factory system – and the burden of this work fell on the backs of working-class women.[14] The time formerly available for leisure was instead used by women to provide the family with subsistence services such as cooking, cleaning and child-rearing. The ideological underpinning of this regime was provided by intense moral pressures on women of all classes that focused on self-sacrifice, modesty and the primacy of their role as wife and mother. The physical enjoyment and the sense of independence that sport could offer women were now viewed as threats to the social order.

For working-class men, the transformation of Britain into an industrial economy imposed a ferocious time-work discipline that led to a change in the conception of what it meant to be a man. Competition, as Engels noted in *The Condition of the Working Class in England in 1844*:

> is the completest expression of the battle of all against all which rules in modern civil society. This battle, a battle for life, for existence, for every-thing, in case of need a battle for life and death, is fought not between the different classes of society only, but also between individual members of these classes. … The workers are in constant competition among themselves as the members of the bourgeoisie among themselves.[15]

To work ten, twelve and even fourteen hours a day required the industrial labourer to be strong, impervious to pain, able to obey orders and work as a cog in a machine (euphemistically known as 'team-working'), precisely the qualities that the emerging sporting world of the mid-nineteenth century promoted. The designation of the male as the 'bread-winner', in contrast to the diminution of female factory workers as working for 'pin-money', meant that competition between men for jobs necessi-tated aggression and 'hardness'. For a male factory worker to succumb to weakness, emotional sensitivity or a lack of willpower – all supposedly 'feminine' qualities – could lead to the loss of wages, dismissal from his job and the destitution of him and his family. The origin of the working-class 'hard man' in life and in sport can be found in the brutal necessities of everyday life in early industrial capitalism.[16]

In this new aggressively masculine world, femininity became an enemy. Of course, hostility towards women was not new. Yet the nineteenth century increasingly saw the English-speaking middle classes around the world become increasingly obsessively fearful of effeminacy. A 'crisis of masculinity' became a regular form of political and social concern, especially in times of military or imperial doubt. 'There is no place in the world for nations who have become enervated by the soft and easy life, or who have lost their fibre of vigorous hardness and masculinity,' wrote Teddy Roosevelt in 1900.[17]

Although accusations of effeminacy had been part of the general discourse of militarism since the mid-eighteenth century, it became a central feature of British political discussion during the French revolutionary wars. In 1805 William Cobbett had linked the progress of the war with Napoleon with warnings about the dangers of outlawing boxing:

> Commerce, Opulence, Luxury, Effeminacy, Cowardice, Slavery; these are the stages of national degradation. We are in the fourth … Of the symptoms of effeminacy none is so certain as a change from athletic and hardy sports, or exercises, to those requiring less bodily strength, and exposing the persons engaged in them to less bodily suffering; and when this change takes place, be assured that national cowardice is at no great distance.[18]

The French themselves came to embody effeminacy for the British, who more and more defined their masculinity in relation to France. 'What! Talk of danger to British boys! To the descendants of those men who were at Waterloo and Trafalgar?' wrote one correspondent to the Rugby School magazine *The New Rugbeian* in 1861 in defence of the violence of rugby football. The game's critics wanted to reduce it to the level of a 'pretty little skirmish in the Champs Elysees' rather than the 'gallant bayonet charge that won the field of Waterloo'.[19] More famously, Blackheath rugby club's F.M. Campbell told one of the meetings that led to the foundation of the Football Association in 1863 that if it banned hacking, it would 'do away with all the courage and pluck of the game, and I will be bound to bring over a lot of Frenchmen, who would beat you with a week's practice'. In the same vein, one of the founders of Wakefield Trinity rugby club told its inaugural meeting in 1872 that 'one Englishman [was] equal to five Frenchmen'.[20]

In the public and grammar schools, the training of the future leaders of the British Empire, whether at home or abroad, was based on an overtly anti-feminine masculinity. Amateurism was by definition masculine, militaristic and patriotic. Sport was essential to British military ascendancy, argued B.F. Robinson in 1896, and a superior substitute for the conscription that was common in European countries.[21] The goal of amateur sports like rugby, argued the headmaster of Loretto school in Edinburgh, H.H. Almond, was to produce 'a race of robust men, with active habits, brisk circulations, manly sympathies and exuberant spirits' who were ready to lead and to follow in defence of the Empire.[22] Charges of effeminacy were not only directed against the French. The British defined many of their colonial subjects, for example, Hindus, as being irredeemably effeminate.[23] By the mid-nineteenth century, this concern to root out all signs of femininity had been extended to adolescent sexuality, particularly in the public schools. The Muscular Christian motto *'Mens sana in corpore sana'* – 'A healthy mind in a healthy body' – referred to not the creation of intellectual minds in healthy bodies, but of morally pure minds, free of the temptations of adolescent sexuality.[24]

Tom Brown's Schooldays, as might be expected from such an overtly propagandistic book, strongly reflected this outlook. The book highlights how new pupils who did not 'fit in' with their schoolmates would sometimes get 'called Molly, or Jenny, or some derogatory feminine name'. In the second part of the book Tom and East are approached by 'one of the miserable little pretty white-handed curly-headed boys, petted and pampered by some of the big fellows, who wrote their verses for them, taught them to drink and use bad language, and did all they could to spoil them for everything in this world and the next'. Unprovoked, they trip him and kick him. In a footnote, Hughes explained that 'many boys will know why [this passage] is left in', implying that physical violence against boys suspected of being homosexual was justified.[25]

The book was published in the midst of a moral panic about masturbation and homosexuality among public schoolboys. In 1854 *The Lancet* published a series on 'spermatorrhea' by John Laws Milton, who recommended the use of strategically placed spiked rings to cure the problem of boys' sexual thoughts. This was the first of three series on the subject over the next four years. In 1857, the year *Tom Brown* was published, William Acton published *The Functions and Disorders of the Reproductive Organs*. Acton recommended lots of physical exercise to discourage the practice – or failing that, tying up the hands of a boy at night to stop it. The following year, Frederick W. Farrar's schoolboy novel *Eric, or, Little by Little* was published with the explicit aim of promoting 'inward purity and moral purpose' among boys. This campaign, which extended throughout the nineteenth century in varying degrees of intensity, was based on the same concerns that animated the drive to place sport at the heart of the school curriculum.[26]

Just as amateurism sought to define and consequently exclude those that sport's leaders felt to be socially undesirable, modern sport was also founded on a rigid differentiation between men and women, the masculine and the feminine, the sexually normative and the transgressive. The link between sport and opposition to transgressive sexual practices was highlighted by the activities of leading sporting figures of the time. Lord Kinnaird, president of the FA for thirty-three years, was a prominent supporter of the Pure Literature Society, the Central Vigilance Society for the Suppression of Immorality, and the National Vigilance Society (which in 1889 was behind the jailing of an English publisher for publishing 'obscene' works by Zola and Flaubert). In 1895, in response to the trial of Oscar Wilde, Kinnaird called for 'something further in the way of repression'.[27] Edward Lyttleton, captain of the Cambridge University cricket team and a first-class batsman with Middlesex, published pamphlets and letters campaigning against the alleged moral, mental and medical dangers of masturbation. And of course it was the Marquess of Queensberry, one of the founders of the Amateur Athletic Association, race-horse owner and the man after whom the laws of modern boxing are named, who was fatefully sued by Wilde in 1895 for calling him in 'Somdomite [sic]'.[28]

Sport was therefore not merely a pastime for men, it was by its very definition masculine. Games were used to define who was and who was not a true, hetero-sexual, man. It was part of the socialisation of boys into men, a central feature of the process of 'making men'. It separated them from girls and femininity. And, as with amateurism, sport also offered its leaders and rule-makers the opportunity to differentiate between the included and the excluded in the realm of gender, a grotesque power that would not be fully exercised until the advent of 'sex-testing' in the 1960s. Thus when middle-class women began to be involved in sport in the latter decades of the nineteenth century, they were met with pathological resistance from sport's male rulers. Women's bodies were unsuited for physical exercise. Stenuous exertion would damage their reproductive organs. Clothing used for sport was immoral. Mixed sports would lead to sexual temptation. Cycling would make women unable to bear children. Competitive sport would make them masculine.[29] Woman, declared Pierre de Coubertin, 'is above all the companion of man, the future mother of a family, and she should be brought up with this fixed destiny in mind'.[30]

Despite this inherent structural bias against women taking part in sport, a significant rise in female sporting activity took place in the latter decades of the nineteenth century. This was part of the widening of middle-class women's social, political and economic rights across Europe and the English-speaking world. In Britain, divorce laws were liberalised in 1878 and three Married Women's Property Acts were passed by parliament between 1872 and 1893 giving married women the right to control their own finances and property. A year after the final act, female property owners were allowed to vote in local elections.[31] In France, the 1804 version of the Napoleonic Code, which had enshrined women as second-class citizens, was slowly being reformed. Divorce was legalised in 1884. Two years later women were allowed to open bank accounts regardless of the consent of their husbands. In 1893 single and separated women were granted full legal rights.[32] By the early years of the twentieth century, both Britain and the United States had significant women's suffrage movements, while in France the struggle for women's rights had strong historic links with the socialist and working-class movement.

The gateway to female sporting involvement was opened by the growth of educational institutions for girls and young women during this period. In Britain, girls' grammar schools had been founded in numerous towns in the two decades following the 1869 Endowed Schools Act.[33] Based on the educational principles of boys' public schools, many of these promoted sports such as hockey and lacrosse, and, in particular, the Swedish system of gymnastics developed by Per Henrik Ling. In the USA, exclusive women's colleges such as Vassar (founded 1861) and Wellesley (1874) also incorporated physical exercise and games into the curriculum.[34] A major impetus to women's physical education was provided by concerns across Europe and North America about the so-called 'crisis of masculinity' in those imperialist nations engaged in the 'scramble for Africa' and other foreign conquests in the Pacific. Much of this was expressed as a renewed fear of effeminacy among the male population. Basil Ransom, a character in Henry James's *The Bostonians* (1886) voiced some of these concerns when he denounced the 'damnable feminisation' of society, declaring that 'the whole generation is womanised; the masculine tone is passing out of the world; it's a feminine, a nervous, hysterical, chattering, canting age'.[35] But the corollary of 'national fitness' for men was a renewed stress on the importance of motherhood and the health of the domestic female population to bear and raise children who would grow up to defend the nation.

In Britain, the leader of the women's physical education movement was Martina Bergman-Österberg. Trained at Stockholm's Royal Gymnastic Institute,

Bergman-Österberg moved to Britain in 1881 to become the superintendent of physical exercises for London girls' and infants' schools, which had been made compulsory by the London School Board in 1876. Arguably the single most influential figure in the history of women's physical education, she introduced Swedish gymnastics into London schools before founding her own private Physical Training College for women at Hampstead, based on on the model of the Royal Gymnastic Institute. Eventually, the college was moved to Dartford, by which time she had both trained an entire generation of women gymnastics teachers and gone a considerable way to establishing her own cult of personality, which eventually led to her forming her own teachers' association eponymously called the Bergman-Österberg Union in 1900.[36] In France, a similar movement arose slightly later, leading to the formation of the Union Française de Gymnastique Féminine in 1912.[37]

As with male sports, middle-class sociability played a major role in the expansion of adult women's sport. Golf and tennis in particular, along with badminton and croquet, became increasingly central to the suburban social and recreational networks of the middle classes, both male and female.[38] Their popularity owed much to the fact that these were individual rather than team sports, which meant that one could pick and choose one's team-mates and opponents without the potential for unwelcome social mixing that team-based league competitions threatened – a key reason why league tournaments have almost entirely been based on team sports. Indeed, tennis, table tennis and badminton had essentially developed in the homes and gardens of the English upper middle classes in the mid-nineteenth century as a form of social recreation.[39] The structure of the club itself was also formidable barrier to indiscriminate social mixing, due to both the cost of membership and, often, the not-so-covert anti-semitism and racism of the British suburban and the American country club.

The first tennis club was formed at Royal Leamington Spa in 1872 and by 1900 there were about 300 clubs affiliated to the Lawn Tennis Association. Golf clubs, the majority of which did not allow women to become full members (or even members at all in some cases) underwent an even greater surge of popularity. This burgeoning popularity laid the basis for the development of elite women's sport. In 1893 the Ladies' Golf Union was founded and the first Ladies' British Amateur Championship won by Lady Margaret Scott, her title indicating the social rank of the leading women golfers.[40] Two years later, the first US Women's Amateur golf championship was won by Mrs Charles S. Brown, known to the rest of the world as Lucy Barnes Brown, the use of her husband's name demonstrating that sporting prowess did not equal emancipation. In 1884 women's tennis was added to the Wimbledon championships, in 1887 to the US Open and ten years after that to the Championnat de France in Paris.[41]

The most prominent champion of this formative era was Lottie Dod, who first won Wimbledon in 1887 at the age of fifteen and went on to triumph in the tournament on another four occasions. The daughter of a cotton magnate whose wealth was so enormous neither she nor her siblings ever had to work, Dod was the very embodiment of the late nineteenth-century middle-class sportswoman, winning the 1904 Ladies golf title, playing international hockey for England, and picking up the silver medal for archery at the 1908 Olympics.[42] But although Dod's achievements would not have been possible without the social and sporting advances made by women at the end of the nineteenth century, she herself was less a women's pioneer than a rather exceptional example of the broadening of sporting opportunities now available to the leisured rich of both sexes.

Indeed, the innovations of Bergman-Österberg and similar reformers were directed at middle-class women and rarely touched the lives of those of the working class. Some wanted nothing to do with working-class women. For example, the All England Women's Hockey Association was founded in 1895 by women graduates of Oxford and Cambridge universities, who proved no less discriminatory than their male counterparts. In one example recounted in 1907 the daughter of a local businessman found herself rejected by a club because its members didn't want to play with someone whose father was 'in trade'.[43] Three years later an article in the *Hockey Field* suggested that working-class girls should play rounders instead of encroaching on hockey. The article demonstrated that women who sought to exclude the working class from their sports were not above using the arguments of those who used pseudo-medical arguments to oppose women's involvement in sport:

> Is not hockey too violent an exercise and too prolonged a strain for those who often spend much of their time in heavy manual work? ... For girls who do this kind of thing daily ... are not violent games unnecessary, and likely to take them 'beyond the health limit of fatigue'?[44]

Nevertheless, this did not deter some working-class women from forming their own hockey clubs and a number of local leagues were set up across industrial towns in the north of England before 1914. Northern industrial towns, especially the cotton towns of Lancashire where women were employed in mills in their thousands, became the centres of working-class women's sports, often based on the recreational facilities provided by paternalist employers. As well as hockey and cricket sides, from around 1916 football teams were formed by women factory workers, although women's soccer suffered an almost mortal blow in 1921 when the Football Association banned women from playing on its affiliated pitches.[45] As if to emphasise the conditional relationship between sport and working-class women, many of these factories stopped women from working once they were married, thus also ending their involvement with organised sport.

Despite her time working with working-class schools in London, Bergman-Österberg came to feel that little could be done with pupils suffering from bad health and poor social conditions, although Swedish gymnastics continued to be taught in London schools after she moved on. She subsequently turned her back on the poor, setting the fees at her colleges sufficiently high to attract only affluent students. Indeed, her underlying philosophy was profoundly conservative: 'I try to train my girls to help raise their own sex, and so to accelerate the progress of the race; for unless the women are strong, healthy, pure and true, how can the race progress?' Echoing the ideologues of masculinity, she argued that gymnastics was 'the best training for motherhood' and a 'vital factor in making manly men and womanly women'.[46]

Bergman-Österberg accepted the social division of the sexes imposed by society and glorified the role of wife and mother. Even leaving aside the eugenicist undertones about improving the race that inflected her statements, her view was that healthy bodies meant healthy mothers. She differed from opponents of women's sport such as Coubertin only in how this goal was to be reached. Few but the most hidebound misogynist could find much to disagree with her about. Even the mouthpiece of the Vatican, *l'Osservatore Romano*, would come to agree: 'it is absurd to think that sport might damage athletes' role as mothers' it wrote in 1934.[47] It has been argued that it is misleading to judge the founders of women's physical education by such ideological standards – yet they themselves were keen to emphasise precisely this aspect of their work. Gymnastics, stressed Bergman-Österberg, 'develop body, mind and morals simultaneously'.[48] The underlying principles of the gymnastics movement did not fundamentally challenge the underlying ideology that legitimised women's subordination to men.

These conservative attitudes put Bergman-Österberg and her followers at odds with other supporters of women's rights at this time. Women in the socialist movement, for example, Eleanor Marx and Dora Montefiore in England, or more influentially, Clara Zetkin and Rosa Luxemburg in Germany, were involved in debates that questioned marriage, the family and the entire basis of women's oppression under capitalism. Leo Frankel, a collaborator of Marx in the First International and a leader of the Paris Commune, argued in 1871 that:

> women are deprived of their rights by the claim that their mental and physical faculties are inferior to those of men because nature designed women to be mother, wife and housekeeper. Thus, in all our laws and in all our institutions, women are considered as inferior to men, as being servants of men.[49]

Moreover, the phenomenon of the 'New Woman' that emerged in the 1890s directly challenged society's restrictions on women's lives in ways that the women's gymnastic movement shied away from. Numerous novels and plays were written that challenged the very idea that a woman's duty was to be a wife and mother. The most famous example was probably Ibsen's *A Doll's House*, the title of which reflected Ibsen's view of marriage for women and ended with its protagonist, Nora Helmer, leaving her husband and children. In Britain, Stanley Houghton's 1910 play *Hindle Wakes* portrayed a young working-class woman having and ending an affair with the son of a factory owner, turning upside down the traditional view of 'master–servant' sexual relations. Many of those who identified with ideas about the New Woman were also involved in sport and physical activity, yet the leadership of women's sport and physical culture remained wedded to conservative notions about gender and sexuality.[50]

The most visible sign of the New Woman was the bicycle craze of the 1890s.[51] In the 1880s technological improvements to bicycles – the development of the chain-driven rear wheel and Dunlop's invention of the pneumatic tyre – made them easier to use and to manufacture. The resulting boom in popularity stretched across America and France and soon spread to Britain. Hundreds of thousands of new cyclists took up the hobby. By 1896 the British magazine *Cycling* was selling 41,000 copies a week, just one of numerous journals devoted to the pastime, and three years later the membership of the Cyclists' Touring Club topped 60,000.[52] Thanks to the relative cheapness of bicycles, it was a phenomenon that was particularly strong among the lower middle and upper working classes. For young women who could afford a cycle, it transformed their lives, offering physical exercise, the ability to travel alone and an unprecedented sense of independence. This was 'the new woman rampant'.[53]

Of course, cycling met with considerable resistance from the opponents of women's rights. The fact that many women cyclists wore trousers (most famously in the style of the 'bloomers' named after the American feminist Amelia Bloomer who popularised them) rather than skirts was felt to be a threat to female modesty. The ability of women to cycle alone or in mixed company was seen, once again, as a threat to morality. This resulted in the formation in the Chaperone Cyclists' Association, whose members would accompany women cyclists to ensure nothing improper occurred, thus guaranteeing sexual propriety at a rate of three shillings and sixpence an hour.[54] The very act of cycling itself was seen as threat to female health. In France a debate broke out among doctors about whether women cyclists could inadvertently masturbate themselves while cycling. Such a thing could not occur accidentally, decided one medical thinker, but suggested that a woman could intentionally do so for the purposes of illicit pleasure.[55] Despite, or one hopes because of, the risk of accidental orgasm, cycling became as popular with French women as it was with women in Britain and America. In the mid-1890s women's professional cycling emerged in Paris and one woman completed the Tour de France in 1908. However, its popularity was not sufficient to stay the hand of the Union Vélocipédique de France, which barred women from competition in 1912.

It was a scenario with which women athletes would be familiar for decades. Bans, restrictions and moral constraints constituted the regime under which they would play and compete. The essential maleness of sport did not diminish. The underlying masculine ideology of sport established in the mid-nineteenth century would not be fundamentally threatened by either female sporting success or the measures of formal equality introduced in the late twentieth century. Women athletes could not escape continuous pressure to prove their femininity, while sport continued to be one of the most important ways in which young men sought to demonstrate their masculinity in the endlessly competitive world of capitalist work and play.

6

THE VICTORIAN SPORTING INDUSTRIAL REVOLUTION

> When people in sporting establishments buy their tickets they know exactly what is going to take place; and that is exactly what does take place once they are in their seats: viz. highly trained persons developing their peculiar powers in the way most suited to them, with the greatest sense of responsibility yet in such a way as to make one feel that they are doing it primarily for their own fun.
>
> Bertolt Brecht, 1926.[1]

In 1876 the FA Cup final between Wanderers and Old Etonians drew a crowd estimated at 3,500 to the Kennington Oval. A generation later, the 1901 FA Cup final between Tottenham Hotspur and Sheffield United attracted 114,815 to the Crystal Palace stadium. Not only was the crowd in 1901 greater by several orders of magnitude, it had arrived at the stadium thanks to a complex matrix of bus, tram and railway journeys specifically organised for the match. And once they had returned home, they could relive their memories through any one of dozens of newspaper reports. Even *The Times* overcame its sniffiness towards professional sport to the extent that an entire column was devoted to a description of the match. In 1876, not even a mention of the final penetrated the Thunderer's pages.

The same exponential growth in mass spectator sport could be seen across the Atlantic. In 1875 just 2,000 spectators had seen the first Harvard–Yale football match in New Haven, yet 40,000 saw 'The Game', as it became known by the press, in 1907. That same year, 35,000 people saw Yale defeat Princeton, 27,000 watched a match in Chicago and 18,000 gathered at Ann Arbor to see Penn inflict the first-ever home defeat on the Michigan Wolverines. Baseball, unashamedly professional and commercial in contrast to nominally amateur college football, had grown from one ill-organised semi-professional league in 1875 to two professional major leagues, underpinned by regional leagues operating across the United States.

In 1905, 91,723 spectators saw John McGraw's New York Giants defeat Connie Mack's Philadelphia Athletics in the first 'best of seven' baseball World Series.[2]

At the bottom of the globe, in the 'new Britannia' of Australia, a complete football world in miniature was being created in the city of Melbourne. Less than twenty-five years after its foundation in 1835, the city began to develop its own football code, derived from the rules of Rugby School football, that attracted thousands of spectators to matches by the 1870s. By the 1900s, 'Australian rules' football had become a commercial juggernaut across the city, the state of Victoria and also South and Western Australia. In 1908, 50,261 people – almost 10 per cent of the city's population – watched the two Melbourne suburbs of Carlton and Essendon fight out the grand final of the Victorian Football League.[3]

In the last three decades of the nineteenth century, sport in the English-speaking world underwent what can only be described as an industrial revolution. It was transformed from what was largely a recreational pastime, with a small commercial fringe of professional sportsmen and promoters, into a hugely popular, mass spectator entertainment industry that commanded the interest of millions. Football, baseball and cricket became the concerns not just of a single class or region but of whole populations and nations.

In France, similar changes were taking place in the nature of sport. In the 1860s France had become the world's leading manufacturer of bicycles and, from a single road-race from Paris to Rouen in 1869, cycling came to dominate French sports culture, its dominance symbolised by the success of the Tour de France, launched in 1903. Like football and baseball, cycling was now watched by hundreds of thousands and followed in the press by millions more. For its promoters and supporters, cycling was not merely a symbol of changes in French life, it was an active participant.[4]

By 1914, 'sports mania' gripped France and the entire English-speaking world. This sporting industrial revolution had an audience of millions, thousands of professional athletes, armies of journalists and an entire industry of sports promoters, sporting goods manufacturers and retailers.[5] And this massive economic expansion of commercial sport had also created a vibrant culture of fans, commentators and proselytisers. Even the meaning of the word sport had changed. Up to the 1870s, 'sport' was invariably used to describe field sports, such as hunting, shooting and fishing. But by 1900, its usage had expanded to encompass all competitive recreations, from the various codes of football, to bat and ball games, to athletics and everything in between. Like the practice itself, the very word had been revolutionised.

Football, of whatever code, baseball and professional cycling had rapidly become part of the late nineteenth-century leisure industries, alongside the music hall, seaside resorts and the emerging popular press. This was due to fundamental shifts in the society and economy of the advanced capitalist nations of Britain, America and France. In the eighteenth and early nineteenth century, commercial sport was confined largely to London and its south-eastern hinterland. The rest of Britain, let alone other parts of the world, had neither the population nor the wealth to support sport as anything more than an occasional or ritual pastime. But by the 1880s, all of these societies were becoming nationally unified, industrial capitalist societies with significant urban working classes that provided the market upon which the sporting industrial revolution was built.

The emergence of mass spectator sport was a development of the embryonic commercialism of the Georgian era and a reassertion of the idea that sport was above all a form of commercial entertainment. Many sociologists and critics today talk about the 'commoditisation' of contemporary sport, yet in reality sport had been a commodity and its practitioners wage-labourers at least since Jack Broughton opened his boxing arena in 1743 and charged the public to watch paid entertainers do battle in the ring.[6] Indeed, one of the common arguments heard against professionalism in soccer and rugby in the 1880s and 1890s was that it made 'football talent a marketable commodity'.[7] The artisan cricketers who were employed to bowl, bat and field for aristocratic teams in the eighteenth century were engaged in a selling of labour power that, in its fundamentals, was no different from that of factory operatives, albeit lacking the dull compulsion of work in the mine, mill or office. But until the 1870s commercial sport found it difficult to develop either a sustainable structure or a national mass market with sufficient surplus disposable income. The rise in real wages for the British working class in the last third of the nineteenth century and the dense urbanisation of the population made possible the creation of such a mass market with the spending power to support regular, continuous sporting events throughout a season. A similar phenomenon took place in the United States after the end of the Civil War. Both countries consequently saw the emergence of league systems for sport, particularly in soccer and baseball but also to a lesser extent in cricket and rugby, which could provide regular high-quality entertainment for an eager and expanding urban audience.

Unlike eighteenth-century sports, football, cricket and baseball in the late nineteenth century could now attract large crowds on a regular and continuous basis. Their regular cycles of matches contrasted with the occasional or one-off events of the earlier period, offering greater opportunities for money to be made from sport. A permanent market for sport was being created. This was a fundamental shift when compared to the commercial sport of the previous century.[8] This is best illustrated by contrasting the professional football clubs that emerged in the 1880s with the professional cricket sides that toured England in the 1850s and 1860s, based largely on the commercial model of Georgian sport. The professional cricket sides were itinerant, with no 'home' ground, and were permanently on tour. Many of the matches they played were against teams comprising more than eleven players (games against 'twenty-twos' of local towns were not unknown). Their economic model was that of the travelling fair, the circus or the touring entertainer. In contrast, the sports teams of the 1880s were symbols of locality, vehicles for civic pride, that placed huge importance of having a home ground of which other clubs would be envious.[9]

The competitive nature of sport enabled it to acquire broader meanings in the advanced industrial capitalist societies of the late nineteenth century. For the middle classes who proselytised for sport, the link between sport and capitalism was obvious, as Walter Camp, the father of American football, made clear:

> Finding a weak spot through which a play can be made, feeling out the line with experimental attempts, concealing the real strength till everything is ready for the big push, then letting drive where least expected, what is this – an outline of football or business tactics? Both of course.

Football, he argued, was 'the best school for instilling into the young man those attributes which business desires and demands'.[10]

Team games in particular became the vehicle for the creation of the modern sports industry because the collective identity of a team could be viewed and promoted as a representative of a locality and so a means of expressing civic pride. In Britain and the USA in the 1850s and 1860s, the formation of sports-based gentlemen's clubs by middle- and upper-class young men gave expression to local economic and municipal rivalries. In a period of mass urbanisation and unprecedented population growth, these clubs soon became seen as representatives of their city, town, suburb or even street.[11] Their games were taken up, either through proselytisation or emulation, by the urban working classes. Football and baseball provided not only entertainment and the opportunity to gamble but also a way for working-class communities to express a sense of belonging, or identity. As Warren Goldstein has noted, in baseball, as in football, there was always a 'home' team.[12]

As competition between clubs intensified through competitions such as soccer's FA Cup (which began in 1871) or baseball's National League (1876), so too did the need to acquire the best players to maintain or improve the status of the club, increasingly seen as a proxy for its locality. In order to attract the leading players, clubs needed to be commercially successful by attracting large crowds, which in turn necessitated the construction of stadia. Such was the extent of capital investment required to build a stadium that a club had to attract paying customers, which meant it had to have a winning team. And a successful side required the best players. This sporting circle of life emerged less than a generation after the first clubs had been established.[13]

Moreover, loyalty to team and locality dovetailed neatly with the business needs of clubs and their financial backers, such as breweries and newspapers, most of whom were at this stage locally based. In the language of capitalism, being a supporter of a local team was a unique form of 'brand loyalty' to a business. And businesses they were. Although it lacked baseball's overtly aggressive business culture, soccer was no less commercial. Limited liability companies were formed by clubs in the 1880s as a way of raising capital for the construction of stadia.[14] Even if club ownership did not necessarily bring profits it did offer other financial opportunities. As the widespread involvement of breweries in sport demonstrates, there was significant money to be made through the sale of refreshments at grounds. The local goodwill generated through financial support of a club could also be converted into business or political capital, a forerunner of modern sponsorship. And ownership or involvement in a local club placed the businessman at the centre of local commercial and social networks, where deals could be done and contacts made. The long-term intangible advantages of team ownership often appeared to outweigh the short-term disadvantages for the ambitious local businessman.[15]

For example, Manchester United owe their existence to one of Manchester's leading brewers. Plagued by financial problems in the 1890s, Newton Heath FC was forced into liquidation in 1902 and was bought for £500 by J.H. Davies, the chairman of Manchester Breweries. Renamed Manchester United, the club became an appendage of the brewery. Its seven-strong board consisted of Davies and six other company employees. The club not only owed its existence to Davies, but also its ground. In 1909 he provided £60,000 so the club could move from Clayton to Old Trafford. Davies' interest in the club was not altruistic. A Football Association enquiry in 1910 discovered that he received rent payments from the club for land it did not use. The centrality of the link between football and business was also illustrated across the city, when Manchester City's attempts to move from its Hyde Road ground were blocked by objections from Chester's Brewery, on the grounds that its financial support to the club would be wasted if the team moved from the brewer's traditional customer base.[16] In Europe, a similar point could be made about the car manufacturer Fiat's ownership of Juventus or electronics manufacturer Phillips' relationship with PSV Eindhoven.[17]

Moreover, clubs that began as local associations of workers, church-goers or neighbourhood residents soon found that to operate at even a semi-professional level meant functioning as a capitalist enterprise. Even a club that was ostensibly controlled by its membership ultimately became reliant on banks and local businesses for financial survival, most notably from those breweries that sought to advertise their products in a regional market. Far from being a 'people's game' – as is often claimed today – it was precisely soccer's ability to create a sustainable business structure that could exploit the new mass sports market of the late nineteenth century that led to it outstripping its rival sports in popularity.

This business imperative was often masked by the fact that sports clubs were rarely profitable. Many soccer and baseball entrepreneurs soon discovered the truth of the quip that the quickest way to make a small fortune was to start with a large fortune and invest in a sports team. The centrality of winning matches and tournaments invariably took precedence over profitability. At best, clubs sought to operate without making a loss; in economic terms they were utility-maximisers, not profit-maximisers.[18] There was great awareness of these problems by team owners. The dominant nineteenth-century leagues in baseball and soccer, the National League and the Football League respectively, both operated as cartels that sought to protect their members' interests and prevent the emergence of rivals that could threaten their market dominance. The National League fought a series of battles that vanquished potential rivals for its title of the major league until it was forced to recognise the major league status of the American League in 1902. The Football League effectively took over its major rival, the Southern League, in 1920.[19] Slightly more paternalistic than its American cousin, soccer's Football

League also sought to protect its members from themselves by restricting the amount of dividend payments that could be received by shareholders and forbidding salaries to be paid to club directors to discourage speculation and profiteering by club owners. In baseball, and later other professional American sports, owners were allowed to move their clubs to new regions if they believed that the grass was greener in a different ball park.[20]

This new model of commercial mass spectator sport could only establish itself because of the social and economic environment of the late Victorian age. In particular, three key elements had to be present for this sporting revolution to take place: an industrial working class, a unified national culture and a mass popular press. The absence of any of these would have severely restricted the growth of modern sport.

The exponential development of capitalism in the nineteenth century led to rapid population growth and, from the 1870s, a rising standard of living for the vast majority of the working population. By 1850, the majority of the British population lived in towns and cities. Fifty years later in 1901, the population of England and Wales had almost doubled from 17.9 million to 32.5 million. Real wages grew and working hours, in Britain especially, declined. The introduction of Saturday half-day working in 1874 not only increased the leisure time of the working class but also presented an afternoon window for the playing and watching of sport.[21]

In the US, the change was no less marked. The victory of the north in the Civil War in 1865 not only freed the black population from slavery but, in doing so, opened the door for America's transformation from a predominantly rural economy to an urban, industrial world capitalist power. Its population doubled from 40 million people on the eve of the Civil War to 80 million in 1900, by which time more of its population worked in industry than in agriculture.[22]

As the working class flooded into the cities, they brought with them a desire for entertainment.[23] In Britain, the newly urbanised proletariat brought with it the games of their rural roots, causing, as we saw in chapter 2, immense friction with the religious and moral reformers who sought to impose 'rational recreation' upon them. The immense waves of immigration into the cities of America brought with them some of the recreations of Europe, especially the Germans who took *Turner* gymnastics with them, but also a huge appetite for spectacle and excitement.[24] Sports like boxing, animal contests and foot-racing were commonplace in mid-nineteenth-century working-class communities on both sides of the Atlantic, but it was the rise in living standards of the final quarter of the century that created the mass market for commercial sport, as it did for all other forms of popular entertainment.[25]

By the 1880s, working-class players and spectators had come to dominate (numerically if not politically) many of those sports most valued by the middle classes: football, rugby, cricket and baseball. This was partially the result of evangelising by those who believed that these sports taught moral and social lessons. But it was not coincidental that it was team sport that became the most popular among the working classes. For those working in factories, mines and shipyards, collective action was the framework of their lives. Their labour was structured by it, their trades unions were based on it, and their communities relied on it. The football or baseball team and the collective struggle of its team members against a hostile world appeared to be a reflection of life as experienced by the working class. And in a hierarchical society that choked opportunity for all but the privileged and the statistically insignificant luckiest, sport offered a way for the athletically gifted to gain respect in their community and a potential route out of a life of manual labour.

The incredible popularity of sport in the late nineteenth century was therefore in large part due to the deep resonance that it found in the daily lives of the urban industrial working classes in Europe and the Americas. Walter Benjamin's description of the appeal of the cinema to the urban masses applied just as much to sport as it did the cinema:

> Our taverns and our metropolitan streets, our offices and furnished rooms, our railroad stations and our factories appeared to have us locked up hopelessly. Then came the film and burst this prison-world asunder by the dynamite of the tenth of a second, so that now, in the midst of its far-flung ruins and debris, we calmly and adventurously go traveling.[26]

The thrill and excitement of the sporting contest offered a weekly respite from the incessant drudgery of the factory or the office. The sports ground was an arena largely free from the restrictions of working life – as can be seen in the verbal and sometimes physical violence visited by the crowd on the authority figure of the referee or umpire. Not only did the sporting arena provide a sense of place – a community seemingly embodied in the local team – but in its mass spectator versions such as soccer, and rugby in certain regions, sport provided a sense of class identity. For the vast majority who watched it, especially in England and Scotland, soccer was part of the separate social sphere that the working class inhabited. Although still played by the middle and working classes, soccer was rarely played between the classes.[27] Professional players were almost always drawn from the working class. Soccer and baseball stadia were situated in the heart of working-class districts, the third element of the urban trinity of home, work and play. The profound social and cultural segregation of the classes was even more marked in rugby, where in England and Australia the sport had split into league and union versions precisely over the issue of class.[28]

Crucially, this world of mass spectator sport was one in which not only supporters and players came from the working class but also its heroes, leaders and team captains. Outside of the trade union and labour movement, working-class people were excluded from leadership positions in society. Sport therefore offered the potential for not only money and fame but also for validation and respect, free from the concerns of status or patronage. Professionalism itself, far from being the social stigma that it was among the middle classes, was a mark of esteem among the working class, a testimony to the skill and prestige of the individual player.[29] Most importantly, sport was a way in which working men could attempt to define themselves and influence the world around them, a possibility they were excluded from in their working lives. For the worker, as Marx argued, 'life for him begins where [work] activity ceases, at the table, at the tavern seat, in bed' and, we might add, at sporting contests.[30] Mass spectator sport offered a stage upon which the masses themselves could become players in the fullest sense of the word.

In France, neither industry nor population grew as rapidly as in the anglophone countries. Between 1801 and 1901 the population grew from just under 30 million to just over 40 million. Nor did urbanisation progress with the same rapidity – it was not until the 1960s that the majority of the French population lived in towns or cities. But its defeat by Prussia in 1870 and the shock of the revolutionary Commune the following year also led to fundamental changes in French society.[31] A drive towards national unity was undertaken, both in communications, through the rapid expansion of the railway and telegraph systems, and the creation of symbols of nationalism, most notably the Eiffel Tower in Paris. The growth of department and chain-stores across France spurred both consumerism and a sense of national unity. And in the main towns and cities, music hall and, from the 1890s, cinema brought commercial leisure to the urban masses. The director of the Folies Bergère, Clovis Clerc, was an early investor in cycling velodromes. Cycling itself was an integral part of the chain that linked industrial capitalism and nation-building.[32] Professional cyclists brought a symbolic unity to the Third Republic as they cycled their way through towns and villages from the Pyrénées to the Pas-de-Calais on the twin-wheeled product of mass consumer industrial capitalism. The organisers of the Tour de France believed, largely correctly, that the race would push forward what they saw as the modernisation of France and help to sell bicycles. To stretch Eugen Weber's memorable phrase, they believed that the bicycle would help turn 'peasants into Frenchmen'.[33]

The role of sport in nation-building could also be seen strongly elsewhere. In Italy, which had been politically but not culturally unified by the Risorgimento, the Giro d'Italia bicycle race replicated the commercial origins and national aims, if not the international prestige, of the Tour de France. 'Far conoscere l'Italia agli Italiani' (Make Italy known to Italians) was the slogan of the Italian Cycling Touring Club, the country's mass participation cycling association.[34] Across the Atlantic, victory over the Confederacy enabled the full unification of the United States, transforming its very name from a plural to a singular noun. Commercial entertainment such as vaudeville and burlesque, coupled with a mass popular press emerged to provide amusement for the working masses of the burgeoning cities. Sport was both a beneficiary and a proponent of this. Despite having teams in a mere eight cities in the east and mid-west of America, William Hulbert had no compunction about calling his new baseball organisation the National League when it was founded in 1876. Tours of the west coast by college football teams in the 1900s underlined the way in which railways, the telegraph and the press were shrinking the continent, and transformed college football from a sport of elite north-eastern colleges to a national game.[35] Britain had also started to become a much more centralised society from the 1870s and its culture increasingly became nationally based. National retail chain-stores, the consolidation of regional organi-sations, such as trade unions, into national bodies, and the growing dominance of national daily newspapers were all signs of the decline of regionalism in favour of singular national culture. Nowhere was this growth of a nation-wide culture more apparent than in the unprecedented rise of the FA Cup and Football League competitions.

In Japan, the Meiji Restoration of 1868 opened the way for the development of capitalism and consequently a modern national state.[36] The creation of a unified education system, a modern army and an industrial economy was accompanied by the importation of baseball and British sports such as rugby. In 1886 the ministry of education introduced elite 'Higher Schools' based on British public schools. Sport was necessarily a vital part of the curriculum. The British model appealed to the Japanese elite because of the apparent success of its constitutional monarchy and the values of the British middle-class masculinity – stoicism, honour, duty and self-sacrifice – infused Japanese concepts of *bushido* and *shitsujitsu gōken* (upright manliness).[37] Such was the importance of modern sport to Japan's new national culture that its traditional sports either faded into inconsequence or reinvented themselves. This was particularly the case with *sumo*, which developed many of its apparently traditional ritual aspects in the early twentieth century. The invention of tradition was yet one more aspect of sporting culture that the Japanese took from the British.[38]

One illustrative example of the importance of national identity to the growth of sport can be seen in the case of cricket in America. Before the Civil War, cricket could claim to be the pre-eminent American summer sport.[39] Based in the north-east, especially around New York and Philadelphia, it was popular largely among English expatriates and those whose families had emigrated from Britain to America.[40] The fact that North America was the destination of the first-ever touring English cricket side in 1859 testifies to its popularity.[41] But it was almost irredeemably middle class. In Philadelphia, three-quarters of cricketers came from the toniest districts of the city. The combination of anglophilia and class elitism did not lend itself to mass popularity in the burgeoning cities of the new world. Most importantly, America's accelerated nation-building in the second half of the century was based on the north's victory in the Civil War. The British government, although formally neutral in the conflict, had a pronounced tilt towards the Confederacy, and the cultural similarities between the highly mannered society of the southern slave-owners and the British upper-classes was acknowledged on all sides. Cricket was thus far too 'southern' for a nation being constructed on the basis of northern industrial capitalism.[42]

Such factors were articulated and promoted in the burgeoning mass circulation press. Indeed, it was print capitalism that provided the electrical charge that was to animate the culture of mass spectator sport. The coming of mass literacy to the English-speaking world and much of Europe in the final third of the nineteenth century created a market for mass circulation newspapers.[43] As many historians have pointed out, sport provided continuous news to feed the demands of journalists and their employers. Drama, speculation, controversy, tragedy, triumph, heroes and villains, the life-blood of the mass market press, was provided continuously by sport. Sport needed the newspapers for publicity and the newspapers needed sport for content. But the relationship went much deeper. In many practical ways, modern sport was a child of the newspaper industry.

In Britain, the importance of newspapers to the advertising and organisation of sport had been established in the eighteenth century. By the end of the Napoleonic wars, not only did daily newspapers regularly carry sporting reports and announcements but weekly and monthly sporting journals had been established.[44] In 1822 perhaps the best known of these was first published, *Bell's Life in London*. Although it was originally a weekly aimed at the London working class that featured crime, scandal and other sensationalist stories, sport came to dominate its pages. By the 1850s it was acting as an arbitrator in disputes between clubs and athletes, turning from a commentator into a participant in the evolving sporting world. Alongside its rival *The Field* (founded in 1853), it played a crucial role in elaborating and publicising the early debates about the codification of the various rules of football. Both weeklies were primarily concerned with horse racing (and the more aristocratic field sports in the case of *The Field*), which led to their eclipse in the 1880s as a plethora of weekly sports newspapers were launched to support the surge in popularity of mass spectator sport. Again, these journals were not merely commentators but active participants in the governance of sport.[45] The most high-profile editor involved in this symbiotic relationship was John Bentley, of the leading football weekly *Athletic News* while also being a committee member, and later president, of the Football League. Alongside the weeklies, national and especially local daily newspapers devoted increasing amounts of space to sport. By the 1900s, the daily newspaper of almost every large town in Britain published a Saturday night sports edition containing all the scores from the day's matches. Many regional reporters also held considerable influence within local sport. The *Yorkshire Post*'s A.W. Pullin, known by his pen-name of 'Old Ebor', attended meetings of the Yorkshire Rugby Union executive committee and sat on the board of directors of Leeds City, the forerunner of Leeds United.[46] In Ireland, the relationship between the Gaelic Athletic Association and the press was even more pronounced. Three of its founding members were journalists, including Michael Cusack, its first secretary and driving force.[47]

Precisely the same points could be made about the relationship between American sport and the news media. The *National Police Gazette* (founded in 1845) and the *New York Clipper* (1853) were both established with a similar but more salacious agenda to *Bell's Life*. Both became important not only to publicising sport but also to its organisation. In the 1850s the *Clipper* served as the clearing house for prize-fighters looking for a match or to challenge others. The *Clipper*'s most famous writer was Henry Chadwick, younger brother of the British Victorian social reformer Edwin Chadwick, who both reported on and shaped the early decades of baseball. Chadwick served on various baseball committees and also published the first annual guide for baseball in 1861, a role mirrored across the Atlantic by Charles Alcock, who also served on the FA executive while publishing his *Football Annual* from 1867. The sports writer's dual role of reporter/participant in baseball was reflected in the fact that local journalists also served as official club scorers, a potential conflict of interest that lasted until the 1980 decision of Major League Baseball to appoint independent scorers. As in Britain, the 1880s saw a wave of sporting weeklies established, most notably the *Sporting News* in 1886 which quickly became the baseball journal of record.[48] As Michael Oriard has meticulously recorded, the huge popularity of college football was encouraged and shaped by the extensive coverage by the major daily newspapers in the 1890s. By the turn of the century most of the major US dailies had introduced sports sections and added full-time sports writers to their payrolls. Sport dovetailed perfectly with the sensationalism and yellow journalism of publishers such as the Hearst press in the US at this time.[49]

But in Japan and France the press played an even more direct role in the establishment of mass spectator sport. In Japan the first national college baseball tournament was organised in 1915 by the *Asahi Shinbun*, the country's leading daily. Baseball had taken root in the college system and the newspaper was merely doing on a national basis what regional newspapers had been doing at a local level. Such was the success of the competition that in 1924 the *Mainichi Shinbun* set up a rival out-of-season tournament. More dramatically, the birth of professional baseball in Japan in 1934 was entirely due to the commercial imperatives of the *Yomiuri Shinbun*, Tokyo's right-wing daily, which in 1931 sponsored a US All Stars team visit to Japan. A similar visit was organised in 1934, this time starring Babe Ruth, and the newspaper formed its own professional side to face the mighty Americans.[50] In 1936 the Japanese Baseball League was founded, comprising seven sides, four of which were owned by newspaper companies. The remaining three were formed by railway companies, inadvertently demonstrating the tight link between modern sport, the media and the communications industry.[51]

This was even more pronounced in France in the creation of commercial sport, especially the Tour de France. Indeed, the development of professional cycling owed its entire existence to the alliance between French newspaper industry and cycle manufacturers. In 1869 the first-ever cycle road-race, between Paris and Rouen, was organised by *Le Vélocipède Illustré* which, as the name suggests, was an illustrated fortnightly dedicated to the promotion of cycling. The popularity of cycling waned in France after the Franco-Prussian war but, as in Britain and America, the invention of pneumatic tyres and the chain-based 'safety bicycle' reignited the boom in the 1890s.[52] The daily *Le Petit Journal* (founded in 1863) organised the Paris–Brest–Paris cycle race in 1891, the first-ever motor car race, from Paris to Rouen (1894) and the Paris–Belfort long-distance running race (1892) and the first Paris marathon (1896).[53]

The Paris marathon had been organised in conjunction with the sports weekly *Le Vélo* (founded 1892), which was selling 80,000 copies a week by the mid-1890s. In 1896 it organised the Paris–Roubaix cycle race in conjunction with the sporting entrepreneur Theodore Vienne. These successful events provided the model for the Tour de France but the catalyst was the Dreyfus Affair, an anti-Semitic witch-hunt against Alfred Dreyfus, a Jewish captain in the French army, who was falsely accused of passing secrets to Germany. Pierre Giffard, the editor of *Le Vélo* and formerly of *Le Petit Journal* supported Dreyfus. In 1899 he reported the arrest of the militantly anti-Dreyfus car manufacturer Comte Jules-Albert de Dion for an anti-Dreyfus attack on the president of France at the Auteuil race course.[54] Furious, Dion withdrew his support for *Le Vélo* and joined with the cycle and motor manufacturer Adolphe Clément and tyre magnate Édouard Michelin to found a rival weekly, *L'Auto-Vélo*, which became known simply as *L'Auto* (the forerunner of today's *L'Équipe*). In 1903, faced with mounting debts and declining sales, *L'Auto* started its own cycle race, the Tour de France.

Thus the press played a central role in the development of mass spectator sport in the nineteenth and early twentieth centuries. It not only provided publicity for and voiced the ideological aspects of sport, but the newspaper industry also initiated and organised the development of competitions and other structures. Print capitalism did not merely articulate an 'imaginary community', to use the phrase of Benedict Anderson[55], it created a real 'community' of sporting events, tournaments and markets, a framework that connected the industry and its products to the masses. It was the artery through which flowed the life-blood of the industrial revolution of modern sport.

7

SPORT AND THE AGE OF EMPIRE

The splendid empires which England has founded in every quarter of the globe have had their origin largely in the football contests at Eton, the boat-races on the Thames, and the cricket-matches on her downs and heaths.

William Mathews, 1876.[1]

On 16 June 1894, seventy-eight assorted noblemen, businessmen, journalists and educationalists gathered in Paris. Together, they represented the majority of the major imperial powers of the world: Britain, France, Belgium, Russia and the USA. Conspicuous by their absence were representatives of Germany, who had not been invited.[2] The meeting was typical of the diplomatic gatherings of the period. In November 1884 the major European powers had met in conference in Berlin to divide Africa among themselves. In 1899 they would meet again in the Hague to agree on 'civilised' behaviour in war and set up an international court of arbitration. In Algeciras in 1906 the imperial nations were to assemble to settle France and Germany's claims to control Morocco.

The Paris delegates assembled in the same spirit but with a different goal: to establish an international sporting body, the International Olympic Committee (IOC), that would organise a revived Olympic Games tournament in 1896. Led by French nobleman Pierre de Coubertin, it sought to promote international harmony through sport. Coubertin's vision of peace was not merely fashionable. It was also an echo of his nation's geopolitical position between 'Albion perfide' across the Channel and an ambitious Germany on its eastern flank. The call for peace was a call to uphold the status quo and ensure France's position in world politics.[3]

The IOC would prove to be no more successful in bringing peace to the world than the Hague Conference. Yet, like all sports in the age of imperialism, the Olympics became both a beneficiary of and an aid to the expansion of imperialism across the globe. The period from 1870 to the outbreak of the First World War in

1914 saw the partition of the world by the major European imperialist powers, the USA and Japan. It was the age of the 'Scramble for Africa', the division of Asia and the economic penetration of Latin America. And it was also the period in which sport as we know it today developed and expanded around the world.[4]

The connection between sport and imperialism was fully appreciated by contemporary commentators. It was a vital element of the culture that held the British Empire together. 'Strong is the bond of nationality, strong are the ties of commerce, but stronger than either is the "union of hearts" which comes from devotion to the same forms of recreation,' explained the St James's Gazette.[5] Rudyard Kipling, the poet laureate of high imperialism, underlined the link when he popularised the phrase that symbolised the competition between Britain and Tsarist Russia for dominance in Central Asia: 'the Great Game'.[6]

This explains why British sports spread beyond the narrow confines of a small group of islands off the north-east coast of Europe to dominate the world. There were no intrinsic reasons why this particular set of sports should be played outside of their original geography. Other European sports, such as Spain's pelota, France's savate or Germany's Turner gymnastics also possessed advantages comparable to British sports, yet did not experience the same global expansion in the last three or four decades of the nineteenth century. Partly this was due to the sheer strength of the British Empire. The Spanish Empire was moribund by the time that organised sports appeared and, despite its global imperial possessions, French capitalism did not develop a mass, commercial sporting industry until the very end of the nineteenth century, much later than Britain.[7] Although German colonists carried their enthusiasm for gymnastics with them, the German Empire itself never amounted to much more than scraps discarded from the high table of European imperialism.[8] The sporting legacy of Japanese imperialism was the establishment of baseball in Taiwan and South Korea.[9]

Only American imperial might was strong enough to deposit sport in its wake, partly thanks to the sporting evangelism of the 'muscular protestants' of the Young Men's Christian Association (YMCA), which itself had been founded in Britain in 1844.[10] Even so, baseball's popularity as a mass spectator sport was confined to the USA's immediate spheres of influence; parts of the Caribbean and Central America, the Philippines and Japan.[11] There was more success for the sports invented directly by the YMCA in the 1890s, basketball and volleyball. These were taken around the world by the YMCA and the US military and became favourites of physical educators, as well as those uncomfortable with commercialised sport, often the same people. In the Philippines the YMCA essentially acted as an arm of the government, with one of its members serving as the national director of education. In 1911 it established the Philippines Amateur Athletic Federation and in 1913 it was responsible for organising the first Far Eastern Games in Manila.[12] Both basketball and volleyball made their way to Europe thanks to the US Army's presence following the First World War and its attempts to use American sports to promote trans-atlantic understanding and social harmony – an impact that received a renewed boost from the US forces in Europe after 1945.[13]

But British sport had two distinct advantages over its rivals. First, as we have seen, the British viewed games as being more than amusement. The interlocking of sport with British nationalism and its subsequent development into the philosophy of amateurism made it an important ideological and moral justification for the empire. Second, the domestic emergence of codified sports coincided with Britain's rise from the mid-eighteenth century to become the world's dominant maritime and imperial power. It was not by chance that the rise of sport was co-terminous with the rise of empire. It was part of the same process. In Georgian England, the wealth generated by imperial trade was one of the major sources of the money that went into sporting wagers and stake money. The fact that many major sporting prizes or bets were measured in guineas – coins originally minted with gold supplied by the slave traders of the Royal African Company and named after the West African region they plundered – underlined the close link between sport and imperial trade, as well as the bloody provenance of much of the wealth of the British aristocracy.

If trade followed the flag, as the supporters of imperialism maintained, a man with a ball was not far behind. The first record of cricket being played in India is by sailors working for the East India Company, who organised an impromptu match in 1721 at Khambat in Gujarat. The first match was played in Australia in 1804, just sixteen years after the establishment of a British colony there. Two years later, in Barbados, the St Anne's Cricket Club had been formed. In 1808 two teams of British Army officers played each other in South Africa. 'Where a score or so of our sons are found,' observed Anthony Trollope in 1868, 'there is found cricket.'[14] As with early horse race meetings in the colonies, these early cricket clubs became part of the social networks of the white colonial administrators and settlers, a source both of recreation and reassurance of their fundamental Britishness, a home away from home to be enjoyed alongside their imported British food, London fashions and ship-delivered copies of *The Times*. This also stimulated the first sporting tours between the metropolitan 'Mother Country' – a term still used in Australia and New Zealand at least until the 1950s – and the colonies of the empire. The first cricket tour from England took place in 1859 when a team of professionals belonging to the All-England and United All-England sides visited Canada and the USA. Two years later, a similar side made the first tour to Australia.[15]

But it was the growth of imperialist rivalries in the second half of the nineteenth century that stimulated the creation of an imperial sporting culture and network. Cricket tours to and from England, Australia, India, South Africa and the West Indies were well established by 1890. In 1888 the first rugby tour to Australia and New Zealand took place, followed in 1891 by a visit to South Africa. Many of these early tours were 'unofficial' tours, organised outside of the control of the sports' governing bodies, and conducted on an entirely commercial basis. But the imperial value of such tours was quickly recognised, to say nothing of their financial success, and so they were taken firmly under official control to establish an imperial sporting structure that included cricket, rugby, rowing and athletics.

By the end of the nineteenth century, a cycle of reciprocal sporting tours between the major colonies was part of the daily cultural life of the empire. J.C. Davis, one of Sydney's leading sports journalists in the early 1900s, summed up their importance. They have, he wrote in 1904, created 'an extended feeling of appreciation and racial sympathy. They have incidentally shown to the muscular Britisher at home that the Britisher abroad and his sinewy colonial descendants are not aliens because thousands of miles of sea intervene.'[16] The RFU's senior administrator, Rowland Hill, felt likewise. Imperial tours, he explained, were 'of great Imperial importance in binding together the Mother Country with the Overseas Dominions'.[17]

The success of these tours also highlighted the strength of sport among the colonial settlers. English visitors found themselves playing against opponents as skilled and just as committed as they. Much of the credit for this can be ascribed to the influence of Arnoldian educators who, alongside their Greek and Latin grammar primers, usually carried with them a cricket bat and ball, and from the 1860s, more often than not, an oval shaped football. They populated the empire with schools and colleges founded on the principles of Rugby School and elaborated in *Tom Brown's Schooldays*, as popular and as influential in the rest of the English-speaking world as it was in Britain. It would not be an exaggeration to claim that every school founded by British educators overseas owed most, if not all, of its educational philosophy to Arnold.[18] So, as in Britain, sport became an essential part of the imperial educational system. Schools like Melbourne Grammar (founded 1858), Cape Town's Diocesan College (1849) and New Zealand's Nelson College (1856) were central to the development of the football codes in their respective countries, thanks to headmasters who placed sport at the core of the curriculum.

The centrality of sport to mid-Victorian imperial education was not merely because it kept boys healthy (as we saw previously, girls were not considered worthwhile subjects by the Muscular Christians) but mainly because of its ideological value. The amateur code of the gentleman, with its belief in social segregation, masculinity and British nationalism, helped not only to cement relations between the centre and peripheries of the empire but also to forge a sense of pan-Britannic identity or membership of a 'Greater Britain'.[19] The importance of amateur ideology to the spread of sport in the colonies can be gauged by the fact that it was only after the full flowering of amateurism in the late 1850s and early 1860s that sport emerges in the British colonies as a crucial component of imperial culture.

To many of Britain's rivals, amateurism also seemed to explain the reasons for her global dominance and offer an educational philosophy that could raise them to similar if not greater heights. For Americans, it appeared to confirm the necessity of Social Darwinism. 'The splendid empires which England has founded in every quarter of the globe have had their origin largely in the football contests at Eton, the boat-races on the Thames, and the cricket-matches on her downs and heaths,' Chicago professor William Mathews told young American males in his guide to *Getting On in the World* (1873).[20] For French anglophiles like Coubertin, it offered not only elitism and hierarchy at home but also a way to enhance France's international standing by promoting sport as a peacemaker. And for the Japanese, hurtling towards capitalist modernisation following the Meiji Restoration of 1868, the games played by the British and American expatriate communities soon became seen as a means to educate its future elite in how to emulate the anglophone empires. Japan's exclusive educational institutions took up both baseball and rugby union – 'this game,' explained a Japanese diplomat, 'seems to singularly reflect the true spirit of the British people. Its encouragement, therefore, in my country will help to bring about a better understanding of that spirit by the Japanese people' – as if in homage to its imperial rivals.[21]

Education was also the artery through which sport was transmitted to the colonial peoples subjugated by the British Empire – or at least to the local elites, the only sections of non-white society that the British thought worthy of education. British-inspired schools to educate the sons of Indian princes were founded in the decades after the Indian Rebellion of 1857. The uprising shocked the British and caused them to invest heavily in fostering a pro-British Indian elite: 'a class of persons Indian in blood and colour but English in tastes, in opinion, in morals, and in intellect,' as had been called for in 1835 by Thomas Macaulay.[22] Sport was an integral part of this project. Universities were founded in Calcutta, Bombay and Madras, as were Arnoldian schools. Chief among these was Rajkumar College (opened in 1868), which was clear in its purpose: 'we shall discipline their bodies in the manliness and hardihood of the English public schoolboy'.[23] *Tom Brown's Schooldays* was read to the boys by the headmaster himself. The school produced two of India's greatest cricketers, the princes Ranjitsinhji and Duleepsinhji, both of whom played for England rather than India, a telling indication of the relationship not only between cricket and empire at this time but also that between the British and Indian elites.[24]

At Mayo College (1875) – the 'Eton of India' – the boys played cricket every day. The largely British teachers at these schools saw themselves as missionaries for imperialism and its values. And sometimes they were actual missionaries. In 1890 Cecil Tyndale-Biscoe – who coxed Cambridge to win the Boat Race in 1884 – was sent to Kashmir by the Christian Missionary Society to teach the sons of the local elite. He established six schools that all had cricket, boxing, rowing and football at the heart of the curriculum. The same pattern was to be found wherever the British sought to maintain their rule through local elites. Private and mission schools were established and spent considerable time and resources playing sport. In Ghana, Achimota College was founded in 1927 and boasted two large cricket ovals, four football fields, three hockey pitches, plus two other fields for netball and rounders.[25] In Trinidad, Queen's Royal College – situated on a square originally called Billiards Orchard – educated future black administrators and sportsmen, in addition to C.L.R. James, who was so profoundly shaped by the education he received there that he remained in thrall to the sentimental cant of amateurism even while writing revolutionary classics like *World Revolution* (1937) and *The Black Jacobins* (1938).[26]

Thus when cricket began to be played outside of the colonial settler milieu, it remained elitist and racially segregated. In India, Parsi cricketers formed the Oriental Cricket Club in 1848, having been brought into contact with it through their trading and commercial links with the British. In 1868 the first Hindu club, Bombay Union, was established, followed by a Muslim club in 1883. It wasn't until 1877 that a native Indian side was invited to play Bombay Gymkhana, the leading European cricket club. The match eventually evolved into the famous Bombay Quadrangular tournament, a contest between European, Parsi, Hindu and Muslim sides. It wasn't until 1932 that India was granted test match – full international – status. The increasingly competitive nature of domestic Indian cricket meant that it began to be taken up across all classes of the Indian population from maharajahs to untouchables. Indeed, the greatest Indian bowler of the Edwardian era was the left-arm spinner Palwankar Baloo, a member of the Dalit, or untouchable, caste. Yet his cricketing prowess – in which he proved himself to be not only equal but superior to cricketers of much higher caste or class, made him a hero to tens of thousands of untouchables. For them, Baloo appeared to use sport to demonstrate that on the supposedly level playing field of cricket, all men started as equals, regardless of colour, class or caste.[27]

In his *Beyond a Boundary* (1963), C.L.R. James made essentially the same point about the game in the West Indies. Growing up in the racially stratified society of colonial Trinidad, James described how 'social and political passions, denied normal outlets, expressed themselves so fiercely in cricket (and other games) precisely because they were games'.[28] For him the dominance of West Indian cricket by a small number of whites symbolised the fate of the islands themselves. This led to his long campaign for a black player to captain of the West Indies cricket side, which eventually resulted in Frank Worrell being appointed the first black captain of the team when it toured Australia in 1960.[29]

The widely accepted idea that sport provides a level playing field on which merit alone can triumph, regardless of class or colour, was an extension of the amateur notion of 'fair play'. But this ignores the question of who controlled access to the playing field. As we have seen, the first decades of colonial cricket were dominated by those educated at elite schools. Moreover, many of the clubs were formed not only on the basis of white/non-white segregation but also by what the British defined as 'race' or 'nationality'. Thus in India, Lord Harris, an England captain and MCC president who was governor of Bombay between 1890 and 1895, refused to allow cricket clubs to be formed on the basis of anything other than religion, declaring that:

> I will steadfastly refuse any more grants once a Gymkhana [club] has been established under respectable auspices by each nationality, and tell applicants that ground having been set apart for their nationality they are free to take advantage of it by joining that particular club.[30]

This was the policy of 'divide and rule' in the sporting arena, the legacy of which devastated the sub-continent in 1947 and scars it today. In the West Indies, access to education and therefore sports facilities, was open only to the rich or those, like James himself, who were both talented enough and lucky enough to win scholarships to elite schools.

It should not therefore be surprising that sport was very rarely a vehicle for anti-imperial sentiment, either of a nationalist or socialist stripe. It played an integrative role within the British and American Empires. Just before the US invasion of the Dominican Republic in 1916, the American ambassador expected baseball to undermine the appeal of the independence movement's guerrilla struggle: 'it satisfies a craving in the nature of the people for exciting conflict, and is a real substitute for the contests in the hillsides with rifles'.[31] It was almost entirely unknown for sports administrators, players or writers to utter anything but politically conservative views. With the exception of the overtly Irish nationalist Gaelic Athletic Association, even those sportspeople at the sharp end of imperial rule were almost always loyal to the British crown. Writing in his 1905 book *Stray Thoughts on Indian Cricket*, the leading Parsi cricketer J.M. Framjee Patel hailed Lord Harris – described by even sympathetic observers as the worst governor of Bombay in a century – as 'a high-minded and sympathetic ruler and a generous and genuine sportsman, who, during his Governorship of Bombay, zealously encouraged physical culture amongst the people'.[32] Welcoming the touring British rugby union team to Wanganui in 1930, the leaders of the local Maori community took the opportunity to praise:

> the home land of the British race, that wonderful country from whence come our knowledge, protection and religion … under the Union Jack, we have come to learn what is meant by the words British justice, British equity and British Christian principles.[33]

The reader will search in vain for any trace of irony. It was only in the 1950s and 1960s, when the British Empire was in terminal decline and its colonies were struggling towards independence, that sport come to be interpreted as reflecting opposition to imperialism. In this, as in everything else, sport followed politics.[34]

Even this late-blooming modicum of anti-imperial sentiment was difficult to locate in what had become known as the 'white dominions' of the British Empire.[35] Despite the claims of nationalist-minded historians, Australian sport remained proudly British until after the Second World War. Melbourne's unique code of football, known today as Australian rules football, was a development of Rugby School's rules of football, and the intensely competitive cricket contests with England were little more than a fierce family rivalry of imperial brothers. The British national anthem 'God Save the Queen' could still be heard on Australian football and rugby grounds into the 1970s. Even the infamous 'Bodyline' controversy between the two in 1932–3 was the result of the Australians' mistaken belief that the English were sincere in their commitment to 'fair play'.[36] During the tour the England captain Douglas Jardine instructed his fast bowlers to bowl directly at the bodies of Australian batsmen. 'There are two teams out there, one is playing cricket. The other is making no attempt to do so,' Australian captain Bill Woodfull complained to Jardine during the third test match at Adelaide.[37] Heated exchanges between the Colonial Office in London and the Australian government followed. But at the heart of the dispute lay not Australia's desire for independence from the 'Mother Country' but frustration that the English seemed to have abandoned the British principles of fair play. As one anonymous pamphleteer noted, Australians felt betrayed by the English:

> we pay our debts and are England's very best customer within the Empire. When danger threatened, we were of the first to respond to the call to arms by the Motherland. … we Australians are at a loss to understand why we, alone of all the Empire, are singled out for these continual attacks.[38]

Tellingly, the drama only came to an end when the Australian cricket authorities succumbed yet again to what was known locally as the 'cultural cringe' and apologised for accusing Jardine of being 'unsportsmanlike', perhaps the ugliest word one could call a chap educated at a public school. Embarrassed by Jardine's undiplomatic behaviour, the English cricket authorities eventually removed him from the England captaincy.

The only example of overt and conscious sporting opposition to imperialism was in Ireland, where the GAA was founded by Irish nationalists in 1884 to establish a specifically Irish sporting culture.[39] Given the level of political opposition to British rule in Ireland, it should not be surprising that the GAA was successful. It barred its members from playing the 'garrison games' of British sports such as soccer and rugby, and waged a vigorous campaign against cricket, which withered away from a position of considerable popularity in post-famine Ireland. But, politics aside, the GAA produced little more than a mirror image of British culture. It was fiercely amateur, and into the space occupied by cricket, soccer and rugby it simply inserted hurling and its own brand of football.[40] Although Ireland was not an industrial economy, it was sufficiently integrated into the British cultural universe to be swept up in the late nineteenth-century sporting revolution. Most importantly, the GAA's coupling of sport with nationalism gave hurling and its football code the same vigorous impetus and appeal that football, baseball and cycling had in the British Empire, North America and France. The GAA's political significance lay less in its choice of sporting activities and more in the fact that its leaders astutely placed it at the centre of the cultural 'Gaelic Revival' of the late nineteenth century. Not to mention that fact that its structures could be used by militant Irish republicans for military training – which, as readers of Henry's Newbolt's *Vitae Lampada* will recognise, was one more thing that the Irish sporting nationalists owed to British sport.[41]

It was supporters of Gaelic football who were the victims of the most brutal example of the relationship between sport and imperialism on 21 November 1920. At the height of the Irish War of Independence, the Royal Irish Constabulary stormed into Croke Park in Dublin and fired into the crowd watching the Dublin versus Tipperary football match, in retaliation for an earlier IRA (Irish Republican Army) operation against British military intelligence officers. When the police had finished shooting, discharging at least 114 rounds of rifle ammunition at the crowd, fourteen civilians were dead and dozens injured. One-time Tipperary captain Michael Hogan was among those killed, as were two boys and a young woman due to be married the following week. In the most visceral way imaginable, sport had once more demonstrated that it was neither an escape from nor immune to the political realities of life.[42]

8

UNFAIR PLAY: THE RACIAL POLITICS OF SPORT

Two negroes are reported killed and a white man was shot in Arkansas and a negro was fatally wounded at Roanoke, Virginia. ... Seven negroes were reported killed in various parts of the country and scores wounded. There were disturbances in eleven large cities, from New York, Pittsburgh and Philadelphia in the Northeast, to New Orleans, Atlanta, St Louis, Little Rock and Houston in the South and South West.[1]

If anything, the *New York Tribune* underestimated the scale of the conflict that broke out on the night of 4 July 1910. Racist mobs attacked black communities across fifty US cities. An estimated twenty-three black men and two white men were left dead and hundreds more injured.

What could provoke such an outpouring of fury? Two men fighting in a ring, something that had been taking place for centuries. Only this time, a black man had defeated a white man to become the heavyweight boxing champion of the world. His name was Jack Johnson and his victory had dealt a knock-out blow to myths of white athletic supremacy.

The development of modern sport was defined by a belief in the superiority of the white 'race'. Sport, believed the *Yorkshire Post*, the organ of the northern English industrial bourgeoisie, had 'done so much to make the Anglo-Saxon race the best soldiers, sailors and colonists in the world'. Across the Atlantic, Harvard football coach, future US governor-general of the Philippines and subsequent ambassador to Japan, W. Cameron Forbes, declared that 'football is the expression of the strength of the Anglo-Saxon. It is the dominant spirit of the dominant race.'[2] The belief that specific 'races' of people are inherently inferior to others was rooted in the development of slavery and colonialism from the seventeenth century. Yet the concept of race is itself a scientific nonsense. As the Human

Genome Project confirmed, regardless of cosmetic differences of skin tone, there are no consistent patterns of genetic similarity that can distinguish one 'race' from another and no genetic basis for ethnic divisions. But if race is a scientifically worthless category, it is an intensely powerful social concept. And there are few places where it is more culturally significant than in sport.

The modern concept of race did not exist before the emergence of capitalism. Thus although slavery existed in classical civilisation, racism did not. Although there was undoubtedly antipathy between nations and peoples, this was not based on skin colour or physical characteristics. Indeed, the slave-owning society of ancient Egypt was at one point ruled by a dynasty of Nubian pharaohs and the Roman Empire governed by a North African emperor, Septimius Severus. Prejudice was directed against those who were believed to have allowed themselves to be captured as slaves, and were thus perceived to be weak and inferior. Indeed, slaves in classical times generally shared the skin colour of their slaveowners.

But the growth of the slave trade in the seventeenth and eighteenth centuries – in which British ships took slaves from West Africa to the Caribbean, and returned to Britain with cash crops such as cotton or sugar – meant that the skin colour of African slaves became a justification for enslaving them.[3] For the slave traders and owners, to have a black skin was to be inferior to those with a white skin, and a torrent of pseudo-scientific, anthropological and biblical scholarship poured forth in order to justify the enslavement of Africans. Yet, as Frederick Douglass, the most important black abolitionist of the nineteenth century, wrote: 'we are then a persecuted people, not because we are colored, but simply because that color has for a series of years been coupled in the public mind with the degradation of slavery and servitude'.[4] A similar point could also be made about the attitudes of the rulers of the British Empire. The conquest of India, Africa and the Far East was justified by imperialist spokesmen on the grounds that people with a darker skin colour were inherently inferior to the pale-skinned inhabitants of Britain. In Rudyard Kipling's words, they were 'the white man's burden'. The ideology of white supremacy arose directly from the need to defend slavery and colonialism.[5]

Modern sport was born at precisely the time that the issue of race had become central to the development of capitalism. The last quarter of the nineteenth century saw the expansion of imperialist domination over almost every corner of the globe and growing tensions between the imperialist powers, as they rushed to acquire territories in Africa and Asia. In the British Empire, imperial rule in key colonies was consolidated through a series of wars that began in the mid-nineteenth century and lasted into the latter decades of the Victorian era: the Indian 'Mutiny' of 1857, the Anglo-Zulu war of 1879 and the New Zealand land wars against Māori peoples, to name just three in countries that were to be seen as part of the British sporting world. In Australia, decades of genocide against Aboriginal peoples and racism towards Chinese and other Asian peoples was crowned by the introduction of an official 'White Australia' policy in 1901. Moreover, between 1861 and 1865 the United States had fought the bloodiest war hitherto in human history over the question of slavery in its southern states. As capitalism sought to expand around the globe, the need for cheap labour and colonial possessions reinforced the racial hierarchy of slavery, in which those with darker skin pigmentation were classified as inferior to those with a white skin. The newly emerging mass commercial sports were not merely products of this period, they were active participants in maintaining this white supremacist world order.

This can be most clearly seen in baseball. Following the end of the Civil War in 1865, the Reconstruction era's attempts to reform the former slave-holding southern states on the basis of legal equality for both black and white had been attacked by white terrorist organisations such as the Ku Klux Klan. The issue of race became a bloody fault-line in American politics – and baseball was firmly in the racist camp. In 1867 the National Association of Base Ball Players barred black players from its teams, a stance that was repeated by successive major baseball leagues. In 1884 catcher Moses Fleetwood Walker became the last black player in the major leagues for over sixty years when his career with the Toledo Blue Stockings in the American Association was ended by injury. A year earlier, Chicago White Stockings' Hall of Famer 'Cap' Anson had refused to take the field against Toledo because of Walker's presence on the team. Like fellow Hall of Famers Tris Speaker, Rogers Hornsby and reputedly Ty Cobb, Anson was a member of the Ku Klux Klan.[6]

From the 1880s black players were excluded from major and minor league baseball due to a 'gentlemen's agreement' between owners and managers. The severity of racism in baseball rivalled anything seen in the 'Jim Crow' states of the segregated south, as was cheerfully admitted by the *Sporting Life* in 1891:

> probably in no other business in America is the color line so finely drawn as in baseball. An African who attempts to put on a uniform and go in among a lot of white players is taking his life in his hands.[7]

The sickening reality of the 'gentleman's agreement' was exemplified in 1908 when, before a New York Giants' exhibition game in Springfield, Illinois, the Giants' manager (and another future Hall of Famer) John McGraw was presented with a piece of a rope used to lynch two black men three days previously. The previous weekend a racist mob had burned down the town's black district, forcing its residents to flee for their lives. When McGraw was handed the piece of the murder weapon, he told his audience that it would 'replace the rabbit's foot as his team's good-luck token'.[8]

In the sporting world of Britain and its empire, a rigorous racial hierarchy was enforced. In 1867 a team of Australian Aboriginal cricketers visited England, who played high-quality cricket yet were treated as an anthropological curiosity, with the press more interested in their dancing and boomerang throwing than their mastery of the game.[9] In 1888 a 'New Zealand Native' rugby team, all but five of whom were Māori, toured the British Isles. Widely acclaimed for their innovative play, their refusal to defer sufficiently to the English Rugby Football

Union inflamed their hosts' racial sensibilities. Māori tour manager Joe Warbrick recalled:

> as long as [the tourists] were losing they were jolly good fellows in the eyes of the crowd. But as soon as they commenced to win they were hooted and the papers were full of the weakness of the home side and the rough play of the visitors.[10]

It was to be seventeen years before another overseas rugby side was invited to tour Britain. When James Peters was selected to play rugby union for England in 1906 – the code's only black England international between 1871 and 1988 – it was remarked that 'his selection is by no means popular on racial grounds'.[11] The British relationship to racial hierarchy was complicated by the obsessions of its upper and middle classes with class and social status. Whereas in America, the overwhelming majority of black people were working class or, in the south, impoverished sharecroppers, the British Empire also contained members of local aristocracies and ruling elites. This was particularly true in India, where the British mission to educate Indian princes in the superiority of the British way of life, including its sports, led to the emergence of talented Indian princely cricketers. K.S. Ranjitsinhji, Maharaja Jam Sahib of Nawanagar, and his cousin K.S. Duleepsinhji both played for England, Indian cricket being thought of as too inferior for men of such status.[12]

By the early 1900s sport was explicitly seen as a confirmation of the racial ideologies of the imperialist world. As part of the 1904 Olympic Games in St Louis, 'Anthropology Days' were staged in which so-called 'primitive' peoples – such as Japanese Ainu, Patagonians, Eskimos, Native Americans and Philippine Moros – took part in athletic contests. The purpose of the events was to compare their performances with those of white athletes, although they were not allowed to compete alongside whites. One hardly needs to note that almost all were peoples subject to US colonial rule or influence. The often unwilling 2,000 participants were no more than humiliated exhibits in a human zoo that served no purpose other than to demonstrate the racist self-satisfaction of the organisers. According to the president of the American Anthropological Association, William McGee, the results of this freak show proved that 'the white man leads the races of the world, both physically and mentally, and in the coordination of the two which goes to make up the best specimen of manhood'.[13]

More than any other sport of the period, it was boxing that was the lightning rod for the issue of race. The black boxers Bill Richmond and Tom Molineaux, both former slaves, had been prominent in bare-knuckle prize-fighting's golden age of the 1790s and 1800s. Molineaux had narrowly lost to world champion Tom Cribb in controversial circumstances in 1810.[14] But the highly charged racial atmosphere of the imperialist era in the early twentieth century meant that black boxers were no longer viewed as cultural curiosities or benign exceptions to the general whiteness of the ring. Boxing itself had been reinvented in the last third of the nineteenth century under the 1867 Marquess of Queensberry rules, although these were actually developed by J.G. Chambers in 1865. It slowly regained its former popularity, having fallen from its Regency heights to become a marginal sport by the start of the modern mass spectator sports boom. Although ostensibly a way of imparting healthy moral values to fighters, the Queensberry rules repackaged boxing as a new commercial mass spectator sport. The size of the ring was regulated, rounds were standardised at three minutes in length and gloves became compulsory. As a consequence, the sport became faster, more athletic and considerably more brutal.[15] It was also unique in that it was the only individual sport of the period that was not only open to urban working-class males – unlike the generally exclusive golf and tennis – but could also offer significant riches to its champions. For black athletes, it offered opportunities that were otherwise closed to them in most team sports.

One such athlete was Galveston longshoreman turned boxer Jack Johnson. Johnson's rise to boxing prominence began as a teenager in the last years of the nineteenth century. In 1903 he won the world 'coloured' heavyweight title. Although he fought both black and white boxers, he was forbidden from fighting for the world heavyweight title, like all black boxers.[16] But on Boxing Day 1908, after two years of stubborn campaigning for the fight, he defeated the Canadian Tommy Burns to be crowned heavyweight champion of the world. It was perhaps the most significant single contest thus far in the history of modern sport. Indicating the global importance of the race question, the fight took place in Sydney, Australia, after negotiations for the fight to take place in the UK broke down. As the poet Claude McKay pointed out, 'in the United States there is not room for a Negro, even in the area of sports. Only in the national American sport called lynching is he assigned the first place.'[17] Such was the shock of Johnson's win that an immediate call for a 'great white hope' to take the title from Johnson was raised by journalists. In 1910 the call proved too strong for former champion Jim Jeffries, who came out of retirement 'for the sole purpose of proving that a white man is better than a negro'. It was to no avail. The fight in Reno on 4 July resulted in Jeffries throwing in the towel at the end of the fifteenth round. The resulting celebrations by black communities across fifty American cities were attacked by rioting racist mobs, leaving twenty-three black and two white citizens dead. Johnson would not relinquish the title until he was defeated aged thirty-seven by Jess Willard in round twenty-six of their fight in Havana.[18]

Johnson was not the first black world title holder. Black Baltimorean Joe Gans had won the lightweight title in 1902.[19] But the heavyweight title was the supreme achievement in boxing. The fact that boxing's most prestigious title could be held by a black man challenged the racial orthodoxies of the time. In Britain, the mere fact that Johnson's victory over Jeffries could be seen on newsreel film was seen as a threat to the imperial order: 'the authorities evidently dread its effect on the relations between the white and coloured population. Of course, this will not be confined to South Africa but may be duplicated in every part of the Empire and elsewhere', complained the Reverend F.B. Meyer in *The Times*.[20] Johnson himself was an extraordinarily courageous man, merely seeking to live what would be an ordinary life for a white celebrity of equivalent fame. He was proud of his talents and saw no reason to defer to racist objections to his relationships with white women. In 1912 he was the first man arrested for violating the Mann Act – an anti-sex piece of legislation that forbade the 'transportation' of women across state lines for so-called immoral purposes that would later be used to ensnare Charlie Chaplin and Chuck Berry among many others.[21] The fact that the woman concerned, his future wife, refused to testify caused the case to be dropped. The following year Johnson was charged again and sentenced to a year and a day in prison. The judge, who ensured the champion's conviction by neglecting to tell the jury that the alleged offence took place before the Mann Act had been passed, was Kenesaw Mountain Landis. From 1920 to 1944, Landis would be the commissioner of Major League Baseball and oversee the last decades of baseball's Jim Crow policies.

Johnson's success had an impact around the world, not least because his rise to fame coincided with the development of the motion picture industry. Not only were Johnson's fights staged around the world, but the new medium meant that he could now be watched by millions who could not see him in person. He became the first global star of sport. Faced with such a clear rebuff to its accepted hierarchy, boxing's authorities sought to reinforce the racial order of imperialism. In Britain, an attempt in 1911 to stage a fight between 'Bombardier' Billy Wells and Johnson was banned by Home Secretary Winston Churchill.[22] Cape Town-born 'coloured' boxer Andrew Japhet won the British welterweight title in 1907 but was the last black boxer to hold a British title until 1948, thanks to a 'colour bar' introduced in response to Johnson's success that banned black boxers from fighting for British titles.[23] Boxing itself became an arena in which racial fantasies of reasserting white supremacy – embodied in 'the great white hope' – would lie permanently below the surface, contradictorily merging with dismissals of the 'primitivism' of the sport. But most importantly, Jack Johnson himself became a permanent symbol of pride, not just for black Americans but for all those who sought self-respect and freedom from oppression, a feeling captured by Harlem Renaissance poet Waring Cuney: 'O my Lord, what a morning,/ O my Lord,what a feeling,/When Jack Johnson turned Jim Jeffries'/Snow-white face to the ceiling.' A similar sense of elation was felt twenty-seven years later when Joe Louis knocked out James J. Braddock to win the world heavyweight title in June 1937. It was, said Malcolm X, 'the greatest celebration of race pride our generation had ever known'.[24]

Johnson's victory also began to undermine contemporary pseudo-scientific justifications for racism. Throughout the nineteenth century, racist ideologues had claimed that dark-skinned athletes were inferior to whites because they were lazy, indolent and lacking in stamina.[25] This was explained supposedly by their origins in the heat of Africa. Yet within forty years, a period which saw not only Johnson but also heavyweight champion Joe Louis and athlete Jesse Owens dominate sport, the racist narrative flipped into its very opposite. Owens' historic four-gold medal haul in the 1936 Berlin Olympics was not seen as demonstrating the reality of racial equality but as proof that black athletes had 'natural' athletic abilities that made them superior in certain physical, but not mental, activities. Now it was claimed that their African origins gave them an advantage over white athletes. 'It was not long ago,' wrote Dean Cromwell, the USA track coach in the 1948 Olympics, 'that [the black athlete's] ability to sprint and jump was a life-and-death matter to him in the jungle.'[26]

This shift in attitude, which nonetheless upheld the supposedly innate intellectual superiority of whites, was not merely a response to the success of black athletes.[27] It was also a reflection of the changing economic position of the black population in the USA and the British Empire. The 1930s and 1940s saw a growth in the demand for industrial labour in America's northern states, much of which was met by black workers from the southern states who made what was known as the 'great migration'. In Britain, a similar labour shortage in the late 1940s and 1950s was met by workers from the West Indies.[28] Moreover, the granting of independence to India in 1947 signalled the beginning of the break-up of the British Empire. Rising political consciousness among black and colonial peoples, sharpened as a result of the allies' often hypocritical rhetoric against Nazi racial policies in the Second World War, also meant that overt racial exclusion was increasingly difficult to defend publicly. Formal legal equality for black people was thus gradually achieved through a combination of economic exigency, political struggle and, in the case of America, sensitivity to the USSR's (Union of Soviet Socialist Republics) highlighting of racism in the USA during the Cold War.[29] In sport this change from overt discrimination to legal, if not social, equality can be seen in Jackie Robinson's debut for the Brooklyn Dodgers in Major League Baseball in 1947, the first black player in the majors for over sixty years, the NFL's (National Football League's) abandonment of its Jim Crow policy in 1949 and the lifting of British boxing's colour bar in the late 1940s.

Despite the end of overt racial exclusion, the old racial hierarchies continued to prevail in sport. It wasn't until the late 1960s that formal and informal exclusion of black athletes ended, with the exception, as we shall see, of apartheid South Africa. Those who thought that the integration of black players into baseball meant the end of racism in the sport were disappointed. Hall of Famer Frank Robinson joined the Cincinnati Reds in 1956 and was shocked. 'I didn't know anything about racism or bigotry until I went into professional baseball,' he later stated. Playing in Greensboro in the minor leagues early in his career, Leon Wagner found himself threatened by a gun-toting racist while he was fielding during a game.[30] Moreover, the sight of a black pitcher or quarterback was a rare event in big-time American sports until the latter decades of the twentieth century. The same could be said of professional soccer players, at least in the anglophone world. In France, Portugal and Latin America, where the imperial relationship with the colonies was less segregated, black players appeared at the higher levels of soccer from the early decades of the twentieth century. Uruguay's José Andrade was perhaps one of the most notable, playing in the 1924 Olympic and 1930 World Cup finals.[31] Yet, even when on the field, racist perceptions of black athletes restricted their opportunities. So-called 'decision-making' positions, such as soccer mid-fielders or rugby half-backs, as well as quarterbacks and pitchers, were portrayed as being beyond the intellectual ability of black players, who found themselves disproportionately represented in those positions that required speed or strength, a self-fulfilling confirmation of racist stereotypes that sociologists came to label as 'stacking'.[32]

The racial hierarchy of modern sport that was established in the nineteenth century would not disappear. And in the late 1960s, thanks to athletes such as Muhammad Ali, Tommie Smith and John Carlos, it was once again an issue that would dominate world sport.[33]

9

SOCCER'S RISE TO GLOBALISM

To say that these men paid their shillings to watch twenty-two hirelings kick a ball is merely to say that a violin is wood and catgut, that Hamlet is so much paper and ink.

J.B. Priestley, 1929.[1]

In the early part of the twentieth century, an adage circulated among the European intelligentsia: 'One Englishman, a fool; two Englishmen, a football match; three Englishmen; the British Empire.'[2] Leaving aside the merits or otherwise of this assessment of the English male character, the maxim was soon overtaken by events. By 1930 – the date of soccer's first World Cup in Uruguay – it could justifiably be said that wherever two or more European or Latin American young men gathered, a football match would take place, or at least be the topic of conversation.

Yet soccer's rise to become the world's most popular sport had little to do with the British Empire as it was formally constituted. Perhaps the greatest paradox in world sport is the fact that, despite being the major beneficiary of the sporting industrial revolution of the late nineteenth century, soccer was the last major British sport to to establish itself outside of the British Isles, Even today, soccer cannot claim to be the undisputed national winter sport of any English-speaking country beyond England and Scotland.

Rugby was the first football code to spread beyond its original geographical location. This should not be surprising in view of the tremendous popularity of *Tom Brown's Schooldays* across the English-speaking world. As well as being a primer for schoolboys and schoolmasters alike, the book also offered an uplifting moral tale for those seeking to justify or emulate British rule around the world. This can be seen clearly in Australia, where a form of organised football was first consistently played in Melbourne, inspired to a greater or lesser extent by former Rugby School pupil Tom Wills. Although its aficionados later claimed that the sport had sprung entirely from Australian sources, the laws of Victorian (later Australian) rules football were entirely drawn from the varying forms of football played in Britain.[3]

In both Canada and the USA, versions of rugby based on the gridiron system emerged as the dominant form of football by the 1880s. The governing body of Canadian gridiron football even continued to call itself the Canadian Rugby Union until 1967, decades after it had abandoned all but the most vestigial links with the rugby union game. Canada's undisputed national sport, ice hockey, owed much to rugby, both in terms of its early rules (originally the puck could not be passed forward) and in the fact that many of its early participants were rugby players, including James Creighton who consolidated the first set of hockey rules in the early 1870s.[4] Despite its belief in its own exceptionalism, most of the elements of American football were present in the early years of rugby in Britain, including blocking and 'downs', until 1906 when the forward pass was introduced. In Ireland, the GAA's own code of football mixed and matched elements from soccer, rugby and, one can assume on the basis of circumstantial evidence, Australian rules.[5]

None of these codes of football would ever be sustained at an at elite level beyond their country of origin. The fact that the name of each was prefaced by its nationality explains their basic lack of appeal to the wider world. And, as they became popular and therefore culturally significant, they became entwined with notions of national identity and character, largely extinguishing their interest for the wider world. Moreover, these local versions of football were viewed by the non-anglophone world as essentially subsets of a British sport known generically as 'football'. As the world's dominant imperialist power for the previous century, it would be largely to Britain itself that the rest of the world would look for sport, not its current or former colonies. This was tacitly acknowledged even by proponents of American sports, such as the journalist Caspar Whitney, the USA's most vocal supporter of amateurism, and right-wing US statesman Henry Cabot Lodge, both of whom saw sport as a key element in the conquest of the world by the anglophone nations.

Conversely, it was this intertwining of national football games with national or regional identity that made it very difficult for rival football codes, especially soccer, to challenge these games in their native settings. The answer to the question why was there no soccer in the United States – or Canada, or Australia or New Zealand, for that matter – is simple. By the end of the nineteenth century, other football codes had emerged and won mass spectator appeal before soccer was seriously established. In the United States, the number of people going to college gridiron games by the 1890s dwarfed even baseball crowds. In Melbourne, the Australian code of football was attracting five-figure crowds as early as the 1870s. Both these styles of football quickly became associated with dominant ideas about national identity, giving them a social resonance that rendered discussion about the comparative aesthetics of other codes immaterial. Of course, soccer existed in all English-speaking countries, yet beyond the British Isles it remained weak and puny, with the exception of the following it gained among the black population of South Africa.[6]

It is this identity of sport with national culture that also explains the failure of baseball to become a global sport, despite the determined efforts of A.G. Spalding.[7] In 1888–9 his world baseball tour visited New Zealand, Australia, Ceylon, Egypt, Italy, France and Britain in pursuit of this goal. It failed despite the business acumen of its initiator, considerable public interest and the presence of future Hall of Famers Cap Anson and John Montgomery Ward in the team.[8] Beyond its immediate colonies, and its unique relationship with its developing junior imperialist rival Japan, America before 1914 was not generally perceived by the wider world as offering an alternative cultural or moral sporting framework to that of the British Empire. Baseball therefore had little of the emulative appeal of British sports.[9]

Soccer alone became a truly global sport. Yet its rise to worldwide pre-eminence was neither simple nor pre-ordained. Today, most historians of soccer attribute its global expansion to what they believe to be its intrinsic qualities. Some believe that it advanced simply because it is 'the beautiful game'. David Goldblatt, one of the sport's premier chroniclers, has argued that its success is due to 'the game's balance of physicality and artistry, of instantaneous reaction and complex considered tactics, [which] is also rare'.[10] But in sport as in love, beauty is in the eye of the beholder and aficionados of other sports also make similar arguments for their objects of admiration. As in most debates about aesthetics, such arguments largely consist of selecting the attractive features of one sport and constructing an argument that supports the desired conclusion. Nor does such an argument fit the historical record. Up until the 1880s, the differences between the association and rugby codes of football were not as distinctive as they are today, as demonstrated by both Preston North End and Burnley easily switching from rugby to soccer and subsequently becoming founding members of the Football League when it was formed in 1888.[11]

A related, yet no less erroneous, argument suggests that soccer is more 'natural' to play than rugby or other codes of football, because it involves kicking and not handling the ball. But this is a circular argument. Soccer appears to be more natural only because the sport is now so popular and ubiquitous – familiarity with a practice does not imply that it is natural. In fact, soccer is unique as the only type of football that does not allow outfield players to handle the ball at all. Moreover, many saw soccer's insistence on the exclusive use of the feet as a novelty or an innovation. When the writer Yuri Oleshare explained soccer to his father in Russia in the early 1900s, his father was incredulous: 'They play with their feet. With their feet? How can that be?'[12] Indeed, soccer's very 'unnaturalness' – and hence its modernity – may have been one of its more appealing features.

This also tends to undermine the argument that soccer's supposed 'simplicity' gave it an advantage over other sports. The exclusive use of the feet make soccer a difficult sport to master. And, as anyone who has tried to explain the subtleties of the off-side rule will know, its rules are not necessarily straightforward. This argument is based on modern examples of today's highly developed code types of football – such as the now fiendishly complex American football – and ignores the historical similarities between the football codes in the late nineteenth century.[13] Nor was soccer less dangerous to play than rugby forms of football. In 1894 and 1907 *The Lancet*, the journal of the British Medical Association, carried out surveys of injuries sustained in soccer and rugby. On both occasions it concluded: 'everything seems to show that the degree of danger incurred by players is greater in the dribbling than in the carrying game'.[14]

So if the global expansion of soccer was not due to its perceived intrinsic merits, what did propel it around the world?

The key is to be found in the development of professsional team sports in Britain in the late nineteenth century. Until the 1880s, rugby was the more popular code of football in Britain. In 1871 *Bell's Life*, the premier sporting weekly of the time, pointed out that since the formation of the Football Association in 1863, 'every year has increased the superiority in point of numbers and popularity of the Rugby clubs over those who are subject to the rule of the Association'.[15] This can be seen in the first issue of C.W. Alcock's *Football Annual*, published in 1868, which records eighty-eight 'football' clubs in existence at the time. Forty-five played under rugby rules and thirty were members of the FA.[16] It was only when the FA Cup became popular in the late 1870s that the FA began to grow. In fact, although the FA and the RFU had drawn up separate rules for their games, there was considerable crossover between the two codes. Many clubs played both, a combination of the two or their own variations. It was only when the football codes acquired a broader social significance, especially through local rivalries in cup competitions in the late 1870s and early 1880s, which in turn spurred the commercialisation of the sport, that the full codification and separation of soccer and rugby was consolidated.

By 1880 interest in soccer and rugby had spread to the working classes of the major British industrial cities, Manchester, Liverpool, Leeds, Birmingham, Cardiff and Glasgow. In these teeming population centres both codes of football began to evolve into a mass commercial entertainment business and rumours spread that working-class soccer and rugby players were being paid to play. In soccer, Fergus Suter was widely believed to be the first player to be paid to play when he moved from Scotland to play for Lancashire's Darwen FC in 1878.[17] A year later, rugby player Teddy Bartram joined Wakefield Trinity in Yorkshire where he was to receive a handsome £52 per year for his services.[18] In soccer, concern over payments to players came to a head in 1884. Preston North End played Upton Park, a London club of middle-class 'gentlemen' in the FA Cup. The match was drawn but the Londoners protested to the FA that Preston had used professional players. Although the FA found no hard evidence to support this claim, they did discover that Preston had arranged jobs for players and therefore expelled them from the FA Cup. Preston maintained that there was nothing wrong in this and, supported by forty other clubs in the north and midlands, threatened to form a breakaway 'British Football Association'. Threatened with a potentially disastrous cleavage, the FA decided to compromise and in January 1885 voted to legalise professionalism under strict controls, many of which were based on cricket's model of professionalism.[19]

The consequences of soccer's move to open professionalism had a crucial impact on its rugby rival. As we have seen, the RFU watched the evolution of soccer with interest and then alarm. Less than two years after soccer legalised professionalism, the RFU decided that the FA's experiment with professionalism was a failure and decided to declare rugby a completely amateur sport. All cases of professionalism were severely punished, with players and clubs suspended or expelled, and resulted in a split in the game in 1895.[20] At precisely the point that 'soccer mania' was sweeping Britain, the RFU's policy led to the creation of two distinct codes of rugby: union and league. Whereas the league version followed in soccer's footsteps and allowed professionalism, the union game rigorously defended the amateur ethos for exactly 100 years until it abandoned the final remnants of its amateur principles in 1995. The union code cherished its exclusivity, whereas the league code was born too late to expand far beyond its industrial heartland. Whether from choice or circumstance, neither form of rugby could counter the popularity of soccer.

The legalisation of professionalism transformed soccer. Most immediately, it meant that no team based on public school- or university-educated players would ever again compete in the FA Cup final. The balance of power in soccer tilted decisively in favour of clubs composed of working-class professionals and organised on commercial lines. This opened the way for the widespread acceptance of league competitions throughout the game, something that amateur sports administrators opposed in the belief that leagues forced clubs to play socially unacceptable opponents. In 1888 the Football League was formed, comprised of the top northern and midlands professional sides. Within a decade, almost every soccer club in Britain was part of a league competition.[21]

Professionalism and the league system gave the sport the appearance of being a meritocracy, unlike amateur sports when selection of players in teams and the choice of opponents for fixtures was often based on social status. Soccer could now claim to be the sporting equivalent of a 'career open to talents', regardless of the social or educational background of the player. The introduction of leagues meant that teams could be assessed objectively on the basis of their playing record rather than their social status. As Jules Rimet, FIFA (Fédération Internationale de Football Association) president and architect of its World Cup, would later write, football 'draws men together and makes them equal'.[22] The game therefore broke from the amateur tradition of informal unwritten regulation based on social and recreational networks and moved towards a system of formal, written objective regulation. This was in marked contrast to sport under amateur regimes. Informal yet tightly knit social networks were central to British middle-class male culture. Amateurism and the 'code of the gentleman' placed the informal understanding of the rules above their formal application, the public-school educated middle classes always favouring the spirit rather than the letter of the law. Amateurism therefore privileged the insider who understood implicit unwritten conventions over the outsider whose understanding was based on the explicit written rules.[23]

But in soccer, professionalism brought continuous competition, precise measurement and the supplanting of personal relationships by the exigencies of the market, so vital to the capitalist economy. Indeed, the culture of professional soccer – and professional baseball in the USA – created a recreational facsimile of the capitalist world, in which capitalism's myths of fair competition, equality before the law and the ability of talent alone to triumph were played out in miniature. Soccer was a living tableau in which the lessons of life under capitalism were illustrated over ninety minutes (or nine innings in baseball). Winners prospered and losers went to the wall.

This new emphasis on rigorous competition also changed the way in which soccer was played. Those educated in the public school spirit played in a different style, priding themselves on their ability to give and take physical violence. Aggressive shoulder charging was their hallmark, as described by a Corinthians FC player of the 1880s:

> our forward with the ball merely dribbled up to the opposing half-back and charged him over, then going on to treat the backs and the goalkeeper in the same way. We got four goals in twenty minutes by this means.[24]

Unlike working-class players, who invariably worked in physically demanding manual jobs, middle-class sportsmen's working lives were generally sedentary and they felt the need to demonstrate their masculinity in the most forceful of ways.[25] Their game was also based on individual dribbling, with passing between players only being used as a last resort. In contrast, when teams from industrial regions met middle-class sides, they were often surprised by the violence of their opponents. The professional style of play was less violent and rested on 'combination' play involving passing between players to move the ball upfield, a style which become known as 'scientific'.[26]

The term 'scientific' is the key differentiator between the old and the new styles of football. It was not only a reflection of the way the professional sides played the game but also indicative of the social stratum from which professional soccer emerged. It was closely linked to the lower middle-class administrators of professional clubs in the industrial north and midlands of England. These were the men who proposed professionalism and created leagues. For example, William Sudell, the manager of Preston North End, was a factory manager and accountant. John Lewis, the founder of Blackburn Rovers, built coaches for railway engines. William MacGregor, the chairman of Aston Villa and the prime mover behind the creation of the Football League, was a shopkeeper. John Bentley, the secretary of Bolton Wanderers and president of the Football League, was a journalist.[27] These were men of the liberal middle classes, who saw themselves as bringing the principles of science to the playing and organising of sport. Their enthusiasm for cup and league competitions, and for the fullest competition between players and teams, reflected their belief in the opportunities that would be available to them, free from restrictions imposed from above.

They represented something very different from the public school men who had hitherto dominated soccer and still led rugby. The leaders of the Football Association and the Rugby Football Union were men largely of the upper middle classes, members of the professions such as solicitors, accountants, doctors, clergymen and higher civil servants. The mid-nineteenth century saw this social layer consolidate their status, forming legally sanctioned associations that allowed them to regulate entry into their professions and exclude those they saw as undesirable or threatening to their status.[28] In business, as in sport, they supported competition yet wished to retain hierarchy and stability. They believed in contests for supremacy but only to the extent that such contests ensured their own supremacy and did not disrupt the social order. Amateurism, their response to working-class encroachment on 'their' sports, was the means by which such contradictions could be kept in check. The leaders of the RFU thus had little interest in seeing rugby develop beyond the domain of the middle classes of the British Empire.[29]

The leaders of professional soccer were perhaps even more parochial, having little interest in anything beyond the welfare of their club and its immediate horizons. They were certainly no less parochial than Major League Baseball. But, although this was not realised at the time, the transformation of soccer by professionalism had detached the game from its organic link to its British middle-class administrators. There was now an external, objective set of rules for the governance of the game. Although the game was still led by the same people, the basis for their control of the game was no longer absolute – it was ultimately controlled by a set of independent laws. Its relationship to British national culture was now a conditional one and, unlike rugby, there was no inherent reason why the game could not be taken up by those who owed no allegiance to the British Empire.

It was primarily the commercial and technical middle classes, men like the founders of the Football League, who took the game overseas. In Germany, it was British tradesmen, businessmen and engineers who took the game there, including sales representatives from textiles factories in the north of England from places like Preston, Blackburn and Bolton.[30] In Brazil, the founders of the game were British gas and railway engineers.[31] This was in stark contrast to rugby – which was used as a marker of Britishness wherever it was played (with the partial exception of France, although here it was a desire to emulate the success of the British Empire that led to rugby's adoption). Soccer became the sport of trade and communication, a way in which British commerce made links with the non-English-speaking world. Those young men who took up the game outside of Britain were largely drawn from the middle-class technical and managerial classes. In France, Germany and Switzerland soccer became the sport of business schools, technical colleges and polytechnics. It became the embodiment of what Chris Young has described as:

> the new forms of physical practice [that] facilitated the genesis of an urban middle class, whose activities found favour with the upper echelons. Technicians, engineers, salesmen, teachers and journalists, who had previously found their personal and professional advancement blocked for lack of the right certificate or university examination, discovered new forms of sociability through sport.[32]

Almost all of those who founded soccer clubs in Europe and Latin America were anglophiles, but their admiration was for what they saw as liberal, modern capitalist

Britain, its legal system and its political constitution. This was the anglophilia of Voltaire, who believed that Britain represented a modern liberal future, rather than the conservative anglophilia of Baron de Coubertin, who admired the tradition and hierarchy of Britain.[33] The men who led the Football League in Britain were almost pathologically not interested in 'abroad' but soccer's professional culture meant that they could do nothing to stop the formation of FIFA in Paris in 1904, with the consequence that British insularity was easily sidelined and the game vigorously promoted around the non-English-speaking world. Likewise, the men who ran FIFA were not dependent on the FA or the Football League for their legitimacy – soccer could exist independently of its British administrators.[34] This was certainly not the case with rugby or cricket, where the British, and more particularly, the English, retained a tight control of the international game until the second half of the twentieth century.

Although amateurism became a minor issue in Europe and Latin America in the 1920s as the game repeated the pattern of late Victorian Britain and became a mass spectator sport, full professionalism was introduced almost painlessly throughout the soccer world. In fact, the version of amateurism upheld by many European and South American associations at that time was not even viewed as true amateurism by its British advocates. There was widespread suspicion in Britain that the Olympics was not a truly amateur organisation, for example, and this distrust helped stimulate the creation of the first British Empire, later Commonwealth, Games in 1930.[35] Many European countries allowed the payment of 'broken time', compensation for wages lost due to time taken off work, anathema to British amateurs and the *casus belli* of the 1895 rugby split. Certainly the elaborate systems of discipline and punishment that the British constructed to defend amateur principles – merely playing a single game of rugby league, paid or unpaid, was enough to earn a lifetime ban from rugby union – were not repeated in soccer. Indeed, one of the reasons that FIFA began the World Cup was a recognition, in the words of FIFA secretary Henri Delauney in 1926, that 'today international football can no longer be held within the confines of the Olympics' because the amateurism of the Olympics, which had hitherto been the pinnacle of international football, excluded those nations that had adopted professionalism.[36]

With this acknowledgement and the consequent staging of the first World Cup in Uruguay in 1930, the last vestiges of soccer's British origins had been overthrown. Soccer was on its way to becoming a truly global sport.

10

THE SECOND REVOLUTION: SPORT BETWEEN THE WORLD WARS

> Through sports, the lure of the war game, the old thrilling magic of national rivalry, was being exercised and maintained ... this was not some harmless venting of bellicose instinct.
>
> Sebastian Haffner, 2002.[1]

What the ideologues of sport saw as the true test came in August 1914. As the rulers of Europe plunged the world into four years of imperial slaughter, few were keener to rush to the front than those schooled in the sporting ideals of duty and subordination. Across Europe young men believed that they now had their chance to 'play up, play up and play the game'. In France, *L'Auto* foamed at the mouth: 'No more Kaiser! No more Agadir! No more bloodsuckers! No more nightmares! No more bastards!'[2] 'Germany has to be smashed,' England rugby union captain Ronald Poulton-Palmer told his parents.[3] In his poem 'The Dead', the poet Rupert Brooke, an old boy of Rugby School and keen rugger fan, captured the feelings of those for whom sport had been preparation for the 'greater game':

> Nobleness walks in our ways again
> And we have come into our heritage.[4]

He was not alone, neither in his desire for military service nor in his later unnecessary death.

Yet the bloody cataclysm that engulfed the world between 1914 and 1918 transformed the face of sport in the industrialised world. From being a minority middle-class interest outside the anglophone and anglophile nations, sport in the post-war world was transformed into a commercial, cultural and political phenomenon that captured the imaginations of tens of millions of people in Europe, Latin America and Asia, and commanded the attentions of governments and politicians.

Sport underwent a second industrial revolution, underpinned by technological developments in the media. As in the past, the commercial development of the newspaper industry helped to promote and popularise sport. As the readership of newspapers continued to grow in the 1920s, a wave of consolidation saw the industry benefit from greater economies of scale and technological innovation. The development of telephotography early in the decade made possible the transmission of photographs over telegraph lines, giving daily newspapers the ability to publish shots from sports events almost immediately they had been taken. The ability to take action photographs was also greatly enhanced by the development of commercial 35 mm cameras and flash bulbs in the second half of the 1920s. And if political power came from the barrel of a gun, celebrity sprang from the lenses of a thousand Leica cameras. Without what became known as photo-journalism, Babe Ruth, Jack Dempsey, Suzanne Lenglen and the other first sporting superstars of the modern age would have been merely famous.[5]

But for the first time in their history, newspapers now had a rival: radio. Public broadcasting began almost immediately after the war and by 1925 all industrialised countries had some form of radio network. As with the newspaper industry, sport was an integral part of the appeal, marketing and business of the new medium. But it was also much more than that. Radio offered an immediacy that newspapers could never match. The millions of Americans who listened to Jack Dempsey take apart Georges Carpentier in defence of his world heavyweight title in July 1921 experienced the atmosphere and action of the fight in a way that was previously impossible, unless they were among the 91,000 crowd in Jersey City. Even more astonishing would have been the experience of the tens of thousands of Buenos Aireans two years later who listened to the live broadcast of Luis Angel Firpo's wild but ultimately unsuccessful assault on Dempsey's crown at the Polo Grounds in New York City, roughly 5,300 miles away from the scene of the action. Even cinema newsreel, which from its earliest days in the 1890s had understood the importance of sport and especially boxing to its audience, could not compete with the shared sense of participation and excitement that live radio broadcasts provided. Newspapers made sports stars household names, but radio made every household an arena, every home a stage for the unscripted drama of the great sporting contest.[6]

Like the cinema and popular music industries, sport was one of the industrial age's new forms of entertainment that offered an emotionally intense experience for a mass audience. Like Hollywood movies, sport provided a collective catharsis of triumph and tragedy, ecstasy and agony, all within the space of a single afternoon. From the 1920s, this experience was also available to those beyond the stadium, thanks initially to radio, then television and eventually satellite broadcasting. Sport was unique in that it could offer a regular collective experience – the millions who attended football and baseball matches every week were part of a real, rather than an imagined, community with its own shared memories, folklore and relationships with local feeling, national pride and sometimes class identification.

The pattern was repeated across the Americas, in Europe and in Japan. In the mid-1920s, the lull that followed the revolutionary upheavals of the Weimar Republic saw German youth possessed by 'a sports craze', in the words of German writer Sebastian Haffner, then a young man in Berlin. Attendances at soccer matches ballooned to previously unheard levels. Tennis and boxing, including women's boxing, became the staple of mass-market dailies. In Japan, radio turned baseball from a passion to a national obsession by the 1930s.[7] In some respects, this second sporting revolution was more pronounced in those countries that had not experienced the first sporting revolution of the 1890s and 1900s. For many of them, the emergence of mass spectator sport coincided with the collapse of monarchy and the sudden appearance of technological, cultural and political modernity. Sport appeared to be part of this shock of the new, a feeling captured in the works of modernist painters such as Robert Delaunay's *Football* (1917), Picasso's *Footballers on the Beach* (1928) and Willi Baumeister's *Fussballspieler* (1929).

The link between sport and modernism, both social and artistic, had emerged shortly before the First World War. Umberto Boccioni's *Dinamismo di un footballer* (1913) was the first major art work on the theme and reflected the Italian Futurists' fascination with sport. In 1914, the founder of Futurism, and future fascist, F.T. Marinetti had attacked English art and demanded that 'sport be considered as an essential element in art', He was especially enamoured with motor racing:

> this wonderful world has been further enriched by a new beauty, the beauty of speed. A racing car, its bonnet decked with exhaust pipes like serpents with galvanic breath. ... We wish to sing the praises of the man behind the steering wheel, whose sleek shaft traverses the Earth, which itself is hurtling at breakneck speed along the racetrack of its orbit.[8]

He was not alone in this enthusiasm. Motor racing emerged in France in the 1890s with the support of motor manufacturers who, like their cycling counterparts, sought to utilise racing as a way to publicise their products. And, once more, following cycling, it was a newspaper, *Le Petit Journal*, that organised the first race in 1894 and it was *New York Herald* owner James Gordon Bennett who provided the stimulus for what became known as Grand Prix racing when he presented a trophy to the Automobile Club de France for an annual race in 1899.[9] The French Grand Prix began at Le Mans in 1906 and motor racing quickly acquired the image of glamour, danger and social cachet. It came into its own in the 1920s as the circuit blossomed across Europe with the establishment of many of the classic Grands Prix: Italy (1921), Spain (1923), Belgium (1925), Britain and Germany (both 1926).[10]

Motor racing became part of the European upper-classes' summer season, with minor races taking place across the tourist resorts of France and Italy. In the socially polarised inter-war years, motor sport represented both a reassertion of pre-war elitism and an embrace of modern technology, symbolised in the heroic masculine figure of the racing driver. This triptych was also part of the ideological canvas of fascism, and the sport was dominated in the 1930s by Italy and Germany, in no small measure due to government support. This link was also highlighted by fascist supporters in the liberal democracies. When, for instance, Malcolm Campbell broke the world land speed record in 1934 he carried the British Union of Fascists' pennant on his car, Bluebird.[11]

But the technological innovations of the 1920s were merely the means by which sport enhanced its popularity and importance. They do not explain why millions of people at this point in history now thought that sport had relevance to their lives and, for the first time ever, took a deep interest in it. For a fuller and deeper explanation, we can identify three major reasons for this extraordinary emergence of sport in the aftermath of the First World War. The first of these was the effects of the war itself. At its most basic, the military authorities of the belligerents realised during the course of the war that sport was a highly effective tool for maintaining morale and staving off boredom. For conscripts who lived outside the great industrial urban centres, the war would often have been the first time that they had come into sustained contact with modern sports. Many of those who managed to survive the slaughter took back home with them an interest in these games.[12]

The biggest beneficiary was soccer. Although there had been jingoistic campaigns in Britain against professional soccer at the outbreak of the war, when it had been accused of being unpatriotic and keeping the fittest young men out of the armed forces, it soon became apparent to the authorities that soccer was both easy to organise and a useful aid to fitness. By 1918, countless networks of soccer competitions were embedded in the Allied Forces in Europe and North Africa.[13] Ten years later, almost every European country had an elite soccer league that commanded the interest of millions of spectators. In France, the number of soccer clubs grew from around 1,000 to over 4,000 between 1920 and 1925. Similar developments took place across the continent.[14] In 1930 Uruguay hosted the first soccer World Cup and the game could now truly be said to be the winter sport of most of the industrialised world. Part of this success was also based on the fact that soccer could offer a symbolic importance that other sports did not have – the memory, often more imagined than real, of the informal games played between British and German troops in No Man's Land during the impromptu truces of Christmas 1914. This was an image of peace and international brotherhood that stood in sharp contrast to the militarism of sports such as rugby union and American football or the national gymnastic movements of Europe. Indeed, Jules Rimet would refer to FIFA as a more successful version of the League of Nations.

Soccer's rise was not completely uncontested in Europe. Handball, which had emerged from the Czech game of *hazena* and Danish game of *hanndbol*, was codified in the 1890s and developed most extensively by the Germans after the war, and was vigorously promoted as an alternative to Anglo-Saxon sport by supporters of gymnastics. It spread rapidly in Europe from the 1920s but failed to slow the soccer juggernaut in the slightest, although as late as the 1950s Swiss aficionados were still promoting handball as a more suitable sport for schoolchildren than soccer.[15] This growth in sporting participation in Europe differed from the anglophone world in that it was usually based on a club structure, largely derived from the gymnastic movements, which themselves had taken their forms of organisation from the military and nationalist clubs of the *Turner*, Sokol and similar movements. In contrast, outside of the professional 'clubs', the British and American sporting model emerged from the schools and universities that had incubated sport as a force for moral education.[16]

The second reason for sport's spectacular emergence was the response of the capitalist world to the 1917 October Revolution in Russia. Although 'welfare capitalism' – the provision of sports and recreation facilities to employees – emerged in the late nineteenth century as a way of building *esprit de corps* between management and labour, the Bolshevik revolution and the revolutionary upheavals that swept across Europe in the aftermath of the First World War accelerated this trend. In France, where the ruling class was probably more acutely aware of the potential for social overturns, the major manufacturers all built extensive sports facilities in the 1920s. Motor manufacturers and their allied trades – Citroën, Peugeot, Renault and Michelin – led the way, with André Citroën declaring: 'I am a firm advocate of sport. I do my best to encourage it and expect the best results from it amongst my workers.'[17] Ernest Mercier, a director of the petroleum conglomerate that would become Total, founded the magazine *Le Muscle*, dedicated to industrial efficiency and social harmony. In Japan, similar developments took place following a national strike wave that swept across the country in 1920. After workers at Yawata Iron & Steel struck for a nine-hour day, the company introduced a company base-ball competition. By the mid-1920s, most major Japanese firms had a representative baseball team that would compete in inter-company tournaments.[18] Italy under-went a huge boom in the provision of company sports and sports facilities in the 1920s as FIAT, Alfa Romeo and Pirelli, among many others, scrambled to build gymnasia and provide playing fields for their rebellious workers.[19] Works-based teams, leagues and cup competitions sprouted up throughout Britain. 'No enterprising firm which aspires to be in the van of progress or which is alive to its own best interests can afford to neglect welfare work for its employees,' wrote a representative of the Birmingham brewers' Mitchell & Butlers. 'For, as health means good work, and recreation means fitness and contentment, welfare is a very efficient synonym for prosperity in every sense of the word.'[20]

These developments had a particularly important impact on women's participation in sport. For the first time, young working-class women had the opportunity to play sport outside of an educational setting. As millions of men were mobilised and moved from the factory to the front, women took their places in industry during the war. The long working hours in munitions and other factories in the war industries led to the provision of welfare and recreation facilities for women. In Britain and France, football became a feature of working life for thousands of women.[21] In the US baseball played the same role. Sides like the 'ladies' team of the Preston-based Dick, Kerr & Co. engineering factory became local celebrities and raised tens of thousands of pounds for war-time charities. Local cup and league competitions emerged in the industrial regions of Britain between 1917 and 1921 but in December 1921, as part of the general move to force women out of the factories and reassert their 'role' as wives and mothers, the Football Association banned its clubs from allowing their grounds to be used by women, reducing the sport to a marginal existence until the 1970s.[22] Women's participation may have been looked upon by the football authorities with amused indulgence during times of national emergency but as soon as the status quo was re-established, football once more became a masculine kingdom.

It was not so easy to re-establish male supremacy in other sports. The example of Bolshevik Russia led to a widespread questioning of social and recreational mores around the world. 'If other women can have themselves elected to parliament,' asked a German woman boxer in 1922, 'why shouldn't we be allowed to box?'[23] In 1920 Dick Kerr's Ladies had played a four-match series against a women's soccer team from Paris. The French side had been organised by Alice Milliat, a rower who was the president of the Fédération des Sociétés Féminines Sportives, which had been founded in France in 1917.[24] As well as soccer, the federation organised women's competitions in field hockey, basketball, swimming and athletics. In October 1921, Milliat led the formation of the Fédération Sportive Féminine Internationale (FSFI). Among its goals was the organisation of a women's Olympic Games for track and field athletes.[25] This was a direct challenge to the International Olympic Committee, which was unequivocally opposed to women's athletics. Coubertin's position was unblinking, stating that 'association with women's athleticism is bad, and that such athleticism should be excluded from the Olympic program ... the Olympiads were restored for the rare and solemn glorification of the individual male athlete'.[26]

The success of the FSFI's first Women's Olympics in 1922 forced the IOC to reconsider its position. This was not because the aristocratic gentlemen's club that was the IOC was becoming liberal. Rather, it was fearful that women's athletics would grow outside of its influence. So in 1923 it advised its affiliated organisations to take control of women's sport to prevent 'abuses and excesses'. It eventually agreed to allow women's track and field events at the 1928 Amsterdam games, but only five events and with no races further than 800 metres.[27] This was too restrictive even for the usually mild-mannered British, whose women athletes did not compete in the 1928 Olympics. By the 1930s, women's participation in sport had increased yet their control over the sports they played had probably diminished. The FSFI had been eclipsed by the IOC's machinations, and physical education, a discipline essentially founded by women such as Martina Bergman-Österberg and an overwhelmingly female profession before the First World War (for example, almost 80 per cent of American PE graduates in 1903 were women), was by the 1930s dominated by men.[28]

Instead of mass participation in sports, women's physical recreation came to be dominated by organisations such as, in Britain, the Women's League of Health and Beauty, which stressed fitness as an aid to motherhood and wifely duty. 'It's your duty to be beautiful' a popular song of the time proclaimed.[29] In Germany and Japan, women's sporting activity was promoted explicitly as a means to improve the race. 'The modern girl is an athlete,' proclaimed the handbook of the Bund Deutscher Mädel, the Nazi women's organisation. Welcoming the Hitler Youth to Japan in 1937, Toyo Fujimura, in her book *Women's Physical Education* argued that 'we have to make women true shitsujitsu gōken [gentlemanly athletes] since they will be mothers and teachers of the future'.[30] Nor was female sporting achievement necessarily congruent with a commitment to women's liberation. Violette Gouraud-Morris, the multi-talented French sportswoman of the 1920s who competed in the Olympics, played international soccer, cycled, boxed and won motor racing's Bol d'Or in 1927 became a fascist and one of the Gestapo's most notorious torturers in war-time France.[31]

Alongside the impact of military service and the impact of the Russian Revolution on social relations, sport's new importance in the inter-war era was directly related to the changed political structure of post-war Europe. The collapse of most European monarchies at the end of the war led to a proliferation of new nation-states in central and eastern Europe, each seeking to create its own national identity and differentiate itself from its neighbours, with whom they often shared a language, culture and counterposed territorial claims. Thus the states of the former Hapsburg Empire – Austria, Hungary, Czechoslovakia and Yugoslavia – were the driving force behind the international development of European football in the inter-war years, organising European club competitions such as the Mitropa Cup and the Central European Cup for national sides, a precursor of the European Championships.[32] These were also the countries that pioneered professional football in Europe. In a similar spirit, Mussolini's fascist regime eagerly promoted sport as a way of asserting Italian international prominence, hosting both the soccer World Cup and the inaugural European Athletic Championships in 1934.

Sport was the ideal cultural medium for nation-building. It was binary, simple and universal. Binary, in that it emphasised us versus them. Simple, in that it required no specialised cultural knowledge to grasp the concept of local and national team loyalties. And universal in that it could not only unite all classes behind a team or athlete but also because it offered personal involvement in the national sporting project as a participant or a spectator. In the pyramid of sport, everyone could be a member of the national team. This was not an 'imagined' nation: the eleven footballers wearing the national shirt or the athlete competing in the Olympics were merely the focal point of a national culture and structures that reached down to every member of society, part of conscious attempts to unify the nation in opposition to competing ethnic, religious and, especially given the threat of revolutionary Bolshevism, class affiliations. As Sebastian Haffner observed about his youth in the Weimar Republic: 'through sports, the lure of the war game, the old thrilling magic of national rivalry, was being exercised and maintained … this was not some harmless venting of bellicose instinct'.[33]

The administrators of sport were willing and active participants in this process. Carl Diem, whose gymnast-like suppleness of principle enabled him to be the leader of the German Olympic movement before, during and after Hitler's regime, shared the opinions of the Nazis on the value of sport: 'for us the measure of sport is the extent to which it makes man able to fight as a soldier and a woman able to bear children'.[34] Such views were not confined to right-wing Germans. Similar attitudes linking sport with militarist vigilance could also be found at the highest echelons of Anglo-Saxon sport, as a 1921 speech by English Rugby Union secretary Rowland Hill highlighted:

> generations yet unborn will enter with spirit into the great games of England and will regard their country with such reverence and keen affection that should she ever again need the services of her young men they will be prepared to follow in the footsteps of the illustrious dead.[35]

Indeed, as we have seen, the Tour de France owed its birth to the anti-Semitic prejudices of opponents of the editor of *Le Vélo*, who started their own newspaper and subsequent cycle race. As the inter-war years once again demonstrated, modern sport was intertwined with nationalism and conservatism, which meant that it inevitably overlapped with militarism. And sometimes much worse.

On 2 June 1933, four months after Hitler came to power in Germany, Nazi education minister Bernard Rust ordered that Jews be excluded from all sports associations. But many German sports' organisations had already pre-empted him. Two months earlier, in April, the German football, boxing and tennis federations had expelled their Jewish members.[36] In May the *Turner* movement purged 20,000 Jews from membership. Some soccer clubs, such as Karlsruhe, Nürnburg and Eintracht Frankfurt did not even bother to wait for the official instruction from their football federation to expel their Jewish members. With the exception of a handful of individuals, sports organisations had few qualms about supporting the Nazi regime.[37] Those outside of Germany showed little inclination to oppose the regime. In December 1935 the German national soccer side travelled to England for a friendly international match, staged provocatively at Tottenham Hotspur, then as now a club known for its large Jewish support. In 1938 the England team, at the urging of the Foreign Office but with no significant opposition, lined up before the kick-off of their match with Germany in Berlin and gave the Nazi salute in honour of their hosts.[38]

The Germany–England match was staged at the Olympic Stadium, which in 1936 had witnessed the most conspicuous display of unity between sport and Nazi ideology. The official narrative of the 1936 Olympics has long been based around the myth that Hitler 'hijacked' the games for his political ends, yet the reality was that the International Olympic Committee were more than willing partners. The IOC swept aside the criticisms of Nazi Germany made by the international campaign to boycott the 1936 Games about the regime's persecution of Jews, gypsies and the labour movement. 'We have no intention of being influenced by agitation originating from a political source,' declared IOC president and Belgian aristocrat Henri de Baillet-Latour. 'It is purely political in nature, being built upon willful assertions, the falseness of which was easily proved.'[39] For those with any doubt about the IOC's sympathies, the Games' official newsletter approvingly quoted Hitler's views on sport: 'Sporting chivalrous contest arouses the best human attributes. It does not sever but unites opponents in mutual understanding and reciprocal respect. It also helps to knit the bond of peace between nations. Therefore may the Olympic flame never expire!'[40]

Indeed, many in the leadership of sport and physical education saw the Berlin Olympics as a model to be emulated.[41] Coubertin himself declared the 1936 Games to be the best ever. Arthur Steinhaus, professor of physiology in Chicago and a future president of the American Academy of Physical Education, gave a speech at the 1936 Olympics' Congress of Physical Education on 'The Science of Educating the Body' in which he called Hitler 'the great leader of the German people' and ended his lecture by quoting from a speech from the Führer.[42] In Britain, as elsewhere, the political nature of the Berlin Games was downplayed. 'Surely one of the greatest sports festivals of all time, [that] made its magnificent contribution towards a fitter youth and more peaceful international relationships', declared Harold Abrahams, himself Jewish, in the British Olympic Association's Official Report. For many in sport, the lustre did not fade even as war approached. In March 1939, the head of the School of Athletics, Games and Physical Education at Loughborough College – Britain's leading sports' college – Captain F.A.M. Webster, extolled the 1936 Games as 'one of the greatest sporting triumphs the world has yet witnessed'. 'As in ancient Greece, so it is today in Germany', he wrote, 'the sports grounds were, and are, places where the young go to train and compete strenuously and the old watch knowledgeably and exercise themselves gently'.[43] Nor was the IOC's enthusiasm undiminished. In the spring of 1939 it awarded the 1940 Winter Olympics to Garmisch-Partenkirchen in Germany, the same venue that had staged the 1936 winter games.

The 'deep politics' of sport had never been so exposed, nor more utilised.

11

REVOLUTIONARY SPORT

Bourgeois sport has a single clear-cut purpose: to make men more stupid than they are. ...
In bourgeois states, sport is employed to produce cannon fodder for imperialist wars.

Maxim Gorky, 1928.[1]

In the 1920s and 1930s hundreds of thousands of working-class men and women across Europe watched and participated in sport. International competitions were organised with the express intention of undermining national rivalries. Women took place in athletic contests free from the shackles of discrimination. In Frankfurt, Vienna and Antwerp, tens of thousands gathered for huge sporting festivals that could attract more spectators and athletes than the Olympic Games. But these activities were not organised by commercial entrepreneurs or moralistic educationalists. This was a sporting culture based on socialism and the labour movement that sought to provide an alternative to the nationalism, male chauvinism and hyper-competition of the commercial and amateur models of sport.

The rise of the workers' sport movement in Europe was inspired by the growth of the socialist and the trade union movements, and spurred by the lack of sports facilities available to working-class people. The German Social Democratic Party (SPD), as with almost everything else in the pre-1914 European workers' movement, provided the model for others to follow. The German workers' sport movement evolved from the left-wing of the *Turner* movement. As a result of the failed democratic revolution of 1848, the *Turner* had split into a constitutional monarchist wing, backed by Friedrich Jahn, and a radical democratic wing. Many of the radicals emigrated to the United States. By the 1890s those who identified with Jahn had become increasingly right-wing and anti-Semitic, having the replaced liberal-national flag of black, red and gold with the imperial flag of black, red and white.[2] The growth of the SPD, which had been founded in 1863 and legalised in 1890, inspired the creation of the Arbeiter Turn-und Sportbund (ATSB, Workers' *Turner* League) in 1893. By 1900 it had 37,000 members, which increased to 153,000 by 1910. Although not formally linked to the SPD, the tenor of the movement can be gauged from the attitude of the leaders of its workers' cycling association: '[if] we consider the party and the trade unions in this class war as the main block of the army, which is marching forward like the infantry and artillery, then we worker cyclists are the red hussars, the cavalry of the class war'.[3]

In Tsarist Russia, where socialist activity was illegal, the social democrats made use of the few workers' sports clubs in existence to educate the working class in Marxist politics and to train them in the art of insurrection.[4] In the more liberal atmosphere of western Europe, the seeds of the French workers' sport movement were sown in 1908 when workers in Paris formed a socialist sports and athletic association. By 1913 the movement had spread throughout France, leading to the formation of the Fédération Socialiste de Sport et de Gymnastique.[5] Similar movements were established in Belgium and Switzerland, and in 1913 the Fédération Sportive Socialiste Internationale in Ghent was founded by Belgian, British, French, German and Swiss socialists.[6]

But the workers' sports organisations were established not only to provide political and practical support to the labour movement, but also to meet the very real need for sport and physical culture among the working class. The demand for healthy working and living conditions was a central plank of the platform of the socialist movement. The demand for leisure time – most memorably elaborated in *The Right to be Lazy*, the 1883 pamphlet by Karl Marx's son-in-law Paul Lafargue – was a necessary corollary to the campaign for a shorter working day. Moreover, sporting facilities were generally available only to the rich and privileged. Sports clubs were part of the recreational and social culture of the middle and upper classes. The working classes were not welcomed. Nor did employers provide sports facilities in any substantial way until the 1920s. Mass working-class parties like the SPD therefore saw themselves as providing the opportunities for physical recreation that capitalism would not supply.[7]

This explains the hostility of much of the socialist movement to the emergence of mass spectator sport. This opposition was also based on internationalist revulsion at the nationalism of modern sport, which produced 'cannon fodder for imperialist wars' in Maxim Gorky's words. And football, boxing and similar spectator sports were organised on an openly capitalist basis, and offered a commercialised alternative to those sports provided by organisations such as the SPD. In Britain, soccer's emergence as the dominant sport of the working class pre-dated the growth of a mass socialist movement. Moreover, much of the leadership of the early British socialist movement shared many of the middle-class prejudices of the administrators of amateur sport – H.M. Hyndman (1842–1921), the patrician leader of the Social Democratic Federation, had played first-class cricket for Cambridge University, Sussex and the MCC.[8]

The other major socialist criticism of modern sport was that it appeared to be a distraction from politics. In 1902 the SPD's leading theoretician, Karl Kautsky, had criticised the British working class for their lack of interest in socialism, blaming it on the fact that 'it is foot-ball, boxing, horse racing and opportunities for gambling which move them the deepest and to which their entire leisure time, their individual powers, and their material means are devoted'.[9] This rather moralistic argument bore more than a passing resemblance to the views of the advocates of rational recreation in the mid-nineteenth century, merely substituting socialism in place of Christianity. So it should be no surprise that the Independent Labour Party, formed in the rugby and soccer hotbed of Bradford in 1893, recoiled from the sports of the industrial working masses. Football, it argued:

> is a spectacle and a debasing spectacle at that … absorbing from year's end to year's end, the minds of the great mass of the workers, rendering them incapable of understanding their own needs and rights. We are in danger of producing a race of workers who can only obey their masters and think football.[10]

In fact, the most militant sections of the British industrial working class were to be found in exactly the same areas where football and rugby were at their most popular: the north of England, south Wales and the west of Scotland. As a writer to the British Communist Party's *Daily Worker* argued in 1930, it was perfectly possible to be both a proletarian revolutionary and a rugby league (or soccer) player.[11] Indeed, in 1915 Lenin himself had pointed to the Christmas truces of 1914 in which British and German troops played informal football matches against each other as an object lesson in internationalist fraternisation.[12] A more subtle criticism of the role of sport was made by Trotsky in his 1925 *Where is Britain Going?*, which argued that 'social conventions, the church and the press, and … sport' had restricted and suppressed the possibilities for cultural enrichment available to the working class under capitalism.[13] In a socialist society, the cultural level of the working class would be raised to such an extent that, for the first time in its existence, the proletariat would have access to, and involvement in, the fullest possible range of cultural engagement, not just sport or commercial entertainment. One of the goals of the revolution, he wrote in 1923, was 'to give the satisfaction of this desire [for amusement] a higher artistic quality, at the same time making amusement a weapon of collective education, freed from the guardianship of the pedagogue and the tiresome habit of moralizing'.[14]

The belief that sport was a prophylactic against workers' revolution was echoed from the opposite direction by supporters of capitalism. G.M. Trevelyan was not alone in his drawing-room assertion that the chateaux of France's aristocracy would not have been burned by the peasantry in 1789 if only the French had played cricket. Robert Bruce Lockhart, a British diplomat stationed in Russia in the early years of the Bolshevik revolution, also believed that if more sport had been played in Russia the Winter Palace would never have been stormed. The introduction of soccer was, he thought, 'an immense step forward in the social life of the Russian worker and, if it had been adopted rapidly for all mills, history might have changed'.[15] Gino Bartali's 1948 Tour de France victory, which took place in the aftermath of the attempted assassination of Italian Communist Party (PCI) leader Palmiro Togliatti, is believed by right-wing commentators to have diverted the attention of outraged workers and dissipated the threat of an insurrection in crisis-torn Italy, although it was actually the PCI itself that stopped the situation esca-lating in order to maintain 'social peace'.[16] As we saw in the previous chapter, the idea that sport could dampen the threat of revolution lay behind the tremendous expansion of work-based welfare and leisure provision across the industrialised world in the 1920s.

Sport became an arena in which the class struggle was being waged, a fact also acknowledged by all wings of the workers' movement. In September 1920 parties belonging to the Socialist, or Second, International met at Lucerne in Switzerland to found the International Association for Sport and Physical Culture, which became known as the Lucerne Sports International (LSI). Its stated goal was to oppose nationalism and militarism while providing sports facilities to workers.[17] To those who remembered the parties of the Second International's support for, or failure to actively oppose, the First World War this seemed disingenuous at least and in August 1921 the third congress of the Communist, or Third, International founded its own network, the Red Sports International (RSI). Unlike the Lucerne International, which had deliberately omitted the word 'socialist' from its title when it was founded, the RSI openly proclaimed that sport was a political battle-ground and that the goal of the workers' sports movement was to contribute to the struggle for a revolution on similar lines to the October Revolution in Russia.[18] Stung by the communists' criticism, the leadership of the Lucerne International effectively abandoned its belief in a unified workers' sport movement and eventually, in August 1927, broke off all relations with the RSI and banned its own members from taking part in the 1928 Moscow Spartakiad. In Germany, tens of thousands of communists were expelled from the Lucerne-affiliated Arbeiter Turn-und Sportbund.[19]

In the Soviet Union itself, debates raged about the nature of sport and physical culture.[20] The demands of the civil war following the 1917 revolution initially subordinated all physical culture to the needs of the military, and sports activity was controlled by the department of universal military training, Vsevobuch. The eventual defeat of the counter-revolution and the stabilisation of the economy at the start of the 1920s decoupled sport from military exigencies, giving rise to several schools of thought about the role of sport in a socialist society.[21] For much of the early 1920s Soviet thinking was dominated by the 'Hygienist' movement, which argued that physical culture for the working masses should be integrated into all aspects of education, and not seen as a separate activity in its own right. Like many in the social democratic movement, they were largely opposed to competitive sport, so much so that at the Trade Union Games of 1925 soccer, boxing and even gymnastics were not staged. Another group, the 'Proletkultists' opposed all sport as bourgeois, instead arguing that the working class had to invent new forms of physical recreation appropriate to a proletarian state. Their alternative to sport was spectacular mass pageants that involved both physical activity and education. Although few records survive of their activities, they appeared to be something like a cross between a military tattoo and a mardi gras, as can be imagined from the titles of some of the Proletkultist events: 'Rescue from the Fascists', 'Indians, British and Reds' and 'Pageant of the Universal October'.[22] It is worth noting that this type of activity was not confined to supporters of the Bolsheviks. At the 1925 Workers' Olympiad, organised by the social democratic LSI, 60,000 people took part in the 'Workers' Struggle for the Earth' pageant.[23]

Many of the debates about sport reflected wider discussions in Soviet society. For example, the Proletkultists were more famous as an artistic movement that rejected all hitherto existing forms of art as bourgeois. Until the consolidation of Stalin's bureaucratic rule, the Soviet state itself was largely agnostic about policy in the sporting sphere, other than to insist on its importance in promoting the health and fitness of the population. Lenin, a keen walker and cyclist, endorsed the idea of 'healthy minds in healthy bodies' and competitive sport flourished alongside the initiatives of the Hygienists and Proletkultists.[24] The first Soviet chess championship was staged in 1920, the first soccer championship in 1922 and the first basketball championship in 1923.

This latter championship was for women's basketball – the men's championship began in the following year – and highlighted a crucial difference between sport in the Soviet Union and the rest of the capitalist world. Unlike elsewhere, the Soviet government actively promoted women's involvement in all forms of sporting activity, integrating physical culture into female education policies and workplace-based welfare facilities. This perhaps can be most notably seen in Dziga Vertov's 1929 film, *Man With a Movie Camera*, in which women can be seen playing a wide variety of sports, including basketball, high jump, discus and shot put. Moreover, in direct contrast to the western sporting model, women's sport was not promoted as an aid to motherhood and wifely duties. In Soviet sports propaganda, Alison Rowley explains, 'the traditional image of womanhood was jettisoned in favour of a more modern woman dressed practically for sport, exuded good health and was the equal of the men around her'.[25] The goals of sport in the early USSR were not aimed at making women better wives and mothers but fit, active workers, who were also physically prepared for military service should the need arise. This contrast with western sport was most starkly highlighted at Moscow's 1928 international Spartakiad, when 4,000 athletes, mainly from Russia but with representatives from fourteen other nations, gathered to stage an alternative to the social democrats' Workers' Olympiads. In contrast to the restrained language of the Lucerne International, there was no mistaking the aims of the Spartakiad, as demonstrated by a speaker at its opening ceremony:

> We take the word Spartakiad from Spartacus – the hero of the ancient world and leader of the insurgent slaves … [our goal is] the common struggle for revolution – classical physical culture and the revolutionary militant culture of Marxism-Leninism.[26]

The workers' sport movement became a major phenomenon in inter-war Europe, comparable to Coubertin's Olympics. By 1931 the German ATSB had 1.2 million members, which included 320,000 members of the Workers' Cycling Association, and the German Communist Party sports group claimed a further 125,000. In Austria, the workers' sport organisation had almost a quarter of a million members in 1931, while the Czech movement had over 200,000. Overall the Socialist Workers' Sports International, the name adopted by the Lucerne International in 1928 in answer to communist criticism that it downplayed its politics, had over 1.8 million members by 1931.[27] The most spectacular demonstrations of the strength of the movement were seen at its Workers' Olympiads. The first was held in Frankfurt in 1925 with athletes from twelve countries, and was watched by 150,000 spectators. It stood in stark contrast to the International Olympic Committee's Paris Olympics of the previous year. Whereas the Paris Olympics barred Germany and its war-time allies from taking part, and refused to allow women to compete in athletic events, the Workers' Olympiad welcomed athletes from all nations and organised women's track and field events. Indeed, a new world record for the women's 100 metres relay was set in Frankfurt, despite the downplaying of record attempts and a focus on non-elite sports. The 1931 Workers' Olympiad, held in Vienna, had 80,000 participants across its events, which included mass gymnastics, and was watched by a quarter of a million people, both numbers in excess of those for the 1932 Los Angeles Olympics.[28] The RSI, forced to stage its own events, responded with international Spartakiads in Moscow in 1928 and Berlin in 1931. By the mid-1930s, Stalin's pursuit of a 'popular front' stretching from himself to liberal capitalist politicians forced a rapprochement between the two workers' sport internationals. The proposed Barcelona workers' games of 1936, staged to counter the Berlin Olympics, was abandoned when the Spanish civil war broke out, but the 1937 Antwerp Workers' Olympiad attracted 27,000 athletes and tens of thousands of spectators, including 50,000 for the closing ceremony.

Given such support, one must ask ask why the workers' sport movement disappeared. The most obvious point is that its two strongest components outside of the USSR were in Germany and Austria. In both countries, the labour movement and its organisations were drowned in blood by fascism. The advent of the Second World War had similar consequences for the rest of Europe. Alongside the physical destruction of the movement and its supporters, the Stalin regime's abandonment of revolutionary politics transformed Soviet sport from an instrument of change to a tool of diplomacy abroad and nationalism at home.[29] In 1934, *Red Sport* signalled a change in official policy when it declared that athletes should now seek 'to win first place in the world for Soviet sport. We want victories, records, success.'[30] With the Soviet integration into international sports organisations such as the IOC and FIFA in the decade after the Second World War, there ceased to be an ideological alternative to sport in the capitalist world.

12

SEX, DRUGS AND SPORT IN THE COLD WAR

We face in the Soviet Union a powerful and implacable adversary. ... To meet the challenge of this enemy will require determination and will and effort on the part of all Americans. Only if our citizens are physically fit will they be fully capable of such an effort.

John F. Kennedy, 1960.[1]

Just six months after the end of the Second World War in Europe, Moscow Dynamo soccer club began a four-match tour of Britain. Conceived in an atmosphere of war-time unity, in which the anti-communist Winston Churchill praised Stalin, and communist parties opposed strikes, the tour's organisers hoped that it would help sustain the alliance into the post-war peace. Dynamo arrived in November 1945 and played Chelsea, Cardiff City, Arsenal and Glasgow Rangers. They drew two matches and won two (one a 10–1 mauling of Cardiff City), attracting enormous crowds and generating controversy that would last for decades. The era of Cold War games had begun – and sport in the western capitalist world would seek to reassert its old moral authority while being forced to change in unexpected ways.[2]

The USSR's entry into the western sporting world had been foreshadowed in the 1930s when Stalin moved towards a strategy of overt peaceful coexistence with capitalist countries. The first fruits of this policy were seen in France, when a 'popular front' government of socialists and liberals supported by the Communist Party came to power in May 1936. In August of that year a Spartakiad was staged in Paris, the first time the event had been staged outside of the USSR.[3] The war-time partnership with Britain and the USA against Nazi Germany was viewed by Stalin as the highest achievement of this policy. He fully expected that this anti-fascist alliance would continue into peacetime and at the end of the war the Soviet sports authorities began to join international sporting federations: most notably FIFA in 1946, the IAAF (International Amateur Athletics Federation) in 1947 and, eventually, the IOC in 1951. Embracing what had formerly been denounced as bourgeois sport, the Soviet leadership declared in 1949 that its sporting mission was to 'win world supremacy in the major sports in the immediate future'.[4]

Although the Soviet leadership had abandoned revolutionary aims in sport as it had in politics, the USSR's planned, centralised economy gave it tremendous advantages over its western sporting rivals. Resources could easily be directed into particular sports. The recreational facilities provided by large factories or administrative offices allowed wide participation, especially for women. There were few social barriers preventing entry into sports that were seen in the West as socially elite, such as equestrianism. Perhaps the most remarkable example of the Soviet Union's ability to focus resources and personnel on sport was ice hockey. The sport was unknown in the USSR before the Second World War but was taken up in the 1940s. The national side played its first game in January 1954 and two months later carried off the world championship, thumping the previously dominant Canadian side 7–1 in the final. They then proceeded to carry off the Olympic gold medal two years later.[5]

The full impact of the USSR's entry into world sport was felt with shock and disbelief at the 1952 Helsinki Olympics. After some hesitation about admitting a self-proclaimed communist country into membership, hubris and the desire to expand its sphere of influence finally got the better of the IOC and it accepted the Soviets' application to join the Olympic movement in May 1951. When the Games took place in July 1952, the USSR finished second in the medals table behind the USA, with twenty-two golds and more silver and bronze medals than any other nation.[6] To underline the new era that had begun, Soviet ally Hungary finished third. Four years later at the Melbourne Games, the Soviets topped the medal table across gold, silver and bronze. Similar seismic shifts were seen in soccer, where the Hungarian team dominated the European game in the mid-1950s, and even in rugby union, where the Rumanians temporarily seemed to threaten the Anglo-French dominance of the sport.

Coming at the height of the Cold War, with actual war raging in Korea and revolution in China consolidating under Mao Zedong, the triumphs of the Soviets and their allies placed a question mark over sport in the West. On the basis of a belief that success at sport reflected a successful society, western dominance of sport had not only been taken for granted but was also symbolic of an underlying cultural confidence. For the US in particular, the Olympics had become the most important international stage on which it could demonstrate its athletic superiority, given the parochial nature of baseball and American football.[7] In response to the Soviet gate-crashing of their arena, western commentators complained about the 'politicisation' of sport, blithely ignoring the political underpinnings of western sport, and accused the Soviets of behaving unfairly.[8] The focus of these attacks was the Soviets' ambiguous stance towards the amateur ethos. Indeed, there had been some professional athletes in the USSR in the 1920s, and in the 1930s the more popular spectator sports, especially soccer, began to pay players. Although some voices raised concerns, there was no systematic ideological opposition to professionalism in Soviet sport.[9] In October 1945, as part of the policy of encouraging sporting competition with the West, the Soviet government decided to pay salaries to all elite athletes and set a sliding scale of bonuses for breaking world or national records.[10] However, this was quickly abandoned in July 1947 when it was discovered that most of the international governing bodies that the Soviets wished to join still pursued some form of amateurism, especially the IOC, the most important organisation of all for the USSR.

This decision to adopt amateurism changed little in practical terms – most Soviet athletes already belonged to clubs that were associated with workplaces – other than elite athletes now declaring their occupations to be students, soldiers or teachers. Hypocrisy, the Russians quickly discovered, was as central to amateurism in the East as it was in the West. Despite the outcries about Soviet shamateurism from sporting cold warriors, Soviet athletes were little different from US college athletes, sportsmen in the British armed forces or even those English cricketers who were made 'assistant secretaries' of county clubs in order to preserve their amateur status while being paid by the club. Some western athletes even viewed the Soviet system with envy. Gordon Pirie, the English 5,000 metres silver medallist at the 1956 Olympics, attacked the 'hypocrisy of British athletics', comparing it unfavourably with the USSR where 'the jobs which amateur athletes have are purely nominal. These jobs keep them with reasonable comfort but do not interfere in any way with their athletics.'[11]

The rhetorical flourishes of conservative sports administrators and politicians aside, disputes over amateurism were little more than storms in an etymological tea cup. From the 1960s, the major focus of western criticism switched to the use of drugs in Soviet sport. How could Russian and East European athletes become so successful? After all, western propaganda insisted that these were totalitarian societies in which individual talent and initiative was rigorously suppressed. It appeared that the only logical explanation was that Soviet athletes had an unfair advantage – and the finger was pointed at 'performance-enhancing' drugs.[12] The USSR, as imagined by the western media, was using drugs to create a race of invincible supermen. This concern over drug use was eventually to reshape the moral landscape of modern sport. In an era when the certainties of the old moral code of amateurism were melting away, the question of drugs offered a paradigm shift through which moral control over sport could be reasserted. Like professionalism in the 1890s, drugs became the evil 'other' to contrast with the alleged natural purity of sport.

It was not always thus. Pharmacological potions had been used by athletes in the ancient Greek Olympics to boost performance. It had been commonplace in the nineteenth century to use drugs in endurance sports such as cycling and long-distance running. More to the point, it was not until the 1920s that opium, heroin and other opiates were banned from sale to the general public.[13] The British had even fought two wars with China in the mid-nineteenth century to retain control of the opium trade in the Far East. The discovery that the coca plant of South America was a powerful stimulant led to numerous scientific experiments in the 1870s and widespread public use of cocaine as a 'pick-me-up' by the turn of the century, perhaps most notably in the invention in 1886 of Coca-Cola, a drink originally based on a cocktail of cocaine and caffeine. Naturally, the use of such stimulants was taken up by athletes and trainers eager to gain an extra advantage. The prevailing attitude can be gauged from the official report of the 1904 Olympic Games:

> The Marathon race, from a medical standpoint, demonstrated that drugs are of much benefit to athletes along the road. … Ten miles from the finish, [the eventual winner Thomas] Hicks began to show positive signs of collapse. When he asked for a drink of water, it was refused him, and his mouth was sponged out with distilled water. He managed to keep up well, until seven miles from the stadium, and then the author was forced to administer one-sixtieth grain of sulphate of strychnine, by the mouth, besides the white of one egg. … As Hicks passed the twenty-mile post, his color began to become ashen pale, and then another tablet of one-sixtieth grain strychnine was administered him, and two more eggs, besides a sip of brandy.[14]

Following the First World War the increasing importance of sport to society led to the emergence of 'sports science' in Germany and America, and with it further investigations of the efficacy of vitamins, hormones, amphetamines and many other chemicals and compounds. In France, the open use of stimulants by cyclists provoked widespread debate, while English football went through a vogue for 'pep pills' and monkey-gland extracts. The widespread use of amphetamines in the Second World War by the military and civilians alike further highlighted the general acceptance of artificial stimulants.

Soviet use of drugs was therefore not unusual. It was part of a wider shift towards the increased use of science and technology to enhance performance in sport.[15] Indeed, Paul Dimeo has demonstrated that both Soviet and American weightlifters and bodybuilders were experimenting with anabolic steroids in the early 1950s, and that the idea that the Americans only took drugs in response to the Russians is incorrect. As is often the case with scientific discovery, both sets of scientists were working at a similarly advanced level in the same field, as demonstrated by the fact that the widespread use of steroids across western sport in the 1960s was made possible by their production by US pharmaceutical companies.

The moral panic that came to dominate discussion about drugs in sport in the 1960s was not only motivated by accusations of Soviet lack of 'fair play'. Drugs of any sort were also associated with the 1960s counter-culture, youth rebellion and student uprisings. The outlawing of opiates and cannabis in the inter-war years had been part of a moral backlash against immigration and relaxed social mores, as can be seen in the unintentionally hilarious 1936 film *Reefer Madness*.[16] The campaign against drugs in sport in the 1960s was a further manifestation of socially conservative opposition to what appeared to be radical changes in society. 'Turn on, tune in and drop out', was not a message that provoked any sympathy among the conservative and often authoritarian leaders of sport. Indeed, in times of social conflict sport was (and is today) seen as an antidote to youthful rebellion, whether in the form of political radicalism or adolescent discontents such as Mods and Rockers in Britain or *blousons noirs* in France.

This anti-drug hysteria was not accompanied by any objective testing of so-called performance-enhancing substances. Although the deaths of cyclists Knud Enemark Jensen in 1960 and Tommy Simpson in 1967 have been claimed as pivotal moments in public perception of the dangers of drugs, Jensen's use of drugs has never been satisfactorily proved and Simpson was just one of thousands of cyclists who traditionally had used stimulants during the Tour de France.[17] In fact, a 2011 study of Belgian, French and Italian riders in the Tour between 1930 and 1964 (two years before drug-testing was introduced in the Tour) suggested that they had a life expectancy eight years greater than their respective general populations. Given that drug-taking was rife among this particular social stratum, the study carried the unspoken implication that the riders' drug-cocktails may even have beneficial health effects.[18]

In fact, it seems quite probable that some drugs used by athletes, including the cyclists' personal elixirs, had no more effect on their ability to win than the lucky charms or game-day superstitions still beloved by many sportsmen and women today. Insofar as they did have an impact, drugs such as anabolic steroids enabled athletes to train more intensely and recover from injury more quickly. Although there are no longitudinal or comparative studies of athletic drug use, the 2007 Mitchell Commission report into steroid use in Major League Baseball offers some insights. The report named twenty-three pitchers and forty-eight batters as steroid users. But sixteen of the pitchers performed worse when using steroids and the batting averages of all forty-eight hitters fell.[19] Even the reports that emerged in the 1990s of the extensive use of drugs within East German athletics demonstrated little more than the prevalence of abuse of athletes by coaches, highlighting that the culture of the physically, sexually and psychologically abusive coach was as common in the East as it was in the West.[20] Indeed, during the 1980s the Italian Athletics Federation was so keen for their athletes to get the benefits of taking anabolic steroids that it made them sign legal waivers in which they stated that they were fully aware of the medical risks.[21]

Viewed within a medical rather than a moral context, drugs are no more and no less than the pharmacological equivalent of the sophisticated medical and technological training expertise – such as customised running shoes, high altitude training camps and hyperbaric chambers – available to the richest elite athletes. It is therefore not surprising that much of the contemporary opposition to the use of drugs in sport echoes the arguments against regular training and specialist coaching used by supporters of amateurism in the nineteenth century. Both insist on 'natural' talent unassisted by outside intervention, both point to the 'immorality' of their opponents and both use arbitrary categories of their own definition to separate the good from the evil.[22]

More to the point, if there is no evidence that drugs boost performance, there is ample evidence that sport itself is not necessarily the healthy lifestyle choice that anti-drugs campaigners claim to promote. Researchers in 2006 discovered that linemen in the NFL had a 52 per cent greater risk of dying from heart disease than the general population. They also found that 56 per cent of all active NFL players were medically obese.[23] At the recreational level, a study in 2009 found that apparently healthy marathon runners had surprisingly high rates of coronary heart disease. 'Strenuous endurance activities, such as marathon running', it warned, 'may even lead to an increased risk of acute cardiac events.'[24] Less catastrophically, chronic hip and joint problems afflict many retired soccer players. Forty-nine per cent of ex-soccer players in their fifties surveyed in the UK in 2000 had been diagnosed with osteoarthritis, a rate two-and-a-half times that of the general population. High jumpers, javelin throwers and handball players have all recorded above-average rates too.[25] And, of course, prohibition of drugs hugely increases the chances of unforeseen health complications due to the lack of medical supervision. Unlike every other sphere of life, sport rejects the progress made by medical and pharmacological science in favour of its own moral certainties. The discourse on drugs in sport was not a debate, but an attempt to define and command the moral high ground.

In the 1960s, it became generally accepted that sport had become so important to national prestige that it was the business of governments everywhere. The intensifying rivalry with the Soviet bloc led western governments to increase state funding of sport, in order to close the so-called 'Muscle Gap', a variation of the Cold War 'Missile Gap' myth used by then Senator John F. Kennedy in the late 1950s.[26] In France, the founding of the Fifth Republic in 1958 was accompanied by a drive by the de Gaulle government to place sport at the centre of French cultural life. 'The best [youths] must be taken in hand to prove the continuity of French vigour and its rebirth in international competition,' wrote de Gaulle in 1960, underlining the strategy of '*La France qui Gagne*'.[27] Even the British Foreign Office, long an exponent of gentlemanly disinterest in international sporting contests, believed by 1959 that 'the Olympic Games have immense prestige and offer a unique stage for the demonstration of national prowess', and bridled at the prospect of British teams losing to opponents from the East.[28]

Throughout North America and western Europe, this governmental interest in sport led to a rapid expansion of state-funded sports facilities, coaching schemes and administrative structures. Sport was no longer only the concern of commercial interests or the legions of volunteers who kept sport alive at a grassroots level. A major beneficiary of increased government attention to sport were women athletes. In all western countries, state funding for women's sports increased. The most notable example of this was in the United States, where Title IX of the Education Amendments of 1972, an amendment to the 1964 Civil Rights Act, mandated that women's sports be funded at the same level as men's sports in high schools and universities.[29] Although most narratives of women's sport imply that this was part of a natural upwards arc of progress, the reality was that women only increased their sporting opportunities either due to struggles by women against sports' existing leaderships, most notably in order to gain admission to Olympic athletic competition, or due to wider social change. The advances women made in the 1960s and

1970s were due to a combination of these elements, driven once more in large part by Cold War concerns in the West about the successes of East European sportswomen.[30]

Although long abandoned by Stalin and his successors, women's rights, including health and physical education, were at the heart of Soviet policy in the early years of the revolution. Not all of this legacy was extinguished and the provision for Soviet women's involvement in sport was far more extensive than in the West. For example, a women's soccer league was established in the USSR in 1940, a time when women's football in the West had no official support whatsoever.[31] The difference between women's sport in the East and the West was thrown into sharp relief at the Helsinki Olympics. Of the forty Russian women at the Games, eighteen won a total of thirty-seven medals. Similar results followed at subsequent Olympics. And between 1958 and 1981, seventeen track and field meetings were staged between Soviet and US women. The USSR won thirteen of these contests.[32]

As could be expected, this domination by East European women was explained by many in the West as due to Soviet cheating, as was the case with their male counterparts. But alongside the usual claims of veiled professionalism and drug-taking, female athletes were also faced with an altogether more personal accusation: that they were not real women. Soviet women's success in strength sports such as the shot put or hammer was highlighted as evidence of their underlying masculinity. The muscular physiques of runners were held up as proof of their lack of femininity. In the mid-1960s the IOC and IAAF introduced compulsory sex-tests for women because, as the *Washington Post* put it, of 'some suspicions that in the last one some of the muscular Russian and Polish babes were not quite as feminine as they declared in the Olympic registry'.[33]

The first testing began in 1966 when international athletics introduced compulsory gynecological inspections for women athletes. Athletes who refused or avoided it were assumed to have something to hide, a reversal of the principle of natural justice and a denial of their right not to undergo what 1972 pentathlon gold medallist Mary Peters described as 'the most crude and degrading experience I have ever known. The doctors proceeded to undertake an examination which, in modern parlance, amounted to a grope.'[34] In 1968 the IOC introduced a smear test to determine whether a woman had two XX chromosomes. This gave a pseudo-scientific veneer to the process, which was based on the IOC's belief that 'hermaphroditism does not exist. One is born a man or a woman and one remains of that sex.'[35] This was scientifically illiterate at best. Although it is usually the case that men have XY chromosomes and women XX chromosomes, sex is determined by the interaction between chromosomes and hormones. Moreover, some women possess a Y chromosome and some men may not. Some possess three or more chromosomes. A number of people can be characterised as intersex, having both or indeterminate genitalia. Like all issues involving human sex and sexuality, reality is both very complicated and infinitely variable.[36]

The IOC's ignorance was matched only by its insensitivity, which meant that women with an unusual genetic make-up or biological disorder who 'failed' the test were publicly humiliated and often confronted with evidence of a medical condition of which they were previously unaware. Not a single man posing as a woman was ever unmasked by a sex-test. Nor was any woman discovered who was being transformed into a man through the use of drugs containing testosterone. This regularly used rationale for testing had even less basis in science. No drugs can alter human chromosomes. And, of course, no-one suggested sex-tests for male athletes. Sports men have never had to prove that they were men – because playing sport was one of the most important ways in which men demonstrated their masculinity. As in the nineteenth century, women who enjoyed or excelled at sports were still suspected of hidden masculinity.[37] When forced into a corner, defenders of sex-testing resorted to the argument that women with higher than usual levels of testosterone had an unfair advantage over other women athletes, an argument that could equally apply to male athletes with high levels of the hormone, and one that ignored the fact that sporting success for both sexes is in large part underpinned by genetic advantage.

As with much else in the Olympic movement, the origins of 'gender paranoia' about successful women athletes emerged at the 1936 Berlin Games, where at least one sex-test was carried out. American Helen Stephens was subjected to a genital inspection after defeating the 1932 gold medallist Stella Walsh of Poland in the 100 metres final.[38] Ironically, it was Walsh who was discovered to have ambiguous sex organs and both XX and XY chromosomes after she died in 1980. Doubts had also been expressed about Germany's Dora Ratjen, who came fourth in the Olympic high jump. Shortly after setting a new world record in 1938 she was arrested by German police after being accused of being a transvestite man, an offence that carried the threat of being sent to a Nazi concentration camp. She admitted that she was a man, but had been mistakenly identified as a girl at birth, and was raised and competed as a female.[39] It should come as no surprise that the first call for regular testing was made by arch-reactionary Avery Brundage, then president of the US Olympic Committee and vice-president of the IAAF, at the very first IOC meeting he attended as a member in 1936. He cited the examples of Czech runner Zdenka Koubkova and English shot putter and javelin thrower Mary Weston. Both were raised as girls and competed as women but opted to have sex-change surgery in their twenties. 'All women athletes entered in the Olympics,' Brundage argued, 'should be subjected to a thorough physical examination to make sure they were really 100 per cent female.'[40]

This outrageous assumption of the right to determine someone's sex, perhaps the most intimately personal part of their identity, was never abrogated by the IOC or any other sporting organisation. But by the end of the 1990s sex-testing no longer had the immediate ideological purpose of the Cold War and had fallen into disuse following the restoration of capitalism in the USSR and eastern Europe. Yet gender paranoia was not dead – indeed, one might say that it was embedded in sport's chromosomes – and it would re-appear once more in the twenty-first century.

13

TAKING SIDES IN THE 1960s

I ain't got no quarrel with them Viet Cong. ... They never called me n–r.

Muhammad Ali, 1966.[1]

On 16 October 1968, the Olympic 200 metres gold medal was won in a world record time of 19.83 seconds. Broadcast live and in colour – the first time the summer Olympics had been generally available in this format – viewers witnessed the most extraordinary event in the history of the Olympics, if not modern sport itself. As the US national anthem played at the medal ceremony, the gold and bronze medallists bowed their heads and raised their clenched fists in protest against racism and poverty in America. Those viewers who looked closely at their screens would also notice that the Australian silver medallist was wearing a badge of solidarity with his brother athletes. Thanks to television, not only sport but politics had been brought into tens of millions of living rooms around the world, ensuring that the protest of Tommie Smith and John Carlos would be seared into the global memory.

Politics had been at the forefront of international sport since the 1950s. One common accusation that the West regularly levelled against the Soviets was that they had made sport political. Of course, as we have seen, nationalist and conservative politics had always been part of modern sport. But the Russians brought a different type of politics. In particular, the USSR campaigned for greater representation in the Olympic movement of the newly independent states of Africa and Asia and for the expulsion of South Africa for its apartheid policies.[2] To a large extent this was because Soviet officials were aware of the growing radicalisation that was taking place around the world and sought to take diplomatic advantage from it. The late 1950s and early 1960s saw the rise of the civil rights movement in the United States, independence struggles in Africa and the Cuban Revolution.

The 1960s became a decade of revolutionary fervour and social change that inspired new generations to challenge the established authorities. And, for the first time, sport was not immune to that challenge.

It is a remarkable fact that before the 1960s there had been no significant internal challenge to the orthodoxies of sport. The workers' sport movement had attempted to build an external alternative to amateur and commercial sport. Those who had suffered at the hands of the leadership or the ideology of mainstream sport had simply accepted it and made the best of their situation. Jack Johnson was not a radical or revolutionary but simply believed in his right to live his life as he chose – and was persecuted for it. But he was not interested in politically challenging the racism of boxing. Jesse Owens, driven out of amateur athletics days after his triumph at the Berlin Olympics by Avery Brundage's demand that he compete in fund-raising exhibition races for the United States Olympic Committee, never questioned Brundage's right to govern athletics.[3]

But as the radicalisation of the 1960s gathered pace, sport became inextricably caught up in its gears. Its inherent nationalism, which had served the western imperial powers so well, now became a weapon in the hands of the national independence movements, whether in power or aspiring to power, of the former colonies of European empires. One of the earliest examples could be seen in the Algerian struggle for independence from France. In 1958 the Front de Libération Nationale organised a national football team in exile – '*l'onze de l'indépendance*' – to represent Algeria, composed of Algerian players active in the French soccer league and captained by 'footballer of the revolution' Rachid Mekloufi.[4] In the West Indies, the demand that its cricket team have a black captain, a position hitherto occupied only by whites, became a reflection of and a conduit for the demand for self-government and an end to British rule.[5] If the axiom that the first governmental decisions of every newly independent country in the 1960s were to join the United Nations, the IOC and FIFA was an exaggeration, it was only a slight one. The creation of the short-lived 'Games of the New Emerging Forces' in 1963 as an alternative to the Olympics – initiated by Indonesia after it had been expelled from the Olympic movement for excluding Israel and Taiwan from the 1962 Asian Games that it hosted – was an attempt to create a sporting equivalent of the Non-Aligned Movement, an association of states formed in 1961 by newly independent and developing nations outside of the western and Soviet blocs. In a similar vein, Ghana's Kwame Nkrumah led African nations in a boycott of the 1966 soccer World Cup in protest at their lack of representation in the finals.[6]

The lightning rod for much of global political campaigns around sport was South Africa. The coming to power of the Nationalist Party in 1949 had codified the racial segregation introduced by the British over the previous century into the system of apartheid. The races were zealously segregated to maintain white supremacy. Sport and other social contact between whites and non-whites was strictly forbidden.[7] This was not so different from other parts of the British Empire nor, in particular, the southern states of the USA, but the collapse of the empire and the civil rights struggle of black Americans had left white South Africa as one of the last bastions of legalised racial segregation. Protests had been raised against sporting contacts with the apartheid regime as early as the mid-1950s but it was the viciousness of the government's repression against the non-white population, most notably when in March 1960 police shot dead sixty-nine unarmed demonstrators and injured 180 others, that sparked an international campaign.[8]

Most sports were highly resistant to breaking their links with apartheid. In 1966 the IAAF voted against a Soviet proposal to expel South Africa. Despite withdrawing its invitation to South Africa to the 1964 Olympics, the IOC invited the apartheid state to the 1968 Games, only to rescind the invitation when African nations threatened a boycott. Both the IAAF and the IOC finally broke their ties in 1970.[9] In 1968 the England cricket selectors initially refused to select Basil D'Oliviera, a 'coloured' South African player who had qualified to play for England, for their tour to South Africa, despite his outstanding feats for England against Australia earlier in the same year. Eventually they were forced to backtrack, and his inclusion in the touring squad led to the South Africans cancelling the tour because they refused to play with non-white cricketers.[10] Two years later, faced with international protests, the international cricket authorities banned official tours to and from South Africa – although 'unofficial' tours of high-profile international players took their place. It was not until 1976 that the all-white Football Association of South Africa was finally expelled from FIFA after years of suspension.[11] Rugby union tours continued until 1984 and South African rugby officials played a leading role on the International Rugby Board throughout the apartheid years. South African golfers such as Gary Player competed as individuals in world golf without sanction.

The reluctance of sports' governing bodies to oppose racial discrimination put them in direct opposition to the international protest movements of the 1960s and 1970s. The 1969 Springbok rugby union tourists to Britain were met with ferocious opposition and two years later in Australia the South Africans found themselves under siege from demonstrators, while the Queensland leg of the tour led to the government declaring a state of emergency. In New Zealand – traditionally an ally of the regime and which had refused to pick Maori players for tours to South Africa until 1969 – massive protests against the Springboks in 1981 caused a governmental crisis that almost forced the National Party government to fall. New Zealand's strong rugby links with apartheid also led to an African boycott of the 1976 Montreal Olympics, following the IOC's refusal to bar the New Zealand team because of its rugby tours to South Africa. With the exception of two British and six Australian players, not a single international rugby union player refused to play against the whites-only, apartheid era South African team.[12]

It was not a coincidence that the question of race came to the forefront of international sporting political protests in the 1960s. The experience of black athletes clashed discordantly with the idea that sport was a level playing field, a haven of equality regardless of class or colour. Moreover, the contrast between the prominence of black athletes in the sporting arena and their powerlessness outside of it could not be sharper. Even when black and other minority athletes had overcome segregation and achieved formal equality with whites, they were still confronted by the racism of team-mates, officials and supporters, together with stereotypical assumptions about the physical and intellectual abilities of those whose skin was not white.

In the United States, the trail blazed in baseball in 1947 by Jackie Robinson when he became the first black player in the major leagues in the twentieth century had been tightly policed. It was no secret that Brooklyn Dodgers general manager Branch Rickey had chosen him not merely because of his outstanding athletic gifts but also because he agreed not to retaliate when faced with racial abuse. Robinson was acutely aware of racism all through his life – 'I know that I am a black man in a white world', he wrote in his autobiography – but decided that the historic opportunity to lead the integration of baseball was more important than confronting individual instances of racism.[13] Rickey himself thought that the biggest threat to Robinson's success was 'the Negro people themselves', who might not appreciate his willingness to turn the other cheek.[14] But baseball was slow to integrate on the field and did little to integrate black managers, coaches or journalists into its structures. When frustration with the economic and social injustices boiled over into riots across American cities in the mid-1960s, one black Philadelphia resident remarked about the Phillies, the local baseball club team:

> The only thing I regret about the riot ... was that we didn't burn down that goddamn [baseball] stadium. ... They had it surrounded by cops, and we couldn't get to it. I just wish we could've burned it down and wiped away its history that tells me I'm nothing but a n–r.[15]

These same feelings of anger and rebellion animated the founders of the Olympic Project for Human Rights (OPHR). Inspired by the militant Black Power movement that emerged from the civil rights movement in the US, the OPHR was founded in 1967 by the sociologist Harry Edwards to organise a boycott of the 1968 Mexico Olympics in protest at the inequality and injustice faced by black American athletes. Although its call for a boycott dissipated, two of its supporters, the sprinters Tommie Smith and John Carlos, made the most courageous and inspiring protest ever seen at a sports event, a statement of pride and rebellion that was seen in every corner of the globe.[16]

The two sprinters had been inspired by the example of Muhammad Ali. Under his birth name of Cassius Clay, Ali had won the world heavyweight boxing championship in 1964 but in early 1966 he became eligible to be drafted in the US Army, which was engaged in an increasingly unpopular war in Vietnam. Ali refused to be drafted, declaring: 'I ain't got no quarrel with them Viet Cong. ... They never called me n–r.'[17] He knew that in all probability this meant that he would be stripped of the title and possibly imprisoned. Sport had never seen anything like this. Here was an athlete, one of the finest ever to practise his art, who put his political principles before sporting glory. This abrogation of the sporting code annoyed his critics almost as much as his opposition to the Vietnam war. This was a man who understood through his very existence that sport and politics were inseparable. He was a sportsman who knew that there were more important things than 'playing the game'.[18]

He was not alone. The 1960s also saw the athletes demanding employment rights and trade union recognition. Partially inspired by the example of Ali, Smith and Carlos, but also by the immense social struggles taking place around the world, a number of professional sports men and women began to question their subordinate position in sport. Tennis star Billie-Jean King was one of the first to speak out in 1967, when she declared that tennis professionals were treated as a 'cross between a panhandler and a visiting in-law. You're not respected, you're tolerated.'[19] Books such as Jim Bouton's *Ball Four*, Dave Meggyesy's *Out of Their League* (both 1970) and Eamon Dunphy's *Only a Game?* (1976) laid bare the reality of daily life of in, respectively, baseball, American football and English soccer, from the viewpoint of the player.

In 1969, Curt Flood, the great center fielder for the St Louis Cardinals, refused to be traded to the Philadelphia Phillies, arguing that 'I do not feel I am a piece of property to be bought and sold irrespective of my wishes', and took legal action against Major League Baseball (MLB) to defend his rights.[20] He argued that its 'reserve clause', whereby a player remained the property of a club even when his contract with it had expired, was a violation of his rights. He was not alone. Bill Veeck, the former owner of three MLB clubs, described baseball as being 'one of the few places in which there is human bondage'.[21] Flood sat out the 1970 baseball season while the Supreme Court eventually found in favour of the reserve clause, and his career ended in 1971. Eventually he was recognised as a hero for his struggle for players' rights, despite the failure of the Major League Baseball Player's Association (MLBPA) to provide more than verbal support.

Curt Flood's struggle for basic labour rights had been foreshadowed with greater success in England. In 1963 Newcastle United's George Eastham had won a High Court ruling that outlawed soccer's 'retain and transfer' system, whereby a player out of contract with his club still needed their consent to transfer to another club. This was a significant victory for the Professional Footballers' Association (PFA), which had also forced the abolition of football's 'maximum wage' pay ceiling of £20 per week in 1961.[22] British footballers had formed the Association Footballer Players' and Trainers' Union as early as 1898, although this had only lasted three years, and the forerunner of the PFA had been formed in 1907 by two Manchester United players, Billy Meredith and Charlie Roberts. In 1961 French World Cup star Just Fontaine and Cameroonian international Eugène N'Jo Léa created the Union Nationale des Footballeurs Professionnels (UNFP). In Italy, the Associazione Italiana Calciatori (AIC) was formed in 1968, the third attempt at creating a players' union after short-lived organisations in 1917 and 1945. In 1965 the PFA, UNFP, AIC, the Scottish PFA and the Dutch players' union founded FIFPro, the international soccer players union.[23]

In America, as was the case with the labour movement in general, the formation of baseball players' unions had a more volatile history. The Brotherhood of Professional Base-ball Players, the first players' union, created its own Players'

League in 1890 in an attempt to improve the life of the professional ball player, but this only lasted one season. There were several subsequent short-lived attempts to form players' unions but it wasn't until 1968 that the MLBPA negotiated the first collective bargaining agreement with club owners.[24] In 1972, confronted with the owners' recalcitrance in providing adequate pension provision for players, the players went on strike. The MLBPA struck again in 1981 over free agency for players, once more in 1985 and, most seriously, in 1994 when the entire post-season was cancelled. The 1994 strike was a response to the owners' attempts to roll-back the gains that the players had made over the previous two decades. The NFL Players' Association, like the MLBPA formed in 1956, also won recognition in 1968 and led its players in strikes in 1974, 1982 and 1987. The players' unions were hardly radical organisations, basing themselves firmly in the tradition of business unionism and rarely venturing beyond salary and contract issues, but their growth demonstrated that, across the sporting world, the era of deferential athlete was coming to an end.[25]

The overt radicalism of the 1960s soon vanished from sport. Cricketers and rugby union players undertook 'unofficial' tours of apartheid South Africa in the 1970s and 1980s with little restraint and a pitifully small number refused to compete against Springbok teams. Yet the undermining of the culture of deference that took place in the West in the 1950s and 1960s also contributed significantly to the rapid decline of the amateur ethos in sport. The apparent meritocracy of sporting achievement began to outweigh its traditional submissiveness to self-appointed authority. In 1962 cricket's distinction between amateur 'gentlemen' and professional 'players' was abolished, ending two centuries of social separation and hypocrisy.[26] In 1968 tennis also scrapped the distinction between amateurs and professionals and the sport went 'open'.[27] The last vestiges of amateurism in elite soccer disappeared in 1963 when the Deutscher Fussball Bund created the fully professional Bundesliga, abandoning its threadbare claim that German soccer was amateur, which was in large part a legacy of the Nazi regime's insistence on amateurism in sport.[28] Even the IOC's amateur grip began to slip and it began to allow athletes to receive various forms of payment, culminating in it allowing open professionals to compete after 1988.

But there was an even stronger force at work dissolving the bonds of amateurism.

14

THE REVOLUTION IS BEING TELEVISED

Television got off the ground because of sports. When we put on the World Series in 1947, heavyweight fights, the Army–Navy football game, the sales of television sets just spurted.

Harry Coyle, NBC.[1]

If the ideals of the 1960s quickly evaporated from the sporting world, a different type of revolution did take place. New sources of revenue were emerging that would transform the economics of sport, destroying the necessity for amateurism and draining the willpower of all but the most ascetic advocates of the amateur ethos. And, as with the development of newspapers and print media in the eighteenth and nineteenth centuries, and the emergence of radio in the inter-war years, it was a new form of media that would be the catalyst for this revolution in sports economics. Television.

In the 1950s, the emergence of television started to transform the traditional sports business model, which had relied on spectators attending matches for the overwhelming bulk of its income. Television technology had become practical in the 1920s and by the late 1930s TV stations had begun broadcasting with varying degrees of success in North America, western Europe and the USSR. As the 1997 film *First Contact* eerily highlighted, the first sporting event to be televised was the 1936 Berlin Olympics by the Nazi government. It was followed by a specially arranged soccer match between Arsenal's first and reserve teams broadcast by the BBC in 1937 and a Columbia versus Princeton college baseball match in 1939 by NBC in America.[2] Nevertheless, until the late 1940s television remained a niche product, the preserve of the rich or the technological intelligentsia, and was dwarfed by the ubiquity of radio.

But as television technology made rapid advances and as the cost of a set became affordable, ownership ballooned. In 1951 TV ownership in the US broke the

10 million mark. By 1953 it had doubled to 20 million. Ten years later there were over 50 million sets in American households, covering over 90 per cent of the population.[3] Growth in the UK was slower but no less profound. There were 10 million TV sets in 1960 and 90 per cent coverage was not reached until 1968. In western Europe by 1970 TVs could be found in 69 per cent of German households, 59 per cent of French and 54 per cent of Italian.[4]

Sport lent itself perfectly to the new media. The football codes' rectangular pitches and boxing's square ring easily fitted the viewing area of the television screen. As if to compensate for their irregularly shaped arenas, baseball and cricket had periods of inaction when the camera could focus on individuals and commentators provide punditry. The quotidian of sport provided material for news and magazine shows – a continuous soap opera for male viewers who would not consider watching a genuine soap opera, sport's gendered television twin. And, of course, matches were cheap to televise, providing unscripted drama at a fraction of the cost of a scripted stage play or a movie.

The relationship between sport and television replicated the same symbiotic relationship that had developed between sport and the print media in the eighteenth and nineteenth century. Sport provided television with compelling content, regular news and a pre-existing market upon which to capitalise. And, as in France at the turn of the century when the bicycle and motor car industries created races to publicise and sell their products, the television networks in the United States were the creation of the manufacturers of radio and television sets. 'Television got off the ground because of sports,' recalled Harry Coyle, an early NBC sports producer. 'When we put on the World Series in 1947, heavyweight fights, the Army–Navy football game, the sales of television sets just spurted.'

The importance of sport to television can be seen most strikingly in Japan.[5] In the early 1950s Japan had almost no television industry. In order to stimulate interest in the new medium, the fledgling Nippon Television erected large screen televisions around Tokyo. In October 1953, Japan's first-ever world boxing champion, Yoshio Shirai, defended his world flyweight title in Tokyo against Englishman Terry Allen. Thousands of people gathered at the screens to watch his victory, bringing parts of the city to a standstill. But individual ownership was still beyond the means of most Japanese and only 16,000 TV sets were in use a year later. The greatest boost to TV ownership came in 1959 with a royal wedding, which saw 2 million sets sold, and the announcement that the 1964 Olympic Games would be held in Tokyo. This stimulated both the sale of televisions and its technological development – the Games were the first to be broadcast in colour and transmitted live by satellite – to the extent that not only did Japan's TV market become one of the biggest in the world, but it also began exporting television sets around the world, a major step towards becoming the leading manufacturer of consumer electronics.[6]

And just as newspapers had transformed sport in the earlier centuries, providing it with publicity, communication and structures, television provided the basis for a revolution in the economics of sport in the second half of the twentieth century.

In 1948 the BBC had offered the British Olympic Association (BOA) 1,000 guineas to televise the London Olympics. The BOA left the cheque un-cashed, demonstrating its amateur lack of interest in commercial opportunity.[7] This attitude was shared by the IOC, although not for long. In 1956 Avery Brundage wrote that 'we in the IOC have done well without TV for 60 years and will do so certainly for the next 60 years too'.[8]

'Facility fees', payments for broadcasting sports events, rarely topped £1,000 in 1950s Britain. As was the case in most of western Europe, the dominance of a state-controlled broadcasting service such as the BBC undermined any bargaining power that sports' organisations had with television companies. This was further curtailed by the fact that the leaders of the BBC and many sports' organisations, such as the RFU, the Amateur Athletic Association and cricket's MCC, shared the same narrow upper middle-class background, preferring 'gentlemen's agreements' in business and disdaining open competition. The advent of the commercial broadcaster ITV in 1955 appeared to open the market, but the lack of unity among football clubs, and on a lesser scale rugby league clubs, sank the potential for major earnings from TV. For example, in 1960 ITV paid the Football League £150,000 for live coverage of twenty-six matches that season. But Arsenal and Tottenham Hotspur refused to play matches on live TV and the deal unravelled. It would be twenty-three years before live league soccer would be broadcast in the UK. Similar state control of television in the rest of Europe held back the financial potential for sport on the continent.[9]

However, in the United States, without a dominant state broadcaster and with three national commercial television networks competing for viewers, the financial rewards for major sports were much greater. Baseball and American football sides sold broadcast rights to their matches to local TV stations and the World Series, NFL Championship and college bowl games were bringing in hundreds of thousands of dollars per match by the mid-1950s. The money paid by broadcasters to American sports grew exponentially over the following decades. In 1970 the NFL received $50 million, MLB $18 million and the up and coming National Basketball Association (NBA) $2 million.[10] In boxing, which had become a staple of sports programming in the 1950s and 1960s, Muhammad Ali and Joe Frazier's 1971 'Fight of The Century' brought them both guaranteed purses of $2.5 million. And despite Avery Brundage's reluctance, the IOC fully embraced the television era in the 1960s.[11] The 1960 Rome Olympics were the first summer games to sell television rights on a commercial basis and raised $1 million. A little over a decade later, broadcasters paid $17.8 million for the Munich Games. By the late 1970s, it was estimated that 97 per cent of the IOC's income came from television.[12]

This televised revolution in sport changed sport in two fundamental ways. First, the regular appearance of sport on television, whether in games, news or documentary programmes, meant that clubs and leagues became a medium for advertising in their own right. Rather than being restricted to their own local markets and those who attended their matches, clubs now had a regional and even a national platform to offer businesses for advertising and sponsorship. Leagues and tournaments could offer businesses opportunities to advertise on television at much cheaper rates than buying advertising directly from the networks. This was especially important in countries where there was little or no commercial television. In France, where television barred advertising until 1968 and was effectively a state monopoly until deregulated by the Mitterrand government in 1982, advertisers took advantage of the many opportunities presented by the Tour de France to promote their products on national television. The stages of the races, timekeeping, jerseys, secondary competitions within the main race, official cars, drinks, laundry, oil, medical facilities, as well as the teams, all acquired sponsors in the 1960s.[13] Not for nothing were the Tour's cyclists seen as 'human advertising hoardings', the most extreme example of the use of athletes as product promoters.

Second, the unprecedented torrent of money liberated clubs and leagues from their previous reliance on spectators as the sole source of income. While crowd revenue remained the biggest source of revenue for most sports – and could not be ignored because television abhorred empty seats on the screen – the television audience became a decisive factor in the sports business.[14] In 1958, the PGA Championship switched its rules from match-play (where the winner is decided by the number of holes won) to stroke-play (where the winner is the player with the least number of strokes) because television producers wanted the last and decisive day of the tournament to feature more golfers. The formation of the American Football League in 1960 as a rival to the NFL was based explicitly on making football more accessible to the needs of broadcasters. It deliberately set out to play a more spectacular brand of passing football, put players' names on their shirts, inaugurated the use of stadium clocks to show the progress of a match and adopted the use of the two-point conversion, whereby a side that had scored a touchdown could attempt to score a two-point touchdown instead of a one-point goal. The introduction of the 24-second shot clock by the National Basketball Association in 1954 made the sport a far more attractive proposition to TV networks.[15] The creation of soccer's European Cup in 1955, and the Cup Winners Cup and European Championship, both in 1960, was a direct consequence of the extension of television coverage across Europe. Even the staid and conservative sport of English cricket, alarmed by falling attendances in the 1960s, introduced television-friendly 'limited over' one-day cricket tournaments such as the Gillette Cup and the John Player Special League.[16]

Indeed, it was cricket that highlighted the shift in the balance of power between sport and the broadcasters. In 1976 Australian media tycoon and owner of the Channel Nine network Kerry Packer offered the Australian Cricket Board (ACB) A\$1.5 million for an exclusive three-year deal to broadcast cricket. Cricket's popularity in Australia had reached new heights in the 1970s, and there was considerable dissatisfaction among players about their low wages.[17] To Packer's astonishment, the patrician ACB awarded the contract to the state-run Australian Broadcasting Corporation for just A\$210,000. Used to getting his own way, he simply decided to start his own competition, World Series Cricket, by signing up fifty of the world's best cricketers, most of whom were only too eager to boost their meagre incomes. The new competition introduced night-time matches, coloured uniforms, white balls and innovative TV coverage, effectively setting the agenda for cricket's future. After initial teething troubles, World Series Cricket was so successful that it forced the ACB to come to terms with Packer in 1979.[18]

In the world of the former British Empire, Packer's success sent shockwaves through sport. After a century of assuming that sport was the rider and the media the horse, the leaders of sport were confronted with the fact that this was no longer the case. Packer had demonstrated the ease with which a sport's governing body could be outflanked by a media corporation. Packer's success provided the inspiration for his rival Australian media mogul Rupert Murdoch to set up his own short-lived 'Super League' rugby league competition in the mid-1990s. It hastened the death of amateurism in rugby union.[19] Fearing that Packer or another media organisation would set up their own professional rugby union competition, the International Rugby Board voted to start its own world cup tournament in 1987. 'If we were to save our game and not lose it to some entrepreneur, we would have to act promptly and organise a world cup,' commented Nick Shehadie, the president of the Australian Rugby Union, preparing the way for his sport's embrace of professionalism in 1995.[20]

In the wake of the Packer coup, and no longer able to resist the lure of the money offered by television, English soccer also faced up to the reality of television, receiving £5.2 million in 1983 from BBC and ITV to show live league matches, a figure that would increase to £44 million from ITV five years later.[21] But it would be the emergence of satellite television that would accelerate this process and take it to a higher level.

15

WINNERS AND LOSERS: SPORT IN THE NEW WORLD ORDER

The Old strode in disguised as the New.

Bertolt Brecht, 1938.[1]

In 1996 Australian newspaper baron Rupert Murdoch addressed shareholders of his News Corporation at an annual meeting in Adelaide. 'Sport absolutely overpowers film and everything else in the entertainment genre,' he told the gathering, adding that he intended to 'use sports as a battering ram and a lead offering in all our pay television operations'.[2] Unwittingly, he was acknowledging the historical importance of sport to media companies of all technologies since the eighteenth century.

Viewing figures around the world underlined this. Eleven of the twenty most watched American network television shows in the twentieth century were sports programmes, ten of which were Super Bowls. San Francisco's 1982 victory over the Cincinnati Bengals in Super Bowl XVI was the fourth most watched programme ever in US television history. Two of the top six most watched programmes ever in the UK were soccer matches, with the England side's 1966 World Cup final triumph the most watched programme ever on British television. In Germany, nine of the top ten most viewed programmes were soccer matches.[3]

As part of his battering ram strategy, Murdoch paid the English Football Association £304 million to televise the newly created Premier League in 1992. The following year his US Fox Network paid $1.58 billion to broadcast the NFL. In 1995 he established his own Super League rugby league competitions in Australia and England. The same year his television deals provided the financial underpinning of international rugby union's decision to abandon amateurism and turn professional.[4]

Similarly lucrative deals took place in baseball, European soccer and, in 2008, Indian cricket created the Indian Premier League (IPL), explicitly as a television product based on soccer's Premier League. This massive increase in exposure allowed sport to attract new sponsors, eager to tie their brands to the popularity of clubs and the enhanced celebrity status of sports stars.[5] Ironically, the model for sports sponsorship was that former bastion of amateurism the IOC, which had learnt in the 1980s that the quickest way to riches was to sell every conceivable space and service to corporate donors and their brands.[6] Almost all of this exponential growth in the value of sport came from television, and more particularly from pay-per-view satellite and cable TV. Deregulation of the European television market had begun in the late 1970s and the technological development of cable and satellite, and subsequently digital delivery of programming, opened the door to new revenue streams and new entrants to the market.[7]

Murdoch's importance to television sport was the most prominent example of the upward shift in popularity, scope and structure that sport underwent in the final decades of the twentieth century. As in the late 1890s, the 1920s and the 1950s, this change was propelled by a growing market and new advances in media technology. And it benefited from an ideological climate in which the competition and nationalism inherent in sport found a new leverage. By the dawn of the twenty-first century, the value of sport could be measured in tens of billions of dollars, its popularity was truly global and it once more offered a metaphor for life in a world in which the capitalist market reigned supreme.

Such developments could not have taken place without similar shifts in wider society. The world changed profoundly in the 1980s and 1990s. The decline of trade union movements, the dismantling of welfare provision, the collapse of the social-democratic project and the implosion of the Soviet Union led to the almost unchallenged supremacy of capitalism and its ideology. Although dubbed neo-liberalism, there was nothing new in the rhetoric of laissez-faire economics and untrammelled competition that was espoused by Ronald Reagan, Margaret Thatcher and their supporters. Indeed, their inspiration was Adam Smith. And just as in the eighteenth century, sport was both a beneficiary of and an ideological buttress for this late twentieth-century counter-reformation. It benefited from the deregulation of markets and provided a gushing font of rhetoric for politicians and ideologues. Its 'deep politics' were now very much on the surface.

Like the newly fashionable 'free market', sport was nothing if not competitive, dividing winners from losers, the most important social distinction of this 'New World Order'. It also taught the lesson that there were many, many more losers than winners in life in capitalist society. Vince Lombardi's infamous saying, 'Winning isn't everything, it is the only thing,' summed up the *Zeitgeist*.[8] The use of sport as a metaphor for life as ceaseless competition became increasingly prevalent. The media giant ESPN even used a US advertising campaign to proclaim that sports aren't a metaphor for life, sports are life in 2002.[9] Business adopted the language of sport. Teamwork, attitude, commitment, contest; the lexicon of the locker room became the badinage of the board room. Sports stars were recruited to tell corporate leaders what athletic prowess could teach them about business. The most ambitious, competitive and scheming corporate executives become known, like the Wall Street bond trader in Sherman McCoy in Tom Wolfe's *Bonfire of the Vanities*

(1987), as 'players'.[10] Supporters' identification with and loyalty to a club or sport, especially that of the most hardcore or 'authentic' fans, became interchangeable with the 'brand' and 'consumer loyalty', as the most astute sports marketers realised.

This shift took place on a global scale, having an impact wherever sport was played. Yet the 'globalisation' of sport was and remains primarily a media phenomenon. Although television coverage of sport clearly possesses a global reach – for those able to afford pay-TV subscriptions almost any sport can be watched in any country of the world today – only soccer can claim to have truly global participation and support. Its only rival is the Olympic Games, but this of course is an event not a sport. Sports themselves remain solidly cemented into the international hierarchy established before the First World War. Only three Latin American and five European nations have won soccer's World Cup. Over a third of the world's nations have never won an Olympic medal. Baseball and cricket remain largely locked into the geographical strongholds that they established over a century ago, and the other football codes have stayed resolutely national – as adjectively demonstrated in American, Australian, Canadian and Gaelic footballs – or as with the two rugby codes, dominated by former 'British' nations and the French. The creation of cricket's IPL, which dealt a serious blow to the domination of cricket by English-speaking white nations, represented not so much an international extension of the sport but a deepening of its commercial exploitation in a traditional heartland of the game. Even the financial behemoth of the NFL could not sustain American football's international expansion through what began as its World League and eventually shrank to NFL Europa.[11] North American and European domination of elite sport was also enhanced by the creation of 'player farms' in Africa, Asia and Latin America which supplied huge numbers of teenage soccer and baseball players to be assessed and, usually, rejected by the major teams.[12] Sport had acquired a global audience yet, with the exception of soccer, its geographical template had not qualitatively changed nor was its traditional hierarchy threatened.

Conversely, soccer's global character, like that of the Olympics, made it an arena for the open parade of national rivalries and ethnic chauvinism. 'There are no black Italians' chanted Juventus fans during their match against Inter Milan in 2009.[13] Across Europe, soccer stadia were the sites for the most appalling displays of public anti-Semitism since the 1930s.[14] The break-up of the USSR and the eastern bloc countries in the 1990s, renewed immigration into Europe and North America from countries impoverished by 'free-trade agreements', and the eagerness of the US, Britain and the West to use their military might in defence of their imperial interests exacerbated national and racial enmities, and found their reflection in sport.

Although the scale and speed of sport's relentless commercial expansion since the 1980s appears to be a new phenomenon, it is merely the latest of several equivalent developments over the past 250 years. As a business, sport in the twenty-first century increasingly resembled its forebears in the eighteenth century. Unashamedly part of the entertainment industry and played for profit, it became a fashionable bauble for super-rich patrons. Baseball, IPL and football clubs of all codes became status symbols for the wealthy in the same way that cricket clubs, race-horses and pugilists were for the British aristocracy in Georgian times. Roman Abramovich at Chelsea and Daniel Snyder at the Washington Redskins in the twenty-first century were little different from the cricketing earls of Tankerville and Winchilsea in the eigtheenth century, apart from the fact that today they do not expect to play alongside their expensively acquired rosters of stars.

Just as in that formative period of modern sport, gambling began to regain its position as a major feature of sporting culture. The development of satellite television and the internet in the 1990s reinvigorated the gambling industry – indeed, it became colonised by dealers and traders who had learnt their skills in the global casino of the financial markets. Clubs and leagues jostled for sponsorship deals with gambling businesses and in-game betting became a feature of televised sport. The emergence of spot-betting and other forms of 'exotic' bets – made possible by the internet and digital technology – was in reality a re-emergence of the sophisticated gambling markets that had once existed at cricket matches and prize-fights in the 1700s.[15] And the spectacular cases of corruption that were now uncovered, most notably in South African, Indian and Pakistani cricket, were little more than a distant echo of similar scandals that had occurred two centuries earlier. The old had returned as the new.

This new economic regime of sport also brought down the final curtain on the *longue durée* of amateurism. For almost a century and a half amateurism had defined the morality of sport. Even professional sport had genuflected to the supposed ethical superiority of the amateur ethos. Yet, with the exception of American college football and basketball, no significant sport in the world described itself as amateur by the end of the twentieth century. The 1984 Los Angeles Olympics were the last Games to wear its diminishingly skimpy fig-leaf. Even rugby union, which had once described amateurism as 'the first principle of the game', had thrown aside its principles to leap aboard the juggernaut of television riches. The pious hypocrisies of amateurism had no place in a world where the only principle was, in the words of Al Davis, the owner of the Oakland Raiders football team, 'just win, baby'.[16]

The naked capitalism of sport now resembled that of the eighteenth century. But the continuing desire of sports administrators to regulate and control their athletes was firmly based on the nineteenth-century model of Victorian sport. Amateurism was dead, but its structures of discipline lived on. In fact, there was no contradiction between the commercial exigencies of sport and the strictures of its administrators. The two went hand in hand, as Clive Woodward, the British Olympic Association's director of sport, made clear to his athletes in 2011:

> it drove me nuts in Beijing [at the 2008 Olympics] because there were a couple of people who took great pride in walking around the village with a Nike T-shirt on. [Adidas] is our sponsor and this is our team kit. All I'll say is that those athletes were nowhere near the podium and I'm not surprised because they didn't have the discipline.[17]

In North America, the NBA and the NFL introduced dress codes and 'personal conduct' policies that applied to their (predominantly black) athletes' lives outside of the playing arena.

As the importance of amateurism declined, the continuing desire to demonstrate the moral value of sport shifted the focus of sports administrators from policing payments to pursuing so-called performance-enhancing drugs. The 'enemy within' for sport was no longer the 'veiled professional' working-class athlete or the Soviet-bloc 'shamateur' but the 'drug cheat'. The arbitrary rejection of certain types of pharmaceuticals – a version of the 'war on drugs' that was started by the Reagan administration in the 1980s – led to increasingly draconian testing and disciplinary measures being taken against athletes in the twenty-first century. In 2004 the World Anti-Doping Agency (WADA), founded at the IOC's initiative in 1999, introduced its 'whereabouts' system that effectively turned elite athletes into prisoners on parole.[18] This forced athletes to nominate one hour per day, seven days a week, when they would be available for unannounced drug-testing. Being somewhere else, failure to complete the required paperwork or providing incorrect details of training schedules were punishable offences. In 2008 the Union Cycliste Internationale took a step further with the introduction of so-called 'biological passports' for its riders. These consisted of regular blood sampling to ascertain, not the presence of drugs but variations in blood chemistry that could be construed as evidence of drug-taking, blood-doping or anything else the UCI chose to classify as cheating.[19] In other words, circumstantial evidence would be used to discipline riders. Informers and spying were also encouraged. At the 2012 London Olympics, cleaning staff and security guards working in the athletes' village were 'educated' so that 'if they come across behaviour that is untoward' they would report it to the IOC.[20] These unapologetic police-state measures were of course justified as being necessary to stop 'cheats'.

The concerns of the nineteenth century could also be heard clearly echoing in twenty-first-century sporting concerns about gender. Although levels of formal equality had risen in the latter part of the twentieth century – by 1984 even the IOC had accepted that women were perfectly capable of running marathons – the boundaries between male and female were more strictly policed than ever. In soccer, FIFA barred female Mexico striker Maribel Dominguez from playing for the Mexican men's second division side Celaya FC in 2004 on the grounds that 'there must be a clear separation between men's and women's football'.[21] In 2009 the case of Caster Semenya, an 18-year-old black South African woman middle-distance runner, once more brought the gender-paranoia of sport to the fore. Having dramatically improved her times for the 800 metres and 1500 metres, the IAAF ordered an investigation, suspecting her of using drugs and/or being a man. She was subsequently forced to undergo an 'examination' in which 'her feet were placed in stirrups, her genitals were photographed and her internal organs were examined'.[22] Following an international outcry, Semenya was eventually allowed to compete again.

The IAAF even granted itself the power to determine the most intimate part of human identity: the sex of an individual. Indeed, any IAAF race-day medical official was given this right. 'The Medical Delegate shall also have the authority to arrange for the determination of the gender of an athlete should he [sic] judge that to be desirable,' read rule 113 of the IAAF *Competition Rules*. The IOC requires transgender athletes to have had sex reassignment surgery at least two years before they compete as women.[23] And despite the fact that similar medical conditions can be found in men as well as women, male athletes are not subject to testing.[24] This is because the underlying yet predominant concern of sports organisations is policing an arbitrary boundary between male and female, just as it was in its formative era of Victorian amateurism. 'Don't you ever talk about home, or your mothers or sisters,' Tom Brown tells a classmate in sport's foundational text, *Tom Brown's Schooldays*.[25] Then as now, modern sport is founded on the affirmation of strict gender division, in which women are subordinate to the masculine ideal, and those who do not conform are condemned.

This inbuilt historic misogyny also explains the continuing deep-seated hostility to gay athletes, both male and female, in almost all sports. Of the thousands of professional football players of all codes around the world in 2011, only one soccer player – Sweden's Anton Hysen – and one rugby player – Welshman Gareth Thomas – felt comfortable enough in their sports to be openly homosexual. In women's soccer, the 2011 World Cup was marked by what one commentator called 'lesbian panic' as Nigeria and Guinea sought to purge players suspected of not being heterosexual.[26] Such a state of affairs marks football in all its forms as probably the most reactionary institution in the world on sexual matters, outside of organised religion.

These restrictive and repressive measures against athletes intensified because of the social conservatism of the post-Reagan/Thatcher world and the drive to roll back the gains of the social and political struggles of the 1960s and 1970s. But sport not only reflected the times, it also played an active role in changing the political climate. From the 1980s the need for 'security' at sporting events increasingly became a rationale for governmental attacks on civil liberties. This too had happened in the past. Ten days before the 1968 Mexico Olympics, police opened fire on a demonstration of 10,000 students, many of whom were chanting '¡No queremos olimpiadas, queremos revolución!' ('We don't want the Olympics, we want revolution!'). The number of dead has never been fully ascertained. Estimates ranged from forty-four to a thousand, with the likely figure being 325. Many more were wounded and thousands jailed. The massacre had been orchestrated by the Mexican government's secret security force, the Brigada Olympica, that had been established to ensure the smooth running of the Olympics.[27]

But it was the 1984 Los Angeles Olympics, dubbed at the time 'the first free enterprise Games' that created the authoritarian template for subsequent 'mega-sporting events'.[28] Combining maximum freedom for corporate sponsors with repressive measures against potential opponents, the organisers of the LA Games ran roughshod over democratic rights, banning demonstrations, 'socially cleansing' the homeless, prostitutes and others, and employing thousands of additional police and military operatives. Olympic precincts became militarised zones.[29] By the time of the 2010 Vancouver Winter Games, the Olympics resembled nothing so much as a travelling totalitarian state that pitched up in a host city every couple of years and subjected the population, especially the poor and racially oppressed, to police-state measures and celebrations of corporate indulgence. As part of the preparations for the 2010 Games, Vancouver's city council enacted laws that banned leaflets, unauthorised placards and megaphones, outlawed demonstrations unless approved by the police, allowed the police to enter homes to take down protest signs hung outside of buildings and authorised the use of military technology, such as a 152 decibel 'sonic gun', against demonstrators. The Canadian secret services identified 'anti-globalization, anti-corporate and First Nations activists' as specific threats to Olympic security.[30] Nor was soccer any different. The introduction and extensive use of closed-circuit television systems at English soccer grounds in the 1990s presaged their almost saturation use across English towns and cities today.[31] During Euro 2008 in Switzerland, private security firms vetted all supporters entering the specially designated 'Fan Zones', police undertook a programme of 'preventative arrests' of those they thought might commit crimes and a database of 'hooligans' was established, entry on to which was based on suspicion rather than criminal conviction. Ominously, elements of these measures were incorporated into Swiss immigration law.[32] In preparation for the 2014 soccer World Cup and the 2016 Olympics, it is estimated that 1.5 million Brazilians will be removed from their homes to make way for the building of new sports stadia.[33] The cost of creating these capitalist utopias – in which free enterprise controls an unfree people in celebration of the glories of competition – is of course borne entirely by the populations of the host nations, not by the IOC, FIFA or other sports bodies. As with so much sport, the 'magic of the marketplace' could only conjure up profit when underpinned by public subsidy.

However, this rarely discouraged governments from bidding for major sporting events. The huge contracts available to builders, suppliers and the ubiquitous advisers were in themselves highly attractive. Most important, and increasingly so, is the fact that since the 1950s the hosting of major sporting tournaments has become a way in which governments can signal to the rest of the world that they are a willing and eager member of the global business community. Rome's 1955 bid for the 1960 Olympics was part of their integration into the European mainstream following the Second World War and came just two years before the Treaty of Rome that led to the creation of what became the European Union. Japan's hosting of the 1964 Games played a similar role, as did West Germany's 1972 Munich Games. The bids of Seoul, Barcelona and Sydney all took place in the context of the liberalisation and privatisation of their economies. China's bid to host the 2008 Olympics took place as it was negotiating to join the World Trade Organisation in 2001.[34]

Thus the global mega-sports event has come to be a passion play of celebration of and deference before the world capitalist order. And sport, like its capitalist progenitor, has established itself 'over the entire surface of the globe. It must nestle everywhere, settle everywhere, establish connexions everywhere'.[35] In the first decade of twenty-first century, the bond between sport and capitalism that was established in the eighteenth century had never been stronger nor more apparent.

CONCLUSION: WHAT FUTURE FOR SPORT?

You know ... what I really hate about cricket is that it is such a damned good game.

From Julian Mitchell's play, *Another Country*, 1981.

On 30 October 1999, early in his innings against Zimbabwe, Hansie Cronje became South African cricket's highest-ever test run scorer. He was captain of the national side and of his state team. Most significantly, he had come to symbolise South Africa's rise back to the elite of test cricket after years of international ostracism under the apartheid regime. He was a national icon.

But less than a year later, he had been banned for life from ever playing or coaching cricket again. He had been found guilty of corruption, accepting bribes and persuading his team-mates to fix matches. As the evidence emerged, it became clear that Cronje had worked closely with bookmakers and acted as their agent within the South African team. The cricket world was stunned and many in South Africa simply refused to believe the evidence. The affair symbolised the nature of sport as it entered the twenty-first century: a potent symbol of nationalism, a major sector of the entertainment business and the focus for a re-emergent gambling industry.

Of course, none of this was new. From its birth in the emerging capitalist economy of eighteenth century England to its global significance today, modern sport owes its growth to its symbiotic relationship with the media industry of print, radio and television, the development of a national economy and nationalism, and the creation of a mass, urbanised working class. As it spread from Britain, to North America, Europe, Japan and eventually the rest of the world, these three factors were crucial in sport acquiring its popularity and influence. It carried with it all the prejudice of capitalism at its rawest. It has always been the plaything of the rich and the authoritarian bureaucrat. It has enthused over war and provided a platform for prejudice of every type. The fact that it is seen by the poor and the oppressed as their only escape from lives of unfulfilled grimness only serves to shed a shameful light on the society which gave birth to it.

Yet, sport is also a unique form of entertainment that offers an immersive emotional experience in which the spectator, like the player, can experience the intensity of joy and despair without the risks that generate such feelings in real life. Unlike its fellow products of the technological entertainment revolution, the cinema and popular music, the sport spectator's experience is not passive – fans can participate in the events they witness, whether through gambling, identification with the participants or simply by contributing to the atmosphere at stadia. Because it offers the opportunity for personal identification with a player, team or sport, it provides a social significance magnified beyond that of other forms of entertainment. And every single match possesses the ever-present possibility of beauty, grandeur, triumph, tragedy and creative self-expression – whether on the diamond, at the wicket, on the track, in the ring or on the football field. There can be little wonder that corporate giants and local businesses alike seek to profit from such a potent cocktail.

The idea that sport has been hijacked by team owners or commodified by corporate interests fails to understand that modern sport is itself a creation of capitalism.[1] There was no prelapsarian era in which football, baseball or any other modern sport was played by people purely for enjoyment. Those such as Jean-Marie Brohm or, more recently, Marc Perelman, who believe that contemporary commercial sport is a perversion of play, share the same idealised view of the past as those middle-class supporters of amateurism who excoriated working-class professionals in the nineteenth century.[2] Sport has never 'belonged' to participants or supporters any more than the movie industry belonged to actors or cinema-goers. Indeed, modern recreational, participatory sport is a facsimile of commercial, elite sport, played under the same rules and regulations, many of which have been introduced for profit-driven reasons. As its evolution over the past 250 years has demonstrated, sport as an activity is not primarily a form of play – corrupted or otherwise – but a type of commercial entertainment, analogous to the theatre, the cinema or popular music. Recreational sport played for fun bears the same relationship to commercial sport as amateur dramatics does to Broadway or a local choir to La Scala. One might further observe that neither drama nor opera arrogate to themselves the moral certitude assumed by sport.

What of its future? The major forces that have historically driven the development of sport – the media, nation-building and urbanisation – will continue to play the decisive role. The growth of the internet, the next stage in media technology, has already begun to play an important role, not only in broadcast rights but also in the way that sports fans communicate and consume. The willingness of national governments to throw themselves at the feet of the IOC and FIFA for the privilege of spending billions for the right to stage the Olympics and the World Cup highlights how national prestige and sporting nationalism have become more important in the twenty-first century than ever before. The quickening pace of urbanisation around the world, especially in Africa and Asia, has further increased the market for sports, particularly those with a global reach and recognition. Yet, as has been the case with the global expansion of 'free trade', the poorer countries will not be the beneficiaries of the rise of global sport, as their sporting competitions become farm systems for European and American sports – the hegemony of the imperial sporting powers will not be fundamentally challenged. The rise of Chinese sport, which has followed broadly the same path as that of the USSR during the Cold War, will perhaps shift the centre of gravity of certain aspects of sporting excellence away from the West, though the major commercial sports will remain controlled by Europe and North America. But the US government's opposition to China will mean that the Olympics will continue to be an arena for sport to remain a form of 'war minus the shooting'.

But these developments will not mean that sport will escape its essential conservatism. The continual extension and strengthening of its disciplinary powers, whether in pursuit of pharmacological or gender 'cheats' or in the imposition of its moral codes, will not be stopped without resistance from athletes and, more importantly, significant social struggle beyond the sporting world. Its willing co-option into the security and intelligence structures of government is to be expected, given its long history as an adjunct to governmental and national policies at home and abroad. In this, sport once more follows current trends in the world capitalist economy, in which growing economic liberalism is accompanied by increasing restrictions on civil liberties – just as was the case in capitalism's formative period in the eighteenth and early nineteenth centuries.

It may also be the case that sport's 'level playing field' as a form of social mobility, insofar as it ever existed, is being eroded. Harry Edwards has argued that Afro-American participation in sport has been in decline, as evidenced most noticeably in boxing and baseball. Despite Michael Jordan's success as a spokesman for corporate America, racial divisions in the US remain as deep as ever. The social and economic devastation wrought by de-industrialisation has meant that prison has replaced school and sports as the US government's primary means of socialising young black men in many of America's inner cities.[3] In Britain, 58 per cent of its gold medal winners at the 2004 Olympics were privately educated, which evened out to 45 per cent of all British medal winners since the 1996 Games. English cricket and rugby union are becoming more elitist, not less.[4] Twenty-first-century sport is not necessarily a career open to all the talented. Indeed, the fight for equality of access to sport and sports facilities for all, regardless of gender, race or class remains as urgent as it has ever been.

Even in areas where change appears to be emerging, in women's and disability sport, the essential masculinity of sport remains paramount. Despite the tremendous advances made by women in the West during the twentieth century, sport remains obdurately male. This is, even when taking into account the burgeoning of women's soccer, arguably the world's fastest growing participation sport of the past generation. The sport remains dominated by male administrators and coaches. Paralympic sport, committed to the same competitive imperative as elite able-bodied sports, employs a dense code of taxonomy to classify and regulate its athletes. Moreover, rather than becoming more integrated, the weight of decades of division and the administrative ambitions of governing bodies have meant that the opportunities for men and women, able and disabled, to play together have diminished rather than increased. The fact that the IAAF could seek to ban the double amputee runner Oscar Pistorius from competing with able-bodied athletes because it claimed he had an unfair advantage over them highlights the extent to which sport is a prisoner of its own desire to categorise and control athletes. The able-bodied, and heterosexual, male still remains the paradigm athlete.

Sport's idealisation of the body, its privileging of physical activity over the intellectual, its fetishisation of blind courage means that the male body is the standard against which everything else is measured. Its worldview is based on a simple binary, and not merely the 'win–lose' of the field of play. Its moral judgements are also derived from antipodes: clean versus dirty, pure versus impure, the cheat versus the role model. This Manichean outlook is or has been applied throughout sport to issues of class, gender, professionalism and drugs. Anything deemed to be aberrant or 'unnatural' falls on the wrong side of the divide. In this, it reflects the everyday, underlying 'deep politics' of capitalism that goes unchallenged as 'common sense'.

As to the future, it is impossible to know how a society that has freed itself from capitalism will play or watch sport. Like many other forms of culture that have emerged out of capitalism, sport is unlikely to lose its appeal, even in a society where unceasing competition has been replaced by cooperation. Its ability to offer the emotional experience of triumph and tragedy to participants and spectators is too potent. But, at the very least, we can hope that in a society in which art, culture and humanity itself have been freed from the exploitation, bigotry and oppression of capitalism, sport may play a positive role in helping men and women to reach the fullest extent of their mental and physical potential.

NOTES

1 Capitalism and the birth of modern sport

1 Anon., *The Jockey Club, or A Sketch of the Manners of the Age*, London, 1793, p. 2.
2 The foremost works on play come from sociologists, most notably Johan Huizinga's *Homo Ludens*, originally published in 1938, and Roger Callois's *Man, Play and Games*, originally published in 1958.
3 V. Gordon Childe, *What Happened in History?* London, 1942. A useful critique can be found in Neil Faulkner, 'Gordon Childe and Marxist Archeology', *International Socialism*, no. 116 (Autumn 2007), pp. 81–106. For a more contemporary discussion of the relationship, see, for example, Keith Thomas's introduction to *The Oxford Book of Work*, Oxford, 1999.
4 For example, see the discussion in Allen Guttmann, *From Ritual to Record*, New York, 1978, ch. 1.
5 Roland Renson, 'Traditional Sports in Europe', in Tony Collins, John Martin and Wray Vamplew (eds), *Encyclopedia of Traditional British Rural Sports*, Abingdon, 2005, pp. 1–19. Alessandro Arcangeli, *Recreation in the Renaissance: Attitudes towards Leisure and Pastimes in European Culture c. 1425–1675*, Basingstoke, 2003, ch. 6.
6 John McClelland, *Body and Mind: Sport in Europe from the Roman Empire to the Renaissance*, Abingdon, 2008. John Marshall Carter, *Medieval Games: Sports and Recreations in Feudal Society*, Connecticut, 1992. Thomas S. Henrick, 'Sport and Social Hierarchy in Medieval England', *Journal of Sport History*, vol. 9, no. 2 (Summer, 1982), pp. 20–37.
7 George Orwell, *The Road to Wigan Pier*, London, 1937, p. 148.
8 Andrew Leibs, *Sports and Games of the Renaissance*, Connecticut, 2004. Jean-François Loudcher, 'The Origins of French Boxing: Bare-knuckle Duelling, Savate and Chausson 1820–45', *International Journal of the History of Sport*, vol. 18, no. 2 (2001), pp. 168–78.
9 For an English-language outline of the history of sport in France see Richard Holt, *Sport and Society in Modern France*, London, 1981.
10 Baseball is referred to in Jane Austen, *Northanger Abbey*, Oxford, 1980, p. 7, written in 1798–99.
11 Elliott Gorn, *The Manly Art*, Ithaca, NY, 1986, pp. 46–68, and Elliott Gorn and Warren Goldstein, *A Brief History of American Sports*, New York, 1993, pp. 49–53.
12 For a more detailed exposition of this view see Eric Hobsbawm, *Industry and Empire*, Harmondsworth, rev. edn 1999, pp. 10–16. For an outline of the debate on the

transition see Perry Anderson, *Arguments within English Marxism*, London, 1980, and Ellen Meiksins Wood, *The Origin of Capitalism: A Longer View*, London, 2002, pp. 11–72.

13 Lawrence Stone, *The Crisis of the Aristocracy, 1558–1641*, Oxford, 1968, p. 383. For aristocratic gambling in general, see pp. 567–72.

14 The Broughton–Slack fight is described in Pierce Egan, *Pancratia, or, a History of Pugilism*, London, 1812, p. 47.

15 For a broad discussion of gambling in eighteenth-century France, see Thomas M. Kavanagh, *Enlightenment and the Shadows of Chance*, Baltimore, 1993, esp. pp. 67–106.

16 Henry Fielding, *An Enquiry into the Causes of the Late Increase of Robbers and Related Writings*, Oxford, 1988, p. 84.

17 Richard Tuck and Michael Silverthorne (eds), *Thomas Hobbes On the Citizen*, Cambridge, 1998, p. 94.

18 Specifically on this, see Joyce Oldham Appleby, *Economic Thought and Ideology in Seventeenth-century England*, Princeton, NJ, 1978 and *The Relentless Revolution: A History of Capitalism*, New York, 2010. For a broader discussion of these developments, see Ellen Meiksins Wood, *The Origin of Capitalism*, New York 1999.

19 Quoted in John Henry, 'Science and the Coming of Enlightenment', in Martin Fitzpatrick (ed.), *The Enlightenment World*, Abingdon, 2004, p. 24.

20 In Bernard Mandeville, *The Fable of the Bees: or, Private Vices, Publick Benefits*, London, 1724, p. 464.

21 Adam Smith, *An Inquiry into the Nature and Causes of the Wealth of Nations*, Chicago, 1976, p. 18.

22 It should be noted that this pre-dated sport's use in the service of Social Darwinism by around 100 years.

23 *Pierce Egan's Book of Sports*, no. XXII (1833), p. 337.

24 Anon., *The Jockey Club, or A Sketch of the Manners of the Age*, p. 2.

25 Pierce Egan, *Pancratia, or, a History of Pugilism*, p. 6.

26 Pierce Egan, *Boxiana*, 1824 edition, London, p. 1.

27 For a broader discussion of the development of leisure, see J.H. Plumb, *The Commercialisation of Leisure in Eighteenth-century England*, Reading, 1973 and Neil McKendrick, John Brewer and J.H. Plumb, *The Birth of a Consumer Society: The Commercialization of Eighteenth-century England*, London, 1982.

28 Raymond Williams, *The Long Revolution*, London, 1961, pp. 202–12. Michael Harris, 'Sport in the Newspapers before 1750: Representations of Cricket, Class and Commerce in the London Press', *Media History*, vol. 4, no. 1 (1998), pp. 19–28.

29 The earliest newspaper advertisement for boxing I have been able to locate is in the *Weekly Journal With Fresh Advices Foreign and Domestick*, 16 April 1715.

30 The Whitacre–Gretton exchange can be found in the *Daily Post* (London), 13 November 1727.

31 Eric Hobsbawm, *Industry and Empire*, pp. 63–5.

32 James Boswell, *The Life of Samuel Johnson*, London, 1907, vol. 2, p. 720. Pierce Egan notes the centrality of London to sport in the 1700s in his *Boxiana*, 1818 edition, p. 136.

33 See, for instance, the examples cited by Wolfgang Behringer, '*Arena* and *Pall Mall*: Sport in the Early Modern Period', *German History*, vol. 27, no. 3 (2009), pp. 331–57.

34 Douglas Hay *et al.*, *Albion's Fatal Tree: Crime and Society in Eighteenth-century England*, London, 2011 (new edition); E.P. Thompson, *Whigs and Hunters*, Harmondsworth, 1975. The fullest discussion of the emergence of rules for sport can be found in Wray Vamplew, 'Playing with the Rules: Influences on the Development of Regulation in Sport', *International Journal of the History of Sport*, vol. 47, no. 7 (May 2007), pp. 843–71.

35 Karl Marx, 'Contribution to the Critique of Hegel's *Philosophy of Law*' (1843), in *Karl Marx and Frederick Engels Collected Works*, Moscow, 1975, vol. 3, p. 106.

36 Wray Vamplew, *The Turf*, Harmondsworth, 1975, pp. 17–25; Dennis Brailsford, *British Sport: A History*, Cambridge, 1992, pp. 53–5.

37 Quoted in James Christie Whyte, *History of the British Turf from the Earliest Period to the Present Day*, London, 1840, vol. 1, p. 389.

38 Warren Goldstein, *Playing for Keeps: A History of Early Baseball*, Ithaca, NY, 1989, p. 143.
39 The best account of early boxing remains Dennis Brailsford, *Bareknuckles: A Social History of Prize Fighting*, Cambridge, 1989.
40 For an outline of Figg's career, see Egan, *Pancratia*, pp. 32–35. *Daily Post*, 21 January 1725.
41 John Broughton, *Proposals for Erecting an Amphitheatre for the Manly Exercise of Boxing*, London, 1 January 1743, p. 2.
42 Broughton, *Proposals for Erecting an Amphitheatre*, p. 3.
43 *Daily Journal*, 26 July 1725. The fullest account of the development of cricket is David Underdown's *Start of Play: Cricket and Culture in Eighteenth-century England*, Harmondsworth, 2000.
44 In 1793 the *Sporting Magazine* reported on nine cricket matches for stake money of 1,000 guineas.
45 *Weekly Journal* or *Saturday's Post*, 16 May 1719.
46 Derek Birley, *A Social History of English Cricket*, London, 1999, p. 18.
47 Underdown, *Start of Play*, p. 88; Harris, 'Sport in the Newspapers before 1750', p. 25. Birley, *A Social History of English Cricket*, p. 27; *Sporting Magazine*, vol. 2, June 1793, p. 134.
48 These are reprinted in the *Sporting Magazine*, vol. 2, June 1793, pp. 134–6.
49 Details of stake money compiled from the 1793 and 1800 editions of Samuel Britcher's *A Complete List of All the Grand Matches of Cricket that Have Been Played in the Year 1793: With a Correct State of Each Innings. And the Articles of Cricket Inserted, with an Old Cricket Song*, London, 1793.
50 Stefan Szymanski, 'A Theory of the Evolution of Modern Sport', *Journal of Sport History*, vol. 35, no. 1 (2008), pp. 1–32.
51 Peter Clark, *British Clubs and Societies 1580–1800: The Origins of an Associational World*, Oxford, 2001.
52 See Gorn and Goldstein, *A Brief History of American Sports*, pp. 40–60.
53 For the rules of golf, see Vamplew, 'Playing with the Rules: Influences on the Development of Regulation in Sport', pp. 846–7.
54 Peter Radford, *The Celebrated Captain Barclay: Sport, Money and Fame in Regency Britain*, London, 2001.
55 P.F. Radford and A.J. Ward-Smith, 'British Running Performances in the Eighteenth Century', *Journal of Sports Sciences*, vol. 21, no. 5 (May 2003), pp. 429–38.
56 For more on changing perceptions of the nature of time, see E.P. Thompson, 'Time, Work-discipline and Industrial capitalism', *Past & Present*, vol. 38, no. 1 (1967), pp. 56–97.
57 D.P. Blaine, *An Encyclopedia of Rural Sports*, London, 1840, p. 1206–12. G. Jobey, 'Cockfighting in Northumberland and Durham during the Eighteenth and Nineteenth Centuries', *Archeologia Aeliana*, vol. 20 (1992), p. 16.
58 J.-F. Loudcher, 'A History of Savate, Chausson and "French Boxing" 1828–1978', *Sport in History*, vol. 27, no. 3 (Sept. 2007), pp. 459–86.
59 Richard Holt, *Sport and Society in Modern France*, p. 142.
60 As is argued, for example, by Allen Guttmann in *From Ritual to Record*, New York, 1978.
61 *London Gazette*, 4–7 April 1719.
62 For White Roding, see Derek Birley, *Sport and the Making of Britain*, Manchester, 1993, p. 115. For Kettering, see E.P. Thompson, 'The Moral Economy of the English Crowd in the Eighteenth Century', *Past & Present*, vol. 50, no. 1 (1971), p. 116.
63 See the wide range of football types in Hugh Hornby, *Uppies and Downies: The Extraordinary Football Games of Britain*, London, 2008.
64 Montague Shearman, *Athletics and Football*, London, 1887, p. 260.

2 Class conflict and the decline of traditional games

 1 *Derby and Chesterfield Reporter*, 7 February 1845, quoted in Anthony Delves, 'Popular Recreation and Social Conflict in Derby, 1800–850', in Eileen Yeo and Stephen Yeo (eds), *Popular Culture and Class Conflict 1590–1914*, Brighton, 1981, p. 94.

2 Martin Walsh, 'November Bull-running in Stamford, Lincolnshire', *Journal of Popular Culture*, vol. 30 (1996), pp. 233–47. Stamford contrasts with the *encierro* in Pamplona, where the bull chases the citizens through the town.

3 Quoted in Robert Malcolmson, *Popular Recreations in English Society 1700–1850*, Oxford, 1973, p. 104.

4 The fullest exploration of the concept of Merrie England can be found in Ronald Hutton, *The Rise and Fall of Merry England: The Ritual Year 1400–1700*, Oxford, 1996.

5 Keith Thomas, 'Work and Leisure in Pre-industrial Society', *Past & Present*, vol. 29 (1964), pp. 50–62.

6 For the debate on recreational continuity, see Hugh Cunningham, *Leisure in the Industrial Revolution, c. 1780–1880*, London, 1980 and Peter N. Stearns, 'The Effort at Continuity in Working-class Culture', *Journal of Modern History*, vol. 52, no. 4 (1980), pp. 626–55.

7 There is a considerable literature on this debate, the most important contributions being Robert W. Malcolmson, *Popular Recreations in English Society*; Eileen Yeo and Stephen Yeo (eds), *Popular Culture and Class Conflict 1590–1914*, and J. Golby and A. Purdue, *The Civilization of the Crowd: Popular Culture in England, 1750–1900*, London, 1984. Two useful contributions to the debate can be found in Emma Griffin, 'Popular Culture in Industrializing England', *Historical Journal*, vol. 45 (2002), pp. 619–35 and Peter Borsay, *A History of Leisure*, London, 2006.

8 For the role of pubs in maintaining traditional sports, see Tony Collins and Wray Vamplew, *Mud, Sweat and Beers: A Cultural History of Sport and Alcohol*, Oxford, 2002.

9 Christopher Hill, *Reformation to Industrial Revolution: A Social and Economic History of Britain 1530–1780*, London, 1967, p. 20.

10 E.J. Hobsbawm and George Rudé, *Captain Swing*, London, 1969, pp. 27–36.

11 See Ellen Meiksins Wood, *The Origin of Capitalism: A Longer View*, London, 2002, pp. 125–46.

12 Quoted in Hobsbawm, *Industry and Empire*, Harmondsworth, rev. edn, 1999, p. 79. The importance of fixed pieces of land for football games can be seen in David Dymond, 'A Lost Social Institution: The Camping Close', *Rural History*, vol. 1, no. 2 (Oct. 1990), pp. 165–92.

13 The classic account of this process is E.P. Thompson, 'Time, Work-discipline and Industrial Capitalism', *Past & Present*, vol. 38, no. 1 (1967), pp. 56–97.

14 *Hansard*, 24 May 1802, quoted in *Cobbett's Weekly Political Register*, 21 September 1805, p. 423.

15 Michael Perelman, *The Invention of Capitalism: Classical Political Economy and the Secret History of Primitive Accumulation*, Durham, NC, 2000. Wray Vamplew, *Pay Up and Play the Game: Professional Sport in Britain 1870–1914*, Cambridge, 1988, p. 39.

16 Douglas A. Reid, 'The Decline of Saint Monday 1766–1876', *Past & Present*, vol. 71, no. 1 (1976), pp. 76–101.

17 Peter Bailey, *Leisure and Class in Victorian England*, London, 1978. R.D. Storch, 'The Policeman as Domestic Missionary: Urban Discipline and Popular Culture in Northern England 1850–80', *Journal of Social History*, vol. 9 (1976), pp. 481–509.

18 *Derby and Chesterfield Reporter*, 23 February 1832, quoted in Malcolmson, *Popular Recreation*, p. 113.

19 Horatio Smith, *Festivals, Games and Amusements*, London, 1831, p. 122. Emma Griffin explores the issue of recreation and changing leisure spaces in her *England's Revelry: A History of Popular Sports and Pastimes, 1660–1830*, Oxford, 2005.

20 E.P. Thompson, *The Making of the English Working Class*, London, 1963, p. 451.

21 However, many Chartists opposed traditional recreations as demeaning and sought to encourage other forms of intellectual and physical improvement. See, for example, Brian Harrison, 'Teetoal Chartism', *History*, vol. 58, no. 193 (1973), pp. 193–217.

22 Malcolmson, *Popular Recreations in English Society*, p. 127.

23 G. Jobey, 'Cockfighting in Northumberland and Durham during the Eighteenth and Nineteenth Centuries', *Archeologia Aeliana*, vol. 5, no. 20 (1992), pp. 1–25.

24 Roger Munting, *An Economic and Social History of Gambling in Britain and the USA*, Manchester, 1996, ch. 1. Mark Clapson, *A Bit of a Flutter: Popular Gambling in English Society c. 1823–61*, Manchester, 1992, ch. 2.
25 Bailey, *Leisure and Class in Victorian England*, ch. 5.
26 Karl Marx, 'Anti-Church Movement', in *Karl Marx and Frederick Engels Collected Works*, Moscow, 1975–2005, vol. 14, p. 303.
27 Dominic Erdozain, *The Problem of Pleasure: Sport, Recreation and the Crisis of Victorian Religion*, Suffolk, 2010, ch. 1.
28 Jonathan Bayes, 'William Wilberforce: His Impact on Nineteenth-century Society', *Churchman*, vol. 108, no. 2 (1994), p. 29.
29 John Wigley, *The Rise and Fall of the Victorian Sunday*, Manchester, 1980. Brian Harrison, 'Religion and Recreation in Nineteenth-century England', *Past & Present*, vol. 38 (1967), pp. 98–125.
30 Adrian Harvey, *The Beginnings of a Commercial Sporting Culture in Britain, 1793–1850*, Aldershot, 2003, p. 64.
31 Brian Harrison, 'Animals and the State in Nineteenth-century England', *English Historical Review*, vol. 88 (1973), pp. 786–820.
32 As is argued by Eric Dunning and other followers of Norbert Elias. See, for example, Eric Dunning and Kenneth Sheard, *Barbarians, Gentlemen and Players*, 2nd edn, Abingdon, 2005.
33 John Emory (ed.), *The Works of the Reverend John Wesley*, London, 1831, vol. 3, p. 612.
34 Keith Thomas, *Man and the Natural World*, Allen Lane, 1983, p. 185. See also Harriet Ritvo, *The Animal Estate: English and Other Creatures in the Victorian Age*, Cambridge, MA, 1989.
35 See Richard Holt, *Sport and Society in Modern France*, London, 1981, pp. 107, 122, 127.
36 Adrian Shubert, *Death and Money in the Afternoon: A History of the Spanish Bullfight*, Oxford, 1999.
37 Jean-Jacques Rousseau, *Discourse on the Origin of Inequality* (Hackett edition), Indianapolis, 1992, pp. 24–5.
38 Reprinted in John Wain (ed.), *The Oxford Library of English Poetry*, vol. 2, p. 223.
39 *Cobbett's Weekly Political Register*, 28 September 1805, p. 442
40 There is a huge literature on this subject. A useful review can be found in Emma Vincent Macleod, 'British Attitudes to the French Revolution', *Historical Journal*, vol. 50, no. 3 (2007), pp. 689–709.
41 *Pierce Egan's Book of Sports*, no. XI (1832), p. 172.

3 Sport, nationalism and the French Revolution

1 Pierce Egan, *Boxiana*, London, 1824 edition, p. i.
2 The gathering is described in *The York Herald, and General Advertiser*, 25 June 1814. The Blucher remark is in *Caledonian Mercury*, 25 June 1814. A description can also be found in Peter Radford, *The Celebrated Captain Barclay: Sport, Money and Fame in Regency Britain*, London, 2001, pp. 223–5.
3 The impetus that the French Revolution gave to nationalism across Europe is of course well documented. For an outline see E.J. Hobsbawm, *Nations and Nationalism Since 1780*, Cambridge, 1990.
4 Christiane Eisenberg, 'Charismatic Nationalist Leader: Turnvater Jahn', *International Journal of the History of Sport*, vol. 13, no. 1 (1996), pp. 14–27. Heikki Lempa, *Beyond the Gymnasium: Educating the Middle-class Bodies in Classical Germany*, Lexington, 2007, pp. 67–111.
5 This is often cited but rarely referenced. It comes from Jahn's 1810 work *Deutsches Volksthum* – see David J. Rosenberg, *Towards a Cosmopolitanism of Self-difference: Heinrich Heine and Madame de Stael between France and Germany*, unpublished PhD thesis, University of Santa Barbara, 2008, p. 4.

6 Roland Naul, 'History of Sport and Physical Education in Germany', in Roland Naul and Ken Hardman (eds), *Sport and Physical Education in Germany*, London, 2002, pp. 15–27.

7 William J. Baker, *Sports in the Western World*, Illinois, 1988, p. 100–1.

8 See, for example, Gertrud Pfister, 'Cultural Confrontations: German *Turnen*, Swedish Gymnastics and English Sport', *Culture, Sport and Society*, vol. 6, no. 1 (2003), pp. 61–91.

9 Fridolín Macháček, 'The Sokol Movement: Its Contribution to Gymnastics', *Slavonic and East European Review*, vol. 17, no. 49 (1938), pp. 73–90.

10 Claire E. Nolte, *The Sokol in the Czech Lands to 1914: Training for the Nation*, London, 2002.

11 John Broughton, *Proposals for Erecting an Amphitheatre for the Manly Sport of Boxing*, London, 1 January, p. 2.

12 Linda Colley, *Britons: Forging the Nation 1707–1837*, Newhaven, CT, 2009, p. 174.

13 *Cobbett's Weekly Political Register*, 10 August 1805, p. 200.

14 Peter Radford, 'Lifting the Spirits of the Nation: British Boxers and the Emergence of the National Sporting Hero at the Time of the Napoleonic Wars', *Identities: Global Studies in Power and Culture*, vol. 12, no. 2 (2005), pp. 249–70.

15 Egan, *Boxiana*, p. ii.

16 Windham letter to A. Hudson, 17 August 1809, in *The Windham Papers*, vol. 2, London, 1913, pp. 351–2.

17 Peter Radford, *The Celebrated Captain Barclay*, pp. 185–6. Carl B. Cone, 'The Molineaux–Cribb Fight, 1810: Wuz Tom Molineaux Robbed?', *Journal of Sport History*, vol. 9, no. 3 (Winter, 1982), pp. 83–91.

18 *The Literary Magazine, and American Register*, vol. 6 (1806), p. 257.

19 *Sporting Magazine*, November 1804, p. 84.

20 *Blackwood's Edinburgh Magazine*, vol. 6, no. 36 (March 1820), p. 610.

21 G.M. Trevelyan, *English Social History: A Survey of Six Centuries from Chaucer to Queen Victoria*, London, 1978, p. 362.

22 Anon., *The Art of Manual Defence*, London, 1799, pp. xiii–xiv.

23 Anon., *The Complete Art of Boxing, etc.*, London, 1788, p. 18.

24 William Wordsworth, *The Complete Poetical Works*, London, 1888, p. 212.

25 Martin Johnes, 'Archery, Romance and Elite Culture in England and Wales, c. 1780–1840', *History*, vol. 89 (2004), 193–208.

26 For Egan, see J.C. Reid, *Bucks and Bruisers: Pierce Egan and Regency England*, London, 1971.

27 William Hazlitt, 'Merry England', in *Sketches and Essays*, Oxford, 1936, p. 51.

28 See Harold Seymour, *Baseball: The Early Years*, Oxford 1960, pp. 8–12; James A. Vlasich, *A Legend for the Legendary: The Origin of the Baseball Hall of Fame*, Wisconsin, 1990, pp. 162–8; Tony Collins, *Rugby's Great Split*, London, 1998, pp. 5–8; and William Baker, 'William Webb Ellis and the Origins of Rugby Football', *Albion*, vol. 13, no. 2 (Summer, 1981), pp. 117–30.

29 See D. Chatziefstathiou, 'Pierre de Coubertin: Man and Myth' and Mark Golden, 'The Ancient Olympics and the Modern: Mirror and Mirage', both in H. Lenskyj and S. Wagg (eds), *The Palgrave Handbook of Olympic Studies*, Basingstoke, 2012, pp. 15–25 and 26–42.

30 For an overview of early cricket literature in its historical context, see David Underdown, 'The History of Cricket', *History Compass*, vol. 4, no. 1 (2006), pp. 43–53. Derek Birley's *The Willow Wand*, London, 1979, handsomely demolishes many of cricket's long-standing myths.

4 The middle-class invention of amateurism

1 Arthur Budd, *Rugby Football*, London, 1899, p. 2.

2 This argument runs counter to that of Adrian Harvey, *The Beginnings of a Commercial Sporting Culture in Britain, 1793–1850*, Aldershot, 2004.

3 Quoted in Anon., 'Review of "Tour in England, Ireland and France in the Years 1828 and 1829" by A German Prince', *The Edinburgh Review*, vol. 54 (Dec. 1831), p. 397.

4 Peter Burke, *Popular Culture in Early Modern Europe*, London, 1978, p. 270.

5 Dennis Brailsford, *A Taste for Diversions: Sport in Georgian England*, Cambridge, 1999, p. 164.

6 Adrian Harvey, *The Beginnings of a Commercial Sporting Culture in Britain, 1793–1850*, pp. 166–7.

7 Quoted in Wray Vamplew, *The Turf*, Harmondsworth, 1975, p. 91.

8 Adrian Harvey, *Beginnings of a Commercial Sporting Culture*, p. 46.

9 Robert Light, 'Ten Drunks and a Parson: The Victorian Professional Cricketer Reconsidered', *Sport in History*, vol. 25, no. 1 (2005), pp. 60–76.

10 Keith A.P. Sandiford, 'Amateurs and Professionals in Victorian County Cricket', *Albion*, vol. 15, no. 1 (Spring, 1983), pp. 32–51; W.F. Mandle, 'The Professional Cricketer in England in the Nineteenth Century', *Labour History*, no. 23 (Nov. 1972), pp. 1–16; Ric Sissons, *The Players: A Social History of the Professional Cricketer*, London, 1988.

11 Eric Hobsbawm, *Industry and Empire*, Harmondsworth, rev. edn, 1999, p. 55.

12 For an overview of this period, see K.T. Hoppen, *The Mid-Victorian Generation 1846–86*, Oxford, 2000.

13 There is a considerable literature on the public schools in this period, most notably J.R. Honey, *Tom Brown's Universe: The Development of the Victorian Public School*, London, 1977; J.A. Mangan's *Athleticism in the Victorian and Edwardian Public School*, London, 1981; and M.J. Bradley and B. Simon (eds), *The Victorian Public School*, London, 1975.

14 Quoted in Lytton Strachey, *Eminent Victorians*, London, 1918 (Folio Society edition), 1986, p. 171; A.P. Stanley, *The Life and Correspondence of Thomas Arnold*, London, 1845, p. 290.

15 *The Rugby Miscellany*, no. 7 (Feb. 1846), p. 226.

16 W.E. Winn, '*Tom Brown's Schooldays* and the Development of Muscular Christianity', *Church History*, vol. 29, no. 1 (1960), pp. 64–73.

17 For a discussion of this relationship, see, Dominic Erdozain, *The Problem of Pleasure: Sport, Recreation and the Crisis of Victorian Religion*, Suffolk, 2010.

18 For the original meaning of 'amateur', see, for example, Pierce Egan, *Boxiana*, London, 1824, pp. 12, 14, 15, 56, 111 and 204.

19 For a detailed discussion, see Richard Holt, 'The Amateur Body and the Middle-class Man: Work, Health and Style in Victorian Britain', *Sport in History*, vol. 26, no. 3 (2006), pp. 352–69.

20 For these and many other examples of amateur regulations, see Appendix 2 of Wray Vamplew, *Pay Up and Play the Game: Professional Sport in Britain 1870–1914*, Cambridge, 1988, pp. 302–7.

21 The process is described in Derek Birley, *A Social History of English Cricket*, London, 1999, pp. 101–8.

22 The best account of amateurism in cricket remains Derek Birley, *The Willow Wand*, London, 1979.

23 Frank Mitchell, 'A Crisis in Rugby Football', *St James's Gazette*, 24 September 1897.

24 For the fullest account of the debate see Dave Russell, 'From Evil to Expedient: The Legalization of Professionalism in English Football, 1884–85', in Stephen Wagg (ed.), *Myths and Milestones in the History of Sport*, Basingstoke, 2011, pp. 32–56.

25 Arthur Budd, 'The Rugby Union Game', in *Football Annual*, London, 1886, p. 52.

26 As is argued in Eric Dunning and Kenneth Sheard, *Gentlemen, Barbarians and Players*, 2nd edn, Abingdon, 2005.

27 The debate is discussed in Tony Collins, *Rugby's Great Split*, London, 1998, pp. 41–51.

28 Tony Collins, *A Social History of English Rugby Union*, Abingdon, 2009, pp. 37–42 and 116–21.

29 Some aspects of this are discussed in J.A. Mangan, *The Games Ethic and Imperialism*, Harmondsworth, 1986.

30 *The Times*, 23 December 1985.
31 See Eugen Weber, 'Pierre de Coubertin and the Introduction of Organized Sports in France', *Journal of Contemporary History*, vol. 5 (1970), pp. 3–26 and 'Gymnastics and Sports in Fin-de-Siècle France: Opium of the Classes?', *American Historical Review*, vol. 76 (1971), pp. 70–98.
32 Quoted in Eugen Weber, 'Pierre de Coubertin and the Introduction of Organized Sports in France', p. 15.
33 Philip Dine, *French Rugby Football: A Cultural History*, Oxford, 2001.
34 See Mike Rylance, *The Forbidden Game*, Brighouse, 1999.
35 Quoted in Elliott Gorn, *The Manly Art*, Ithaca, NY, 1986, p. 188.
36 Clifford Putney, *Muscular Christianity: Manhood and Sports in Protestant America, 1880–1920*, Cambridge, MA, 2003, p. 20.
37 Parke H. Davis, *Football: The American Intercollegiate Game*, New York, 1911, p. 24.
38 These issues are explored in J.A. Mangan and James Walvin (eds), *Manliness and Morality: Middle-class Masculinity in Britain and America, 1800–1940*, Manchester, 1987.
39 Warren Goldstein, *Playing for Keeps: A History of Early Baseball*, Ithaca, NY, 1989, pp. 122–3.
40 Michael Robidoux, 'Imagining a Canadian Identity through Sport', *Journal of American Folklore*, vol. 115, no. 456 (Spring, 2002), pp. 209–26.
41 Caspar Whitney, *A Sporting Pilgrimage*, New York, 1894, p. 164.
42 Birley, *A Social History of English Cricket*, p. 108.
43 Holt, *Sport and Society in Modern France*, London, 1981, p. 79.
44 Donal McAnallen, '"The Greatest Amateur Association in the World?" The GAA and Amateurism', in Mike Cronin, Paul Rouse and William Murphy (eds), *The Gaelic Athletic Association, 1884–2009*, Dublin, 2009, pp. 157–82.
45 The classic account is Michael Oriard, *Reading Football*, North Carolina, 1998.
46 Steve Pope, *Patriotic Games*, New York, 1997, pp. 89–90; David L. Westby and Allen Sack, 'The Commercialization and Functional Rationalization of College Football', *Journal of Higher Education*, vol. 157, no. 6 (Nov./Dec. 1976), p. 630.
47 Steve Pope, *Patriotic Games*, pp. 89–90.
48 There is a wide literature on this subject, the most recent overview being Billy Hawkins, *The New Plantation: Black Athletes, College Sports, and Predominantly White NCAA Institutions*, London, 2010.
49 There is a huge literature on this subject. For more recent analyses see Michael Oriard, *Bowled Over: Big-time College Football from the Sixties to the BCS Era*, North Carolina, 2009; Charles Clotfelter, *Big-time Sports in American Universities*, New York, 2011; and Taylor Branch, 'The Shame of College Sports', *The Atlantic*, October 2011.

5 Women and the masculine kingdom of sport

1 *L'Emancipation*, 1 January 1872, quoted in Eugene Schulkind, 'Socialist Women during the 1871 Paris Commune', *Past & Present*, vol. 106 (1985), p. 137.
2 *The Yorkshireman*, 18 December 1889.
3 See, for example, Philip Mason, *The English Gentleman: The Rise and Fall of an Ideal*, London, 1992.
4 For an overview of women's sport and recreation in the eighteenth and nineteenth centuries, see Catriona M. Parratt, *More Than Mere Amusement: Working-class Women's Leisure in England, 1750–1914*, Lebanon, NH, 2001. See also Nancy L. Struna, 'Gender and Sporting Practice in Early America, 1750–1810', *Journal of Sport History*, vol. 18, no. 1 (Spring, 1991), pp. 10–30, and Allan Guttmann, *Women's Sports*, New York, 1991.
5 Dennis Brailsford, *A Taste for Diversions: Sport in Georgian England*, Cambridge, 1999, pp. 149.
6 David Underdown, *Start of Play: Cricket and Culture in Eighteenth-century England*, Harmondsworth, 2000, p. 81; *Pierce Egan's Book of Sports*, no. XI (1832), p. 341.
7 Brailsford, *A Taste for Diversions*, p. 143, 149.
8 *London Journal*, 31 August 1723.

9 *The Life and Surprising Adventures of Mary Anne Talbot, in the Name of John Taylor*, transcribed by Mary Anne Talbot and edited by Paul Royster, Lincoln, NE, 1809, Faculty Publications, UNL Libraries. Paper 32, http://digitalcommons.unl.edu/libraryscience/32.

10 Adrian Harvey, *The Beginnings of a Commercial Sporting Culture in Britain, 1793–1850*, Aldershot, 2003, pp. 196–7.

11 *Sporting Magazine*, July 1793, pp. 245–6.

12 Brailsford, *A Taste for Diversions*, p. 152.

13 Robert W. Malcolmson, *Popular Recreations in English Society 1700–1850*, Oxford, 1973, pp. 77–9.

14 This argument broadly follows that of Engels in 'The Origin of the Family, Private Property, and the State', in *Karl Marx and Frederick Engels Collected Works*, Moscow, 1975–2005, vol. 26, pp. 129–276.

15 *Karl Marx and Frederick Engels Collected Works*, vol. 4, p. 374.

16 On the relationship between work and masculinity, see the special issue of *Labour History Review*, vol. 69, no. 2 (2004). For a broader discussion see David D. Gilmore, *Manhood in the Making: Cultural Concepts of Masculinity*, New Haven, CT, 1990.

17 Teddy Roosevelt, 1900, 'The Strenuous Life', quoted in Kasia Boddy, *Boxing: A Cultural History*, London, 2008, p. 95.

18 *Cobbett's Weekly Political Register*, 10 August 1805, p. 197.

19 *The New Rugbeian*, vol. 3, no. 8 (Nov. 1861), pp. 296, 313.

20 *Wakefield Express*, 23 November 1872.

21 B.F. Robinson, *Rugby Football*, London, 1896, pp. 49–50.

22 H.H. Almond in Reverend Frank Marshall (ed.), *Football: The Rugby Union Game*, London, 1892, p. 55.

23 Paul Dimeo, 'Colonial Bodies, Colonial Sport: "Martial" Punjabis, "Effeminate" Bengalis and the Development of Indian Football', *International Journal of the History of Sport*, vol. 19, no.1 (2002), pp. 72–90.

24 The key work on this question remains Bruce Haley, *The Healthy Body and Victorian Culture*, Cambridge, MA, 1990.

25 Thomas Hughes, *Tom Brown's Schooldays*, OUP World's Classics edition, Oxford, 1989, pp. 218 and 233–4. See also Paul M. Puccio 'At the Heart of *Tom Brown's Schooldays*: Thomas Arnold and Christian Friendship', *Modern Language Studies*, vol. 25, no. 4 (Autumn, 1995), pp. 57–74.

26 Jeffrey Weeks, *Sex, Politics and Society*, 2nd edn, London, 1989, pp. 49–51.

27 Quoted in Richard Sanders, *Beastly Fury: The Strange Birth of British Football*, London, 2009, p. 77. See also Andy Mitchell, *Arthur Kinnaird: First Lord of Football*, Edinburgh, 2011.

28 Roy Porter and Lesley Hall, *The Facts of Life*, New Haven, CT, 1995, pp. 141–4.

29 The fullest account of this pseudo-scientific nonsense can be found in Patricia Vertinsky, *The Eternally Wounded Woman*, Manchester, 1989.

30 Pierre de Coubertin, *Textes Choisies*, ed. G. Rioux, Zurich, 1986, vol. 1, p. 261.

31 Kathryn Gleadle, *British Women in the Nineteenth Century*, Basingstoke, 2001.

32 Claire Goldberg Moses, *French Feminism in the Nineteenth Century*, Albany, 1984; Tiffany K. Wayne, *Women's Roles in Nineteenth-century America*, Connecticut, 2007.

33 Sheila Fletcher, *Feminists and Bureaucrats: A Study in the Development of Girls' Education in the Nineteenth Century*, Cambridge, 1980, pp. 192–217.

34 Gerald Gems and Gertrud Pfister, *Understanding American Sports*, Abingdon, 2009, ch. 11.

35 Henry James, *The Bostonians*, Digireads edition, Kansas, 2007, p. 176.

36 For Bergman-Osterberg see Jennifer Hargreaves, *Sporting Females: Critical Issues in the History and Sociology of Women's Sports*, London, 1994, pp. 74–83 and Anne Bloomfield, 'Martina Bergman-Osterberg (1849–1915): Creating a Professional Role for Women in Physical Training', *History of Education*, vol. 34, no. 5 (2005), pp. 517–34.

37 For the UFGF, see Mary H. Leigh and Thérèse M. Bonin, 'The Pioneering Role of Madame Alice Milliat and the FSFI', *Journal of Sport History*, vol. 4, no. 1 (1977), pp. 72–83. For the USA, see Linda J. Borish, 'The Robust Woman and the Muscular Christian',

International Journal of the History of Sport, vol. 4, no. 2 (Sept. 1987), pp. 139–54 and for Canada see Helen Lenskyj, *Out of Bounds: Women, Sport and Sexuality*, Toronto, 1986.

38 See, for example, Richard Holt, 'Golf and the English Suburb: Class and Gender in a London Club, c. 1890–c.1960', *The Sports Historian*, vol. 18, no. 1 (1998), pp. 76–89.

39 Rob Lake, 'Gender and Etiquette in "Mixed Doubles" Lawn Tennis 1870–1939', *International Journal of the History of Sport*, vol. 29, no. 5 (2012), pp. 691–710.

40 Jane George, Joyce Kay and Wray Vamplew, 'Women to the Fore: Gender Accommodation and Resistance at the British Golf Club before 1914', *Sporting Traditions*, vol. 23, no. 2 (2007), pp. 79–98.

41 For a discussion on middle-class women's sports in this period, see Catriona M. Parratt, 'Athletic "Womanhood": Exploring Sources for Female Sport in Victorian and Edwardian England', *Journal of Sport History*, vol. 16, no. 2 (1989), pp. 140–57.

42 Dod awaits a full-scale biography but an outline can be found in Jeffrey Pearson, *Lottie Dod: Champion of Champions*, Birkenhead, 1989.

43 Katherine E. McCrone, *Playing the Game: Sport and the Physical Emancipation of English Women, 1870–1914*, Kentucky, 1988, pp. 133–4.

44 'A Few Thoughts on Working Girls', *Hockey Field*, 22 December 1910, quoted in Katherine McCrone, 'Class, Gender, and English Women's Sport, c. 1890–1914', *Journal of Sport History*, vol. 18, no. 1 (Spring, 1991), p. 171.

45 See Jean Williams, *A Game for Rough Girls?*, London, 2003, pp. 25–44 and Alethea Melling, *'Ladies' Football': Gender Roles and the Socialisation of Women Football Players in Lancashire, 1917–c.1960*, unpublished PhD thesis, University of Central Lancashire, 2000.

46 Quoted in Catriona M. Parratt, *More Than Mere Amusement*, p. 204.

47 *L'Osservatore Romano*, 16 May 1934, quoted in Simon Martin, *Sport Italia: The Italian Love Affair with Sport*, London, 2011, p. 79.

48 Quoted in Jennifer Hargreaves, *Sporting Females*, p. 86. See Patricia Vertinsky, *The Eternally Wounded Woman*, p. 20, for an alternative view.

49 Quoted in Eugene Schulkind, 'Socialist Women during the 1871 Paris Commune', p. 137. For the Marxist movement's struggle for women's emancipation see Werner Thonessen, *The Emancipation of Women: The Rise and Decline of the Women's Movement in German Social-Democracy 1863–1933*, London, 1973; and Richard Stites, *The Women's Liberation Movement in Russia*, Princeton, NJ, 1978.

50 Sheila Rowbotham, *A Century of Women: The History of Women in Britain and the United States in the Twentieth Century*, London, 1999.

51 Patricia Marks, *Bicycles, Bangs, and Bloomers: The New Woman in the Popular Press*, Kentucky, 1990.

52 David Rubinstein, 'Cycling in the 1890s', *Victorian Studies*, vol. 21 (1977), pp. 47–71.

53 The phrase is used in Holbrook Jackson, *The Eighteen Nineties*, London, 1913, p. 32.

54 David Rubinstein, 'Cycling in the 1890s', p. 61.

55 Richard Holt, 'Women, Men and Sport in France, c. 1870–1914: An Introductory Survey', *Journal of Sport History*, vol. 18, no. 1 (Spring, 1991), p. 125.

6 The Victorian sporting industrial revolution

1 Bertolt Brecht, 'Emphasis on Sport', in John Willett (ed.), *Brecht on Theatre*, London, 1978, p. 6. The phrase 'sporting industrial revolution' is borrowed from Wray Vamplew, *Pay Up and Play the Game: Professional Sport in Britain 1870–1914*, Cambridge, 1988, p. 281.

2 For the growth of American football, see Michael Oriard, *Reading Football*, North Carolina, 1998. For baseball, see Harold Seymour and Dorothy Z. Seymour, *Baseball*, vols 1 and 2, New York, 1989 and 1990.

3 For Australian rules football, see Geoffrey Blainey, *A Game of Our Own*, Melbourne, 1990.

4 Christopher Thompson, *The Tour de France: A Cultural History*, Berkeley, 2006.

5 For a discussion on the 'sporting entrepreneur', see Stephen Hardy, 'Entrepreneurs, Organizations, and the Sport Marketplace: Subjects in Search of Historians', *Journal of Sport History*, vol. 13, no. 1 (1986), pp. 14–33.

6 For one of the earliest discussions of sport and commodification, see John J. Stewart, 'The Commodification of Sport', *International Review for the Sociology of Sport*, vol. 22, no. 3 (1987), pp. 171–92.

7 See, for example, 'Letter from an Old Player', *Yorkshire Post*, 11 September 1895.

8 For more on this see Wray Vamplew, *Pay Up and Play the Game*, pp. 44–72.

9 Ric Sissons, *The Players: A Social History of the Professional Cricketer*, London, 1988; Rowland Bowen, *Cricket: A History of its Growth and Development*, London, 1970.

10 Quoted in David L. Westby and Allen Sack, 'The Commercialization and Functional Rationalization of College Football', *Journal of Higher Education*, vol. 157, no. 6 (Nov./Dec. 1976), p. 644.

11 For example, see Charles P. Korr, 'A Different Kind of Success: West Ham United and the Creation of Tradition and Community', in Richard Holt (ed.), *Sport and the Working Class in Modern Britain*, Manchester, 1990, pp. 142–58.

12 Warren Goldstein, *Playing for Keeps: A History of Early Baseball*, Ithaca, NY, 1989, p. 101.

13 As an example, see Tony Mason, *Association Football and English Society, 1863–1915*, Brighton, 1980, ch. 5, 'The Crowd'.

14 See Wray Vamplew, *Pay Up and Play the Game*, pp. 54–6.

15 R. Day, 'The Motivations of Some Football Club Directors: An Aspect of the Social History of Association Football, 1890–1914', unpublished MA Dissertation, University of Warwick, 1976.

16 See Tony Collins and Wray Vamplew, *Mud, Sweat and Beers: A Cultural History of Sport and Alcohol*, Oxford, 2002, p. 47.

17 Paul Dietschy and Antoine Mourat, 'The Motor Car and Football Industries from the early 1920s to the late 1940s: The Cases of FC Sochaux and Juventus', in Alan Bairner, Jonathan Magee and Alan Tomlinson (eds), *The Bountiful Game? Football Identities and Finances*, Aachen, 2005, pp. 43–62.

18 This debate is explored in Wray Vamplew, *Pay Up and Play the Game*, ch. 8, pp. 77–111 and in Steven Tischler, *Footballers and Businessmen: The Origins of Professional Soccer in England*, New York, 1981.

19 For soccer, see Matthew Taylor, *The Leaguers: The Making of Professional Football in England, 1900–939*, Liverpool, 2005, pp. 15–17. For baseball, Warren N. Wilbert, *The Arrival of the American League: Ban Johnson and the 1901 Challenge to National League Monopoly*, North Carolina, 2007.

20 For the contrast between soccer and baseball economics, see Stefan Szymanski and Andrew Zimbalist, *National Pastime: How Americans Play Baseball and the Rest of the World Plays Soccer*, Washington, DC, 2005.

21 G.R. Searle, *A New England? Peace and War 1886–1918*, Oxford, 2005.

22 Eric Foner, *Reconstruction*, New York, 2002; John W. Chambers, *The Tyranny of Change: America in the Progressive Era, 1890–1920*, Piscataway, NJ, 2000.

23 Richard Holt, 'Working-class Football and the City: The Problem of Continuity', *British Journal of Sports History*, vol. 3, no. 1 (1986), pp. 5–17.

24 Elliot Gorn and Warren Goldstein, *A Brief History of American Sports*, New York, 1993, pp. 64–80.

25 Gerald R. Gems, 'The City', in John Nauright and S.W. Pope (eds), *The Routledge Companion to Sports History*, Abingdon, 2010, pp. 51–70. See also Stephen Hardy, *How Boston Played: Sport, Recreation, and Community, 1856–1915*, 2nd edn, Memphis, 2003.

26 Walter Benjamin, 'The Work of Art in the Age of Mechanical Reproduction', in *Illuminations*, New York, 1968, p. 236.

27 See for example, Dilwyn Porter, 'Revenge of the Crouch End Vampires: The AFA, the FA and English Football's "Great Split", 1907–14', *Sport in History*, vol. 26, no. 3 (2006), pp. 406–28.

28 See Tony Collins, *Rugby League in Twentieth-century Britain*, Abingdon, 2006.
29 For parallels with the life of jazz musicians, see Eric Hobsbawm, *The Jazz Scene*, New York, rev. edn, 1993, p. 294.
30 Karl Marx, 'Wage Labour and Capital', in *Karl Marx and Frederick Engels Collected Works*, Moscow, 1975–2005, vol. 9, p. 203.
31 Jean-Marie Mayeur and Madeleine Rebirioux, *The Third Republic from its Origins to the Great War, 1871–1914*, Cambridge, 1988.
32 Jonathan Morris, 'Europe versus America', *European Review*, vol. 19, no. 4 (2011), p. 612.
33 Eugen Weber, *Peasants into Frenchmen: Modernization of Rural France, 1870–1914*, Stanford, CA, 1976.
34 Simon Martin, *Sport Italia: The Italian Love Affair with Sport*, London, 2011, p. 34.
35 See Michael Oriard, *Reading Football*, pp. 128–31.
36 E.H. Norman, *Japan's Emergence as a Modern State: Political and Economic Problems of the Meiji Period*, British Columbia, 2000.
37 Keiko Ikeda, 'Rysai-kembo, Liberal Education and Maternal Feminism under Fascism: Women and Sport in Modern Japan', *International Journal of the History of Sport*, vol. 27, no. 3 (March 2010), pp. 537–52.
38 Allen Guttmann and Lee Thompson, *Japanese Sports: A History*, Hawaii, 1998, pp. 142–6.
39 George Kirsch, 'American Cricket: Players and Clubs Before the Civil War', *Journal of Sports History*, vol. 11, no. 1 (1984), pp. 28–49.
40 Gerald Howat, 'Cricket in the United States: Puritan and Nationalist Attitudes, 1776–1893', *The Sports Historian*, vol. 14, no. 1 (1994), pp. 13–20.
41 George Kirsch, *The Creation of American Team Sports: Baseball and Cricket 1838–72*, Urbana, IL, 1989.
42 See Allan Guttmann, *Games and Empires*, New York, 1994, pp. 18–22.
43 As well as Oriard, *Reading Football*, see also John Rickards Betts, 'Sporting Journalism in Nineteenth-century America', *American Quarterly*, vol. 5, no. 1 (1953), pp. 39–56.
44 For an outline, see Raymond Williams, *The Long Revolution*, Harmondsworth, 1965.
45 Adrian Harvey, *The Beginnings of a Commercial Sporting Culture*, Abingdon, pp. 32, 40.
46 The sporting press is a relatively unexplored field. See Tony Mason, 'Sporting News, 1860–1914', in Michael Harris and Alan Lee (eds), *The Press in English Society from the Seventeenth to the Nineteenth Centuries*, London, 1986, pp. 168–86.
47 Paul Rouse, 'Journalists and the Making of the Gaelic Athletic Association 1884–87', *Media History*, vol. 17, no. 2 (2011), p. 120.
48 Tony Mason, 'All the Winners and the Half Times … ', *The Sports Historian*, vol. 13, no. 1 (1993), pp. 3–13.
49 Michael Oriard, *Reading Football*, ch. 2.
50 Sayuri Guthrie-Shimizu, *Transpacific Field of Dreams: How Baseball Linked the United States and Japan in Peace and War*, Chapel Hill, NC, 2012.
51 Allen Guttmann and Lee Thompson, *Japanese Sports*, pp. 135–7.
52 Richard Holt, 'The Bicycle, the Bourgeoisie and the Discovery of Rural France, 1880–1914', *British Journal of Sports History*, vol. 2, no. 2 (1985), pp. 127–39.
53 Christopher Thompson, *Tour de France*, pp. 16–18.
54 Christopher Thompson, *Tour de France*, pp. 18–20.
54 Beredict Anderson, *Imagined Communities: Reflections on the Origin and Spread of Nationalism*, London, 1983.

7 Sport and the age of empire

1 William Mathews, *Getting On in the World*, Toronto, 1876, p. 61.
2 Allen Guttmann, *The Olympics: A History of the Modern Games*, Illinois, 1992, pp. 12–15. Coubertin was merely one of many nineteenth-century enthusiasts who sought to 'revive' the ancient Greek Olympics, including William Penny Brooks of Much Wenlock in England and the Greeks themselves, who organised Olympics in Athens in 1859, 1870 and 1875.

3 For Coubertin's vision, see John MacAloon, *This Great Symbol: Pierre de Coubertin and the Origins of the Modern Olympic Games*, Chicago, 1984.

4 For a useful overview of writings on sport and imperialism see, S.W. Pope, 'Imperialism', in S.W. Pope and John Nauright (eds), *The Routledge Companion to Sports History*, Abingdon, 2010, pp. 229–47.

5 Quoted in J.A. Mangan, *The Games Ethic and Imperialism*, Harmondsworth, 1986, p. 53.

6 There is as yet no single study of the relationship between sport and the British Empire in English; Sébastien Darbon's *Diffusion des sports et impérialisme anglo-saxon*, Paris, 2008 is currently the sole monograph on the subject.

7 For a rare English-language discussion of sport in the French Empire, see Philip Dine, 'Shaping the Colonial Body: Sport and Society in Algeria, 1870–1962', in Patricia M.E. Lorcin (ed.), *Algeria and France, 1800–2000: Identity, Memory, Nostalgia*, Syracuse, 2006, pp. 33–48.

8 See Gertrud Pfister, 'Colonialism and the Enactment of German National Identity', *Journal of Sport History*, vol. 33, no. 1 (2006), pp. 59–83.

9 For an overview see Allan Guttmann, *Games and Empires*, New York, 1994.

10 Gerald R. Gems, *The Athletic Crusade: Sport and American Cultural Imperialism*, Nebraska, 2006.

11 Joseph A. Reaves, *Taking in a Game: A History of Baseball in Asia*, Nebraska, 2002.

12 Janice A. Beran, 'Americans in the Philippines: Imperialism or Progress through Sport?', *International Journal of the History of Sport*, vol. 6, no. 1 (1989), pp. 62–87.

13 Wanda Ellen Wakefield, *Playing to Win: Sports and the American Military, 1898–1945*, Albany, NY, 1997.

14 Anthony Trollope, *British Sports and Pastimes*, London, 1868, p. 290. For the early history of imperial cricket see Rowland Bowen, *Cricket: A History of its Growth and Development*, London, 1970 and Ramachandra Guha, *A Corner of a Foreign Field*, London, 2002.

15 W. Frost, 'Heritage, Nationalism, Identity: The 1861–62 England Cricket Tour of Australia', *International Journal of the History of Sport*, vol. 19, no. 4 (2002), pp. 55–69.

16 J.C. Davis, *Official Souvenir – English Team of Rugby Football Players*, Sydney, 1904, p. 3.

17 *Rugby Football: A Weekly Record of the Game*, 17 November 1923, p. 273.

18 See J.A. Mangan, *The Games Ethic and Imperialism*.

19 On the idea of 'Pan-Britannia' see Duncan Bell, *The Idea of Greater Britain: Empire and the Future of World Order, 1860–1900*, Princeton, NJ, 2007.

20 William Mathews, *Getting On in the World*, p. 61.

21 *Rugby News* (Sydney), 3 September 1927.

22 Quoted in Benedict Anderson, *Imagined Communities: Reflections on the Origin and Spread of Nationalism*, London, 1983, p. 93.

23 Quoted in J.A. Mangan, 'Eton to India: The Imperial Diffusion of a Victorian Educational Ethic', *History of Education*, vol. 7, no. 2 (1978), p. 109.

24 For a broader discussion of the emergence of British sports in India see James Mills, 'A Historiography of South Asian Sport', *Contemporary South Asia*, vol. 10, no. 2 (2001), pp. 207–21.

25 J.A. Mangan, *The Games Ethic and Imperialism*, p. 185.

26 The literature on James is of course legion, see for example, David Renton, *C.L.R. James: Cricket's Philosopher King*, London, 2007.

27 Ramachandra Guha, 'Cricket and Politics in Colonial India', *Past & Present*, vol. 161 (Nov. 1998), pp. 155–90.

28 C.L.R. James, *Beyond a Boundary*, London, 1963, p. 72.

29 James's writings on cricket are collected in his *A Majestic Innings: Writings on Cricket*, London, 2006.

30 Quoted in Guha, *A Corner of a Foreign Field*, p. 61.

31 Quoted in Allen Guttmann, *Games and Empires*, p. 87.

32 Quoted in Guha, *A Corner of a Foreign Field*, p. 56.

33 *Wanganui Chronicle*, 21 May 1930.

34 For a useful discussion on this point, see Brian Stoddart, 'Sport, Cultural Imperialism, and Colonial Response in the British Empire', *Comparative Studies in Society and History*, vol. 30 (1988), pp. 649–73.

35 See Patrick McDevitt, *May the Best Man Win: Sport, Masculinity, and Nationalism in Great Britain and the Empire, 1880–1935*, London, 2004.

36 The definitive account of Bodyline remains Ric Sissons and Brian Stoddart, *Cricket and Empire: The 1932–33 Bodyline Tour of Australia*, London, 1984.

37 Vic Marks and Bill Frindall, *The Wisden Illustrated History of Cricket*, London, 1989, p. 110.

38 Anon., *The Sporting English? A Commentary by a 'Man in the Street'*, Sydney, c. 1933, p. 18.

39 There is a large and vibrant literature on the GAA. For the evolution of the debate see W.F. Mandle, *The Gaelic Athletic Association and Irish Nationalist Politics, 1884–1924*, London, 1987; Mike Cronin, *Sport and Nationalism in Ireland: Gaelic Games, Soccer and Irish Identity Since 1884*, Dublin, 1999; and Mike Cronin, Paul Rouse and William Murphy (eds), *The Gaelic Athletic Association, 1884–2009*, Dublin, 2009.

40 See Patrick McDevitt, 'Muscular Catholicism: Nationalism, Masculinity and Gaelic Team Sports, 1884–1916', *Gender and History*, vol. 9, no. 2 (1997), pp. 262–84.

41 See, for example, Paul Rouse, 'Gunfire in Hayes' Hotel: The IRB and the Founding of the GAA', in Fearghal McGarry and James Mcconnel (eds), *The Black Hand of Republicanism: The Fenians and History*, Dublin, 2009, pp. 72–85.

42 David Leeson, 'Death in the Afternoon: The Croke Park Massacre, 21 November 1920', *Canadian Journal of History*, vol. 38, no. 1 (2003), pp. 43–67.

8 Unfair play: the racial politics of sport

 1 *New York Tribune*, 5 July 1910. A full account is given in Randy Roberts, *Papa Jack: Jack Johnson and the Era of White Hopes*, New York, 1985, pp. 107–10.

 2 *Yorkshire Post*, 29 November 1886; W. Cameron Forbes, 'The Football Coach's Relation to the Players', *Outing*, vol. 37, no. 3 (Dec. 1900), p. 339.

 3 For an illustration of the change in racial attitudes see Andrew S. Curran, *The Anatomy of Blackness: Science and Slavery in an Age of Enlightenment*, Baltimore, MD, 2011.

 4 Philip S. Foner (ed.), *The Life and Writings of Frederick Douglass: Pre-Civil War Decade, 1850–60*, New York, 1975, p. 129.

 5 See, for example, the argument of Nell Irvin Painter, *The History of White People*, New York, 2010.

 6 See Leslie Heaphy, 'Baseball and the Color Line', in Leonard Cassuto and Stephen Partridge, *The Cambridge Companion to Baseball*, Cambridge, 2011, pp. 61–75.

 7 *Sporting Life*, 11 April 1891.

 8 *Sporting Life*, 29 August 1908. The full story is recounted in Cait Murphy, *Crazy '08: How a Cast of Cranks, Rogues, Boneheads, and Magnates Created the Greatest Year in Baseball History*, New York, 2008, p. 172.

 9 David Sampson, 'Culture, "Race" and Discrimination in the 1868 Aboriginal Cricket Tour of England', *Australian Aboriginal Studies*, no. 2, (2009), pp. 44–60.

10 Quoted in Greg Ryan, *Forerunners of the All Blacks*, Canterbury, 1994, p. 94.

11 *Yorkshire Post*, 17 March 1906.

12 This reflected a wider trend in elite relationships within the British Empire; see David Cannadine, *Ornamentalism: How the British Saw Their Empire*, Harmondsworth, 2001.

13 Quoted in Mark Dyreson, 'American Ideas about Race and Olympic Races from the 1890s to the 1950s', *Journal of Sport History*, vol. 28, no. 2 (2001), p. 179. The whole affair is covered in detail in Susan Brownell (ed.), *The 1904 Anthropology Days and Olympic Games: Sport, Race, and American Imperialism*, Nebraska, 2008.

14 For the fight, see Carl B. Cone, 'The Molineaux–Cribb Fight, 1810: Wuz Tom Molineaux Robbed?', *Journal of Sport History*, vol. 9, no. 3 (1982), pp. 83–91.

15 Kasia Boddy, *Boxing: A Cultural History*, London, 2008, ch. 5.

16 For Johnson's life, see Geoffrey Ward, *Unforgivable Blackness: The Rise and Fall of Jack Johnson*, London 2006.

17 Claude McKay, *The Negroes in America*, Moscow, 1923, p. 53.

18 For the broader cultural context of race and boxing, see Kasia Boddy, *Boxing: A Cultural History*.
19 Colleen Aycock and Mark Scott, *Joe Gans: A Biography of the First African American World Boxing Champion*, North Carolina, 2008.
20 *The Times*, 21 September 1911. For a discussion on the relationship between boxing and the early film industry, see Dan Streible, *Fight Pictures: A History of Boxing and Early Cinema*, California, 2008.
21 David J. Langum, *Crossing Over the Line: Legislating Morality and the Mann Act*, Chicago, 2007, pp. 179–86.
22 Jeffrey P. Green, 'Boxing and the "Colour Question" in Edwardian Britain: The "White Problem" of 1911', *International Journal of the History of Sport*, vol. 5, no. 1 (1998), pp. 115–19.
23 Chris Golby, 'A History of the Colour Bar in British Professional Boxing, 1929–48', unpublished MA thesis, University of Warwick, 1998.
24 Rosey E. Pool (ed.), *Beyond the Blues, New Poems by American Negroes*, New York, 1962, p. 81; Malcolm X with Alex Haley, *The Autobiography of Malcolm X*, Harmondsworth 1966, p. 103.
25 Jeffrey T. Sammons, '"Race" and Sport: A Critical, Historical Examination', *Journal of Sport History*, vol. 21, no. 3 (1994), pp. 203–78.
26 Dean Cromwell and Al Wesson, *Championship Techniques in Track and Field*, New York, 1941, p. 6. The absurdity of these ever-changing 'scientific' racist arguments is laid to bare in Dyreson, 'American Ideas about Race and Olympic Races from the 1890s to the 1950s'.
27 For the shifting sands of racism in sport and society, see Ben Carrington, *Race, Sport and Politics: The Sporting Black Diaspora*, London, 2010.
28 Joe William Trotter Jr (ed.), *The Great Migration in Historical Context*, Bloomington, 1991; Peter Fryer, *Staying Power – The History of Black People in Britain: Black People in Britain Since 1504*, London, 1984.
29 Damian Thomas, 'Playing the "Race Card": U.S. Foreign Policy and the Integration of Sports', in Stephen Wagg and David L. Andrews (eds), *East Plays West: Sport and the Cold War*, Abingdon, 2006, pp. 207–21; Mary L. Dudziak, *Cold War Civil Rights: Race and the Image of American Democracy*, Princeton, NJ, 2000.
30 Leslie Heaphy, 'Baseball and the Color Line', p. 76.
31 Tony Mason, *Passion of the People? Football in South America*, London, 1995, pp. 35–6.
32 There is a huge literature on stacking, which extends almost without exception across all sports. As an example, see Earl Smith and Keith C. Harrison, 'Stacking in Major League Baseball', *Journal of African American Studies*, vol. 2, nos 2–3 (1996), pp. 113–29.
33 For a discussion on the historiography of race and sport, see John Nauright and David K. Wiggins, 'Race', in John Nauright and S.W. Pope (eds), *The Routledge Companion to Sports History*, Abingdon, 2010, pp. 148–61.

9 Soccer's rise to globalism

1 J.B. Priestley, *The Good Companions*, London, 1929, p. 3.
2 Salvador de Madariaga, *Englishmen, Frenchmen, Spaniards: An Essay in Comparative Psychology*, Oxford, 1928, p. 19, I am grateful to Peter Mandler's *The English National Character*, New Haven, CT, 2006, p. 171, for bringing this to my attention.
3 Rob Hess, Matthew Nicholson, Bob Stewart and Greg de Moore, *A National Game: The History of Australian Rules Football*, Melbourne, 2008, ch. 1.
4 For the relationship between rugby and hockey, see Michel Vigneault, *La Naissance d'un sport organisé au Canada: Le hockey à Montréal, 1875–1917*, PhD thesis, L'Université Laval, 2001, pp. 72–7.
5 Despite, or perhaps because of, the heritage industries surrounding these sports, the are no definitive historical works on their origins.

6 For black South Africa, see John Nauright, *Sport, Cultures, and Identities in South Africa*, Leicester, 1997, ch. 3.

7 Peter Levine, *A.G. Spalding and the Rise of Baseball: The Promise of American Sport*, New York, 1987, ch. 6.

8 Tony Mason, 'When Professional Baseball nearly came to Britain', *Revue française de civilisation britannique*, vol. 10, no. 4 (1997), p. 37–46

9 Donald Roden, 'Baseball and the Quest for National Dignity in Meiji Japan', *American Historical Review*, vol. 85, no. 3 (1980), pp. 511–34.

10 David Goldblatt, *The Ball is Round: A Global History of Football*, London, 2006, p. 178.

11 For this early period of British soccer, see Matthew Taylor, *The Association Game*, London, 2008, chs 1 and 2.

12 Goldblatt, *The Ball is Round*, p. 118.

13 For the relative similarity of the early football codes, see Tony Collins, 'History, Theory and the Civilizing Process', *Sport in History*, vol. 25, no. 2 (2005), pp. 289–306.

14 *The Lancet*, 16 November 1907, p. 1402.

15 *Bell's Life in London*, 7 January 1871.

16 For detailed figures see Adrian Harvey, *Football: The First Hundred Years*, Abingdon, 2005, ch. 3.

17 The classic work on this period remains Tony Mason, *Association Football and English Society 1863–1915*, Brighton, 1980.

18 Tony Collins, *Rugby's Great Split*, London, 1998, pp. 41–2.

19 Dave Russell, 'From Evil to Expedient: The Legalization of Professionalism in English Football, 1884–85', in Stephen Wagg (ed.), *Myths and Milestones in the History of Sport*, London, 2012, pp. 32–56.

20 Tony Collins, *A Social History of English Rugby Union*, Abingdon, 2009, ch. 2.

21 Dave Russell, *Football and the English*, Preston, 1997, pp. 25–35.

22 Jules Rimet, *Le Football et le rapprochement des peuples*, Zurich, 1954, p. 47.

23 The importance of shared informal attitudes to amateurism is discussed in Collins, *A Social History of English Rugby Union*, pp. 147–50.

24 W.N. Cobbold quoted in Richard Sanders, *Beastly Fury: The Strange Birth of British Football*, London, 2009, p. 161.

25 Richard Holt, 'The Amateur Body and the Middle-class Man: Work, Health and Style in Victorian Britain', *Sport in History*, vol. 26, no. 3 (2006), pp. 352–69.

26 For these changes in playing styles, see Mason, *Association Football*, ch. 7.

27 For a comprehensive examination of the backgrounds of soccer's early administrators, see Simon Inglis, *League Football and the Men Who Made It*, London, 1988.

28 See Geoffrey Best, *Mid-Victorian Britain 1851–75*, London, 1979.

29 For example, France was not accepted as a full member of the International Rugby Board until 1978!

30 For a broader discussion of the British and German middle classes' attitude to sport, see Christiane Eisenberg, 'The Middle Class and Competition: Some Considerations of the Beginnings of Modern Sport in England and Germany', *International Journal of the History of Sport*, vol. 7, no. 2 (1990), pp. 265–82.

31 For an outline of the expansion of soccer beyond Britain, see, Christiane Eisenberg, Pierre Lanfranchi, Tony Mason and Alfred Wahl, *One Hundred Years of Football*, London, 2004, chs 2 and 3.

32 Kay Schiller and Chris Young, 'The History and Historiography of Sport in Germany: Social, Cultural and Political Perspectives', *German History*, vol. 27, no. 3 (2009), p. 321.

33 For a broader discussion of anglophilia, see Ian Buruma, *Voltaire's Coconuts, or Anglomania in Europe*, London, 1999.

34 Alfred Wahl, 'La Fédération internationale de football association (1903–30)', in Pierre Arnaud and Alfred Wahl (eds), *Sports et relations internationales*, Metz, 1994, pp. 31–45.

35 Daniel Gorman, 'Amateurism, Imperialism, Internationalism and the First British Empire Games', *International Journal of the History of Sport*, vol. 27, no. 4 (2010), pp. 611–34.
36 Quoted in Tony Mason, *Passion of the People: Football in Latin America*, London, 1995, p. 38.

10 The second revolution: sport between the world wars

1 Sebastian Haffner, *Defying Hitler: A Memoir*, London, 2002, p. 74.
2 Quoted in Richard Holt, *Sport and Society in Modern France*, London, 1981, p. 195.
3 Quoted in Tony Collins, 'English Rugby Union and the First World War', *The Historical Journal*, vol. 45, no. 4 (2002), p. 801.
4 Rupert Brooke, '1914' in Marcus Claphan (ed.) *The Wordsworth Book of First World War Poetry*, Wave, 1995, p. 17.
5 A useful summary of the emergence of sporting celebrity in the USA can be found in Michael K. Bohn, *Heroes and Ballyhoo: How the Golden Age of the 1920s Transformed American Sports*, Washington, DC, 2009.
6 See, for example, Mike Huggins, 'BBC Radio and Sport 1922–39', *Contemporary British History*, vol. 21, no. 4 (2007), pp. 491–515; Ronald A. Smith, *Play-by-Play: Radio, Television, and Big Time College Sport*, Baltimore, MD, 2001; and Matthew B. Karush, 'National Identity in the Sports Pages: Football and the Mass Media in 1920s Buenos Aires', *The Americas*, vol. 60, no. 1 (2003), pp. 11–32.
7 Haffner, *Defying Hitler*, p. 74. For an English-language overview of sport in the Weimar Republic see, Erik Jensen, *Body by Weimar: Athletes, Gender, and German Modernity*, New York, 2010. For Japan, see Allen Guttmann and Lee Thompson, *Japanese Sports: A History*, Hawaii, 1998, pp. 135–8.
8 Quoted in Alex Danchev (ed.), *100 Artists' Manifestos*, Harmondsworth, 2011, p. 74 and p. 5.
9 James M. Laux, 'Some Notes on Entrepreneurship in the Early French Automobile Industry', *French Historical Studies*, vol. 3, no. 1 (1963), pp. 129–34.
10 David Hassan (ed.), *A Case Study Analysis of the History of World Motor Sport*, Abingdon, 2011; Michael L. Berger, *The Automobile in American History and Culture: A Reference Guide*, Westport, CT, 2001, esp. ch. 9.
11 *The Blackshirt*, 20 July 1934.
12 See, for example, Tony Mason and Eliza Reidi, *Sport and the Military*, Cambridge, 2010.
13 See, for example, Arnaud Waquet and Thierry Terret, 'Ballons ronds, Tommies et tranchées: l'impact de la présence britannique dans la diffusion du football-association au sein des villes de garnison de la Somme et du Pas-de-Calais (1915–18)', *Modern & Contemporary France*, vol. 14, no. 4 (2006), pp. 449–64.
14 Richard Holt, *Sport and Society in Modern France*, p. 70.
15 Gerd von der Lippe, 'Handball, Gender and Sportification of Body-cultures: 1900–1940', *International Review for the Sociology of Sport*, vol. 29, no. 2 (1994), pp. 211–34.
16 For a contrasting discussion of these themes, see Maarten Van Bottenburg, *Global Games*, Illinois, 2001, ch. 5.
17 Quoted in Holt, *Sport and Society in Modern France*, p. 203.
18 Guttmann and Thompson, *Japanese Sports*, pp. 130–34.
19 Simon Martin, *Sport Italia: The Italian Love Affair with Sport*, London, 2011, p. 48.
20 Mitchells & Butlers, *Fifty Years of Brewing*, Birmingham, 1929, p. 101. For the USA, see Steven M. Gelber, 'Working at Playing: The Culture of the Workplace and the Rise of Baseball', *Journal of Social History*, vol. 16, no. 4 (1983), pp. 3–22.
21 Wendy Michallat, 'Terrain de lutte: Women's Football and Feminism in "Les anneés folles"', *French Cultural Studies*, vol. 18, no. 3 (2007), pp. 259–76.
22 Alethea Melling, *'Ladies' Football': Gender Roles and the Socialisation of Women Football Players in Lancashire, 1917–c.1960*, unpublished PhD thesis, University of Central Lancashire, 2000 and Jean Williams, *A Beautiful Game: International Perspectives on Women's Football*, Oxford, 2007.

23 Quoted in Erik Jensen, *Body by Weimar*, p. 72.
24 Kari Fasting, Gertrud Pfister, Sheila Scraton and Benilde Vazquez, 'Women and Football – A Contradiction? The Beginnings of Women's Football in Four European Countries', *European Sport History Review*, vol. 1, no. 1 (1999), pp. 1–26.
25 Mary H. Leigh and Thérèse M. Bonin, 'The Pioneering Role of Madame Alice Milliat and the FSFI', *Journal of Sport History*, vol. 4, no. 1 (1977), pp. 72–83.
26 Pierre de Coubertin, 'Forty Years of Olympism', in Norbert Müller (ed.), *Olympism: Selected Writings*, Lausanne, 2000, p. 704.
27 Florence Carpentier and Jean-Pierre Lefèvre, 'The Modern Olympic Movement, Women's Sport and the Social Order during the Inter-war Period', *International Journal of the History of Sport*, vol. 23, no. 7 (2006), pp. 1112–27.
28 S.W. Pope, *Patriotic Games*, New York, 1997, p. 128.
29 J.J. Matthews, 'They Had Such a Lot of Fun: The Women's League of Health and Beauty Between the Wars', *History Workshop Journal*, vol. 30, no. 1 (1990), pp. 22–54; Ina Zweiniger-Bargielowska, 'Raising a Nation of "Good Animals": The New Health Society and Health Education Campaigns in Interwar Britain', *Social History of Medicine*, vol. 20, no. 1 (2007), pp. 73–89.
30 Quoted in Erik Jensen, *Body by Weimar*, p. 138. Fujimura quoted in Keiko Ikeda, 'Rysai-kembo, Liberal Education and Maternal Feminism', *International Journal of the History of Sport*, vol. 27, no. 3 (March 2010), p. 546. For Nazi Germany see Erik Jensen, *Body by Weimar*. For British attitudes see Ina Zweiniger Bargielowska, *Managing the Body: Beauty, Health and Fitness in Britain, 1880–1939*, Oxford, 2010.
31 Jean-François Bouzanquet, *Fast Ladies: Female Racing Drivers 1888–1970*, Dorchester, 2009, pp. 22–5. I am grateful to Dr Jean Williams for bringing this to my attention.
32 Matthias Marschik, 'Between Manipulation and Resistance: Viennese Football in the Nazi Era', *Journal of Contemporary History*, vol. 34, no. 2 (1999), pp. 215–29
33 Sebastian Haffner, *Defying Hitler*, p. 74.
34 Quoted in Erik Jensen, *Body by Weimar*, p. 101.
35 Quoted in Tony Collins, *A Social History of English Rugby Union*, Abingdon, 2009, p. 63.
36 Udo Merkel, 'The Hidden Social and Political History of the German Football Association (DFB), 1900–950', *Soccer and Society*, vol. 1, no. 2 (2000), pp. 167–86.
37 Ulrich Hesse-Lichtenberger, *Tor! The Story of German Football*, London, 2003, p. 63.
38 The England team also gave the fascist salute before the match against Italy in Milan in May 1939. For the full background to both incidents see Peter Beck, *Scoring for Britain*, London, 1999, chs 1 and 9.
39 *Olympic Games 1936 – Official Organ of the XI Olympic Games*, no. 7 (1936), p. 28.
40 *Olympic Games News Service*, no. 7 (30 March 1935), p. 1.
41 For a transnational exploration of the 1936 Olympics, see Arnd Kruger and William Murray (eds), *The Nazi Olympics: Sport, Politics, and Appeasement in the 1930s*, Illinois, 2003.
42 A pamphlet copy of this speech distributed at the games can be found in the archives of Leeds Metropolitan University. A delegation of Carnegie College, one of the constituent parts of the university, attended the 1936 Games.
43 *Sport in Industry*, March 1939, pp. 9–13.

11 Revolutionary sport

1 *Pravda*, 14 August 1928, quoted in James Riordan, *Sport in Soviet Society*, Cambridge, 1977, p. 351.
2 Eric Hobsbawm, *Nations and Nationalism since 1780*, Cambridge, 1990, p. 121.
3 *Arbeiter Turn Zeitung*, 15 August 1910, quoted in Arnd Kruger and James Riordan (eds), *The Story of Worker Sport*, Champaign, IL, 1996, p. 7.
4 James Riordan, *Sport in Soviet Society*, p. 33
5 Eugen Weber, *France, Fin de Siècle*, Cambridge, MA, 1986, p. 225.
6 Kruger and Riordan, *The Story of Worker Sport*, pp. 30–2.

7 Frank Trommler, 'Working-class Culture and Modern Mass Culture before World War I', *New German Critique*, no. 29 (1983), pp. 57–70.
8 Chris Waters, *British Socialists and the Politics of Popular Culture, 1884–1914*, Manchester, 1990.
9 Karl Kautsky, *The Social Revolution*, Chicago, 1910, p. 102
10 Quoted in Tony Mason, *Association Football and English Society, 1863–1915*, Brighton, 1980, p. 237.
11 *Daily Worker*, 17 September 1930.
12 V.I. Lenin, 'The Slogan of Civil War Illustrated', *Collected Works*, Moscow, 1974, pp. 181–2.
13 L. Trotsky, *Where is Britain Going?*, London, 1926, p. 175.
14 L. Trotsky, 'Vodka, the Church and the Cinema', in *Problems of Everyday Life*, New York, 1973, p. 32.
15 Robert Bruce Lockhart, *Giants Cast Long Shadows*, London, 1960, pp. 173–4.
16 For a full deconstruction of the Bartali myth see chapter 8 of John Foot, *Pedalare! Pedalare! A History of Italian Cycling*, London, 2011, pp. 125–44.
17 Robert F. Wheeler, 'Organized Sport and Organized Labour', *Journal of Contemporary History*, vol. 13, no. 2 (April 1978), pp. 191–210.
18 André Gounot, 'Sport or Political Organization? Structures and Characteristics of the Red Sport International, 1921–37', *Journal of Sport History*, vol. 28, no. 1 (2001), pp. 23–39.
19 David A. Steinberg, 'The Workers' Sport Internationals 1920–28', *Journal of Contemporary History*, vol. 13, no. 2 (April 1978), pp. 233–51.
20 For a cross-disciplinary perspective, see Mike O'Mahoney, *Sport in the USSR: Physical Culture – Visual Culture*, London, 2006.
21 Susan Grant, 'The Politics and Organization of Physical Culture in the USSR during the 1920s', *Slavonic and East European Review*, vol. 89, no. 3 (2011), pp. 494–515.
22 Maurice Roche, 'Modernity, Cultural Events and the Construction of Charisma: Mass Cultural Events in the USSR in the Interwar Period', *International Journal of Cultural Policy*, vol. 7, no. 3 (2001), pp. 493–520.
23 James Riordan, *Sport in Soviet Society*, pp. 96–110.
24 James Riordan, 'Marx, Lenin and Physical Culture', *Journal of Sport History*, vol. 3, no. 1 (1976), pp. 152–61.
25 Alison Rowley, 'Sport in the Service of the State: Images of Physical Culture and Soviet Women, 1917–41', *International Journal of the History of Sport*, vol. 23, no. 8 (Dec. 2006), p. 1315.
26 *Pravda*, 14 August 1928, quoted in James Riordan, *Sport in Soviet Society*, p. 110.
27 Figures taken from Gounot, 'Sport or Political Organization? Structures and Characteristics of the Red Sport International, 1921–37', p. 24.
28 Kruger and Riordan, *Worker Sport*, p. vii.
29 André Gounot, 'Between Revolutionary Demands and Diplomatic Necessity: The Uneasy Relationship between Soviet Sport and Worker and Bourgeois Sport in Europe from 1920 to 1937', in Pierre Arnaud and James Riordan (eds), *Sport and International Politics: The Impact of Fascism and Communism on Sport*, London, 1998, pp. 184–209.
30 Quoted in Barbara Keys, *Globalizing Sport: National Rivalry and International Community in the 1930s*, Cambridge, MA, 2006, p. 165.

12 Sex, drugs and sport in the Cold War

1 John F. Kennedy, 'The Soft American', *Sports Illustrated*, 26 December 1960.
2 Dilwyn Porter and Ronald Kowalski, 'Political Football: Moscow Dynamo in Britain, 1945', *International Journal of the History of Sport*, vol. 14, no. 2 (1997), pp. 100–21.
3 William Murray, 'The French Workers' Sports Movement and the Victory of the Popular Front in 1936', *International Journal of the History of Sport*, vol. 4, no. 2 (1987), pp. 203–30; Gary Cross, 'Vacations for All: The Leisure Question in the Era of the Popular Front', *Journal of Contemporary History*, vol. 24, no. 4 (1989), pp. 599–621.
4 James Riordan, *Sport in Soviet Society*, Cambridge, 1977, p. 364.

5 Robert F. Baumann, 'The Central Army Sports Club (TsSKA): Forging a Military Tradition in Soviet Ice Hockey', *Journal of Sport History*, vol. 15, no. 2 (1988), pp. 151–66.

6 Jennifer Parks, 'Verbal Gymnastics: Sports, Bureaucracy, and the Soviet Union's Entrance into the Olympic Games, 1946–52', in Stephen Wagg and David L. Andrews (eds), *East Plays West: Sport and the Cold War*, Abingdon, 2006, pp. 27–44.

7 For the importance of the Olympics to the USA see Mark Dyreson, *Crafting Patriotism: America at the Olympic Games*, Abingdon, 2008.

8 See for example, John Massaro, 'Press Box Propaganda? The Cold War and *Sports Illustrated*, 1956', *Journal of American Culture*, vol. 26, no. 3 (2003), pp. 361–70.

9 Robert Edelman, *Serious Fun – A History of Spectator Sports in the USSR*, Oxford, 1993, pp. 51–3.

10 Riordan, *Sport in Soviet Society*, p. 132–3.

11 Quoted in John Bale, '"Oscillating Antagonism": Soviet–British Athletics Relations, 1945–60', in Stephen Wagg and David Andrews (eds), *East Plays West: Sport and the Cold War*, p. 89.

12 Paul Dimeo, *Beyond Good and Evil: A History of Drug Use in Sport: 1876–1976*, Abingdon, 2007, chs 4 and 5.

13 Dimeo, *Beyond Good and Evil*, ch. 2.

14 C.J.P. Lucas, *The Olympic Games 1904*, St Louis, 1905, pp. 51–3. I am grateful to Dr Martin Polley for bringing this quote to my attention.

15 See John Hoberman, *Mortal Engines: The Science of Performance and the Dehumanization of Sport*, New York, 1992.

16 Larry Sloman, *Reefer Madness: The History of Marijuana in America*, New York, 1998.

17 Verner Møller, 'Knud Enemark Jensen's Death during the 1960 Rome Olympics: A Search for Truth?', *Sport in History*, vol. 25, no. 3 (2005), pp. 452–71.

18 F. Sanchis-Gomar, G. Olaso-Gonzalez, D. Corella, M.C. Gomez-Cabrera and J. Vina, 'Increased Average Longevity among the "Tour de France" Cyclists', *International Journal of Sports Medicine*, vol. 32, no. 8 (Aug. 2011), pp. 644–7.

19 See www.baseball-reference.com for the statistics of players named in the report: http://www.baseball-reference.com/friv/mitchell-report-players.shtml (accessed Dec. 2011). See also Adam Hadhazy, 'Do Anabolic Steroids Make You a Better Athlete?', *Scientific American*, 11 February 2009.

20 For the West, see for example, Joan Ryan, *Little Girls in Pretty Boxes: Making and Breaking of Elite Gymnasts and Figure Skaters*, London, 1996. For the UK, see Celia Brackenridge, 'Fair Play or Fair Game? Child Sexual Abuse in Sport Organisations', *International Review for the Sociology of Sport*, vol. 29, no. 3 (1994), pp. 287–97.

21 Simon Martin, *Sport Italia: The Italian Love Affair with Sport*, London, 2011, p. 223. See pages 229–31 for a discussion of widespread doping in Italian soccer.

22 For the relationship between drugs and amateur ideology see John Gleaves, 'Doped Amateurs and Clean Professionals', *Journal of Sport History*, vol. 38, no. 2 (2011), pp. 237–54.

23 'Heavy NFL Players Twice as Likely to Die Before 50', http://sports.espn.go.com/nfl/news/story?id=2313476 (accessed Dec. 2011).

24 Frank Breuckmann *et al.*, 'Myocardial Late Gadolinium Enhancement: Prevalence, Pattern, and Prognostic Relevance in Marathon Runners', *Radiology*, vol. 251 (April 2009), pp. 50–7.

25 Jordana Bieze Foster, 'Playing for Pain: Athletes and Osteoarthritis', *BioMechanics*, February 2009, available online: http://www.jordanafoster.com/article.asp?a=/sportsmed/20060 401_Athletes_and%20osteoarthritis (accessed 16 August 2011).

26 Jeffrey Montez de Oca, 'The "Muscle Gap": Physical Education and U.S. Fears of a Depleted Masculinity, 1954–63', in Stephen Wagg and David L. Andrews (eds), *East Plays West: Sport and the Cold War*, pp. 123–48.

27 Quoted in Lindsay Sarah Krasnoff, 'The Evolution of French Sports Policy', in Richard Holt, Alan Tomlinson And Christopher Young (eds), *Sport and the Transformation of Modern Europe*, Abingdon, 2011, p. 70. See also Philip Dine, 'Sport and the State in Contemporary France: From La Charte des Sports to Decentralisation', *Modern & Contemporary France*, vol. 6, no. 3 (1998), pp. 301–11.

28 Quoted in Peter Beck, 'Britain and the Cold War's "Cultural Olympics": Responding to the Political Drive of Soviet Sport, 1945–58', *Contemporary British History*, vol. 19, no. 2 (2005), p. 170.

29 For an overview of women's sport see, for example, Susan K. Cahn, *Coming on Strong: Gender and Sexuality in Twentieth-century Women's Sport*, Cambridge, MA, 1994; Allen Guttmannn, *Women's Sports*, New York, 1991 and Susan J. Bandy, 'Gender', in John Nauright and S.W. Pope (eds), *The Routledge Companion to Sports History*, Abingdon, 2010, pp. 129–47.

30 For US women's athletics in this period, see Ying Wushanley, Playing Nice and Losing: The Struggle for Control of Women's Intercollegiate Athletics, 1960–2000, Syracuse, 2004, pp. 19–32.

31 Riordan, *Sport in Soviet Society*, p. 138.

32 Jim Riordan, 'The Rise, Fall and Rebirth of Sporting Women in Russia and the USSR', *Journal of Sport History*, vol. 18, no. 1 (1991), pp. 183–99.

33 *Washington Post*, 5 February 1968, quoted in Stefan Wiederkehr, '"We Shall Never Know the Exact Number of Men who Have Competed in the Olympics Posing as Women": Sport, Gender Verification and the Cold War', *International Journal of the History of Sport*, vol. 26, no. 4 (2009), p. 560.

34 Quoted in Alison Turnbull, 'Woman Enough for the Games?', *New Scientist*, 15 September 1988, p. 61.

35 Quoted in Wiederkehr, 'We Shall Never Know the Exact Number … ', p. 565.

36 For a full discussion see Gerald N. Callahan, *Between XX and XY: Intersexuality and the Myth of Two Sexes*, Chicago, 2009.

37 Susan K. Cahn, 'From the "Muscle Moll" to the "Butch" Ballplayer: Mannishness, Lesbianism, and Homophobia in U.S. Women's Sport', *Feminist Studies*, vol. 19, no. 2 (1993), pp. 343–68.

38 *Time*, 24 August 1936.

39 For the full story see Stefan Von Berg, 'Die wahre Dora', *Der Spiegel*, 14 September 2009, pp. 150–4.

40 *Time*, 10 August 1936.

13 Taking sides in the 1960s

1 Thomas Hauser, *Muhammad Ali: His Life and Times*, London, 1991, p. 145.

2 James Riordan, 'Soviet Sport and Soviet Foreign Policy', *Soviet Studies*, vol. 26, no. 3 (1974), pp. 322–43.

3 For the enforced end of Jesse Owens' amateur career see William J. Baker, *Jesse Owens: An American Life*, Illinois, 2006, pp. 112–18. Owens was also used by Brundage to criticise athletes proposing a boycott of the 1968 Olympics.

4 Pierre Lanfranchi, 'Mekloufi, un footballeur français dans la guerre d'Algérie', *Actes de la recherche en sciences sociales*, vol. 103 (June 1994), pp. 70–4. For a broader view, see also Pierre Lanfranchi and Alfred Wahl, 'The Immigrant as Hero: Kopa, Mekloufi and French Football', *International Journal of the History of Sport*, vol. 13, no. 1 (1996), pp. 114–27.

5 See C.L.R. James, *Beyond a Boundary*, London, 1963, pp. 225–52.

6 T.P. Ross, 'Sukarno's Lavish Ganefo Was Mostly Snafu', *Sports Illustrated*, 2 December 1963. See also Rusli Lutan and Fan Hong, 'The Politicization of Sport: GANEFO – A Case Study', *Sport in Society*, vol. 8, no. 3 (2005), pp. 425–39.

7 John Nauright, *Sport, Cultures, and Identities in South Africa*, Leicester, 1997; Douglas Booth, *The Race Game: Sport and Politics in South Africa*, London, 1998; Robert Archer and Antoine Bouillon, *The South African Game: Sport and Racism*, London, 1982.

8 There is a huge amount of work on sport and apartheid. A good starting point is Robert Archer and Antoine Bouillon, *The South African Game: Sport and Racism*.

9 Bruce Kidd, 'The Campaign against Sport in South Africa', *International Journal*, vol. 43, no. 4 (1988), pp. 643–4; Marc Keech, 'The Ties that Bind: South Africa and Sports Diplomacy 1958–63', *The Sports Historian*, vol. 21, no. 1 (2001), pp. 71–93.

10 Peter Oborne, *Basil D'Oliveira: Cricket and Controversy*, London, 2005.

11 Chris Bolsmann, 'White Football in South Africa: Empire, Apartheid and Change, 1892–1977', *Soccer and Society*, vol. 11, no. 1 (2010), pp. 29–45.

12 Peter Hain, *Don't Play with Apartheid: Background to the Stop the Seventy Tour Campaign*, London, 1971; Trevor Richards, *Dancing on Our Bones: New Zealand, South Africa, Rugby and Racism*, Wellington, 1999.

13 Jackie Robinson with Alfred Duckett, *I Never Had It Made*, New York, 1972, p. 12.

14 Rickey quoted in Elliott Gorn and Warren Goldstein, *A Brief History of American Sports*, New York, 1993, p. 215.

15 Quoted in Leslie Heaphy, 'Baseball and the Color Line', in Leonard Cassuto and Stephen Partridge, *The Cambridge Companion to Baseball*, Cambridge, 2011, p. 78.

16 For the background, see Harry Edwards, *The Revolt of the Black Athlete*, New York, 1969.

17 Thomas Hauser, *Muhammad Ali: His Life and Times*, p. 145.

18 As indeed had the hero of Alan Sillitoe's 1959 story, and 1962 film, *The Loneliness of the Long Distance Runner,* London, 1959.

19 *Oakland Tribune*, 26 September 1967.

20 Curt Flood and Richard D. Carter, *The Way It Is*, New York, 1971, p. 236.

21 Quoted in Brad Snyder, *A Well-paid Slave: Curt Flood's Fight for Free Agency in Professional Sports*, New York, 2006, p. 187.

22 Matthew Taylor, *The Association Game*, London, 2008, pp. 224–33.

23 John Harding, *For the Good of the Game: Official History of the Professional Footballers Association*, London, 1998.

24 Lee Lowenfish, *The Imperfect Diamond: A History of Baseball's Labor Wars*, New York, 1991.

25 Charles P. Korr, *The End of Baseball as We Knew It: The Players Union, 1960–81*, Illinois, 2002.

26 Stephen Wagg, '"Time Gentlemen Please": The Decline of Amateur Captaincy in English County Cricket', *Contemporary British History*, vol. 12, no.2 (2000), pp. 31–59.

27 Kevin Jeffreys, 'The Triumph of Professionalism in World Tennis: The Road to 1968', *International Journal of the History of Sport*, vol. 26, no. 15 (2009), pp. 2253–69.

28 Ulrich Hesse-Lichtenberger, *Tor! The Story of German Football*, London, 2003, p. 146.

14 The revolution is being televised

1 Quoted Stanley J. Baran, 'Sports and Television', in Scott R. Rosner and Kenneth L. Shropshire (eds), *The Business of Sports*, Ontario, 2004, p. 143.

2 Richard Haynes, 'A Pageant of Sound and Vision: Football's Relationship with Television, 1936–60', *International Journal of the History of Sport*, vol. 15, no.1 (1998), pp. 211–26.

3 Jeff Neal-Lunsford, 'Sport in the Land of Television: The Use of Sport in Network Prime-time Schedules 1946–50', *Journal of Sport History*, vol. 19, no. 1 (1992), pp. 56–76.

4 US figures from Elliot Gorn and Warren Goldstein, *A Brief History of American Sports*, New York, 1993, p. 238. European figures from Garry Whannel, *Fields in Vision: Television Sport and Cultural Transformation*, London, 1992, p. 71.

5 John Horne, 'Sport and the Mass Media in Japan', *Sociology of Sport Journal*, vol. 22, no. 4 (2005), pp. 415–32

6 Anne Cooper-Chen, *Mass Communication in Japan*, Iowa, 1997, ch. 7.

7 Richard Haynes, 'The BBC, Austerity and Broadcasting the 1948 Olympic Games', *International Journal of the History of Sport*, vol. 27, vol. 6 (2010), pp. 1029–46.

8 IOC, *The IOC Official Olympic Companion: The Complete Guide to the Games*, Virginia, 1996, p. 473.

9 Stefan Szymanski and Andrew S. Zimbalist, *National Pastime: How Americans Play Baseball and the Rest of the World Plays Soccer*, Washington, DC, 2005, pp. 154–9.

10 Robert V. Bellamy Jr, 'Impact of the Television Marketplace on the Structure of Major League Baseball', *Journal of Broadcasting & Electronic Media*, vol. 32, no. 1 (1988), pp. 73–87.
11 John Slater, 'Changing Partners: The Relationship Between the Mass Media and the Olympic Games', in Robert K. Barney, Kevin B. Wamsley, Scott G. Martyn and Gordon H. MacDonald (eds), *Fourth International Symposium for Olympic Research*, Ontario, 1998, pp. 49–68.
12 Joan M. Chandler, *Television and National Sport*, Illinois, 1988.
13 Christopher Thompson, *The Tour de France: A Cultural History*, Berkeley, 2006, pp. 39–49; Fabien Wille, 'The Tour de France as an Agent of Change in Media Production', *International Journal of the History of Sport*, vol. 20, no. 2 (2003), pp. 128–46.
14 Gary Whannel, 'The Unholy Alliance: Notes on Television and the Remaking of British Sport 1965–85', *Leisure Studies*, vol. 5, no. 2 (1986), pp. 129–45.
15 Benjamin G. Rader, *In Its Own Image: How Television Has Transformed Sports*, New York, 1984.
16 Gary Whannel, 'Television and the Transformation of Sport', *Annals of the American Academy of Political and Social Science*, vol. 625, no. 1 (2009), pp. 205–18.
17 Bob Stewart, 'Seeing is Believing: Television and the Transformation of Australian Cricket, 1956–75', *Sporting Traditions*, vol. 22, no. 1 (2005), pp. 39–56.
18 The best account of Packer's coup d'etat is Gideon Haigh, *The Cricket War*, Melbourne, 1993.
19 Tony Collins, *A Social History of English Rugby Union*, Abingdon, 2009, pp. 202–5.
20 *Sydney Morning Herald*, 16 October 2003.
21 Stephen Dobson and John Goddard, *The Economics of Football*, 2nd edn, Cambridge, 2011, pp. 171–8.

15 Winners and losers: sport in the New World Order

1 Bertolt Brecht, 'Parade of the Old New', in *Poems 1913–56*, London, 1987, p. 323.
2 *The Independent*, 16 October 1996.
3 Sources: USA: http://tvbythenumbers.zap2it.com/2009/01/18/historical-super-bowl-tv-ratings/11044/ (accessed August 2011); UK: http://www.barb.co.uk/facts/since1981 (accessed August 2011); Germany: http://community.junar.com/datastreams/20477/most-watched-telecasts-germany/ (accessed August 2011).
4 For soccer, See David Conn, *The Football Business*, Edinburgh, 2nd edn, 2002. For the NFL see Michael Oriard, *Brand NFL*, North Carolina, 2010. For rugby, see Collins, *A Social History of English Rugby Union*.
5 For India, see Prashant Kidambi, 'Hero, Celebrity and Icon: Sachin Tendulkar and Indian Public Culture', in Jeff Hill and Anthony Bateman (eds), *The Cambridge Companion to Cricket*, Cambridge, 2011, pp. 187–202.
6 Robert K. Barney, Stephen R. Wenn and Scott G. Martyn, *Selling the Five Rings: The International Olympic Committee and the Rise of Olympic Commercialism*, Salt Lake City, 2004.
7 Garry Whannel, 'Television and the Transformation of Sport', *Annals of the American Academy of Political and Social Science*, vol. 625, no. 1 (2009), pp. 205–18.
8 For the origins and use of Lombardi's saying, see Steven J. Overman, '"Winning Isn't Everything. It's the Only Thing": The Origin, Attributions and Influence of a Famous Football Quote', *Football Studies*, vol. 2, no. 2 (1999), pp. 77–99.
9 Sean Mehegan, 'ESPN's New Message: Sports Is not a Metaphor for Life, Sports Is Life. So Name Your Child ESPN', *New York Times*, 19 December 2002.
10 Tom Wolfe, *Bonfire of the Vanities*, New York, 1987, p. 64 and passim.
11 Maarten van Bottenburg, 'Thrown for a Loss? (American) Football and the European Sport Space', *American Behavioral Scientist*, vol. 46, no. 11 (2003), pp. 1550–62.
12 See, for example, Bente O. Skogvang, 'African Footballers in Europe', in C.J. Hallinan and S.J. Jackson (eds), *Social and Cultural Diversity in a Sporting World*, Bingley, 2008, pp. 33–41, and Paul Darby, Gerard Akindes, Matthew Kirwin, 'Football Academies and

the Migration of African Football Labor to Europe', *Journal of Sport and Social Issues*, vol. 31, no. 2 (2007), pp. 143–61.

13 *The Guardian*, 22 November 2011.

14 Yves Pallade, Christoph Villinger and Deidre Berger, *Antisemitism and Racism in European Soccer*, Berlin, 2007.

15 For a journalist's account of these developments, see Colin Cameron, *You Bet: The Betfair Story and How Two Men Changed the World of Gambling*, London, 2009.

16 Glenn Dickey, *'Just Win, Baby': Al Davis and his Raiders*, New York, 1991, p. 147.

17 Quoted in *The Guardian*, 12 July 2011.

18 WADA, Q&A: Whereabouts Requirements, undated pdf at http://www.wada-ama. org/rtecontent/document/qa_whereabouts_requirements_en.pdf (accessed Dec. 2012).

19 UCI Cycling Anti-Doping Foundation, *The Biological Passport and the UCI's Anti-Doping Measures*, Aigle, 2008.

20 'Cleaners to Act as Doping Spies at London Olympics', *The Guardian*, 4 October 2011.

21 Jo Tuckman, 'It's a Man's Game', *The Guardian*, 5 January 2005.

22 *The Guardian*, 17 September 2009.

23 IAAF, *Competition Rules 2010–11*, Monaco, 2009, p. 112; IOC, 'IOC Approves Consensus with Regard to Athletes who Have Changed Sex', press release, 18 May 2004, www.olympic.org/media?articleid=56234; IOC, 'IOC Addresses Eligibility of Female Athletes with Hyperandrogenism', press release, 5 April 2011, http://www.olympic.org/ medical-commission?articleid=124006 (both accessed Sept. 2011).

24 For an exhaustive discussion of the issue, see Gerald N. Callahan, *Between XX and XY: Intersexuality and the Myth of Two Sexes*, Chicago, 2009.

25 Thomas Hughes, *Tom Brown's Schooldays*, OUP World's Classics edition, Oxford, 1989, pp. 233–4.

26 Jeré Longman, 'In African Women's Soccer, Homophobia Remains an Obstacle', *New York Times*, 21 June 2011.

27 The fullest account of these events can be found in Elena Poniatowska, *Massacre in Mexico*, Missouri, 1991.

28 R. Gruneau and R. Neubauer, 'A Gold Medal for the Market: The 1984 Los Angeles Olympics, the Reagan Era, and the Politics of Neoliberalism', in S. Wagg and H. Lensyi (eds), *The Palgrave Handbook of Olympic Studies*, London, 2012.

29 Helen Lenskyi, *Inside the Olympic Industry: Power, Politics, and Activism*, New York, 2000, pp. 108–12.

30 *The Province* (British Columbia), 8 October 2008.

31 David Lyon, *Surveillance Society: Monitoring Everyday Life*, Milton Keynes, 2001, pp. 51–8.

32 Gabriel Kuhn, *Soccer versus the State*, Oakland, CA, 2011, pp. 68–9.

33 *The Guardian*, 26 April 2011.

34 Andrew Rose and Mark Speigel, 'The Olympic Trade Effect', *Finance and Development*, vol. 47, no. 1 (March 2010), pp. 12–13.

35 Karl Marx and Frederick Engels, 'Manifesto of the Communist Party (1848)', in *Karl Marx and Frederick Engels Collected Works*, Moscow, 1976, vol. 6, p. 487.

Conclusion: what future for sport?

1 Perhaps the best example of this view can be found in Dave Zirin, *Bad Sports: How Owners Are Ruining the Games We Love*, New York, 2010.

2 Jean-Marie Brohm, *Sport: A Prison of Measured Time*, London, 1987; Marc Perelman, *Barbaric Sport: A Global Plague*, London, 2012.

3 See, for example, Michelle Alexander, *The New Jim Crow*, New York, 2010.

4 David Wiggins, *The Unlevel Playing Field: A Documentary History of the African American Experience in Sport*, Illinois, 2003, p. 438; *The Times*, 16 August, 2008; Ed Smith, *Luck*, London, 2012, pp. 27–30.

BIBLIOGRAPHY

Selected newspapers and magazines

Bell's Life in London
The Blackshirt
Blackwood's Edinburgh Magazine
Caledonian Mercury
Cobbett's Weekly Political Register
Daily Journal
Daily Post (London)
Daily Worker (London)
Derby and Chesterfield Reporter
The Guardian
The Independent
The Lancet
The Literary Magazine, and American Register
London Gazette
London Journal
The New Rugbeian
New York Tribune
Oakland Tribune
Pierce Egan's Book of Sports
The Province (British Columbia)
Rugby Football: A Weekly Record of the Game
The Rugby Miscellany
Rugby News
Sport in Industry
Sporting Life

Sporting Magazine
Sydney Morning Herald
The Times
Time
Wakefield Express
Wanganui Chronicle
Weekly Journal With Fresh Advices Foreign and Domestick
York Herald, and General Advertiser
The Yorkshireman
Yorkshire Post

Books, book chapters and articles

Alexander, Michelle, *The New Jim Crow*, New York, 2010.
Anderson, Benedict, *Imagined Communities: Reflections on the Origin and Spread of Nationalism*, London, 1983.
Anderson, Perry, *Arguments within English Marxism*, London, 1980.
Anon., *The Complete Art of Boxing, etc.* London, 1788.
——, *The Jockey Club, or a Sketch of the Manners of the Age*, London, 1793.
——, *The Art of Manual Defence*, London, 1799.
——, 'Review of "Tour in England, Ireland and France in the Years 1828 and 1829" by A German Prince', *Edinburgh Review*, vol. 54 (Dec. 1831).
——, *The Sporting English? A Commentary by a 'Man in the Street'*, Sydney, c. 1933.
Appleby, Joyce Oldham, *Economic Thought and Ideology in Seventeenth-century England*, Princeton, NJ, 1978.
——, *The Relentless Revolution: A History of Capitalism*, New York, 2010.
Arcangeli, Alessandro, *Recreation in the Renaissance: Attitudes towards Leisure and Pastimes in European Culture c. 1425–1675*, Basingstoke, 2003.
Archer, Robert and Bouillon, Antoine, *The South African Game: Sport and Racism*, London, 1982.
Austen, Jane, *Northanger Abbey*, Oxford, 1980.
Aycock, Colleen and Scott, Mark, *Joe Gans: A Biography of the First African American World Boxing Champion*, North Carolina, 2008.
Bailey, Peter, *Leisure and Class in Victorian England*, London, 1978.
Baker, William J., 'William Webb Ellis and the Origins of Rugby Football', *Albion*, vol. 13, no. 2 (Summer, 1981), pp. 117–30.
——, *Sports in the Western World*, Illinois, 1988.
——, *Jesse Owens: An American Life*, Illinois, 2006.
Bale, John, '"Oscillating Antagonism": Soviet–British Athletics Relations, 1945–60', in Stephen Wagg and David Andrews (eds), *East Plays West: Sport and the Cold War*, Abingdon, 1986.
Bandy, Susan K., 'Gender', in John Nauright and S.W. Pope (eds), *The Routledge Companion to Sports History*, Abingdon, 2010, pp. 129–47.
Baran, Stanley J., 'Sports and Television', in Scott R. Rosner and Kenneth L. Shropshire (eds), *The Business of Sports*, Ontario, 2004.
Barney, Robert K., Wenn, Stephen R. and Martyn, Scott G., *Selling the Five Rings: The International Olympic Committee and the Rise of Olympic Commercialism*, Salt Lake City, 2004.
Baumann, Robert F., 'The Central Army Sports Club (TsSKA): Forging a Military Tradition in Soviet Ice Hockey', *Journal of Sport History*, vol. 15, no. 2 (1988), pp. 151–66.
Bayes, Jonathan, 'William Wilberforce: His Impact on Nineteenth-Century Society', *Churchman*, vol. 108, no. 2 (1994).
Beck, Peter, *Scoring For Britain*, London, 1999.

Beck, Peter, 'Britain and the Cold War's "Cultural Olympics": Responding to the Political Drive of Soviet Sport, 1945–58', *Contemporary British History*, vol. 19, no. 2 (2005).

Behringer, Wolfgang, '*Arena* and *Pall Mall*: Sport in the Early Modern Period', *German History*, vol. 27, no. 3 (2009), pp. 331–57.

Bell, Duncan, *The Idea of Greater Britain: Empire and the Future of World Order, 1860–1900*, Princeton, NJ, 2007.

Bellamy, Robert V., 'Impact of the Television Marketplace on the Structure of Major League Baseball', *Journal of Broadcasting & Electronic Media*, vol. 32, no. 1 (1988), pp. 73–87.

Benjamin, Walter, *Illuminations*, New York, 1968.

Beran, Janice A., 'Americans in the Philippines: Imperialism or Progress through Sport?', *International Journal of the History of Sport*, vol. 6, no. 1 (1989), pp. 62–87.

Berger, Michael L., *The Automobile in American History and Culture: A Reference Guide*, Westport, CT, 2001.

Best, Geoffrey, *Mid-Victorian Britain 1851–75*, London, 1979.

Betts, John Rickards, 'Sporting Journalism in Nineteenth-century America', *American Quarterly*, vol. 5, no. 1 (1953), pp. 39–56.

Birley, Derek, *The Willow Wand*, London, 1979.

——, *Sport and the Making of Britain*, Manchester, 1993.

——, *A Social History of English Cricket*, London, 1999.

Blaine, D.P., *An Encyclopedia of Rural Sports*, London, 1840.

Blainey, Geoffrey, *A Game of Our Own*, Melbourne, 1990.

Bloomfield, Anne, 'Martina Bergman-Osterberg (1849–1915): Creating a Professional Role for Women in Physical Training', *History of Education*, vol. 34, no. 5 (2005), pp. 517–34.

Boddy, Kasia, *Boxing: A Cultural History*, London, 2008.

Bohn, Michael K., *Heroes and Ballyhoo: How the Golden Age of the 1920s Transformed American Sports*, Washington, DC, 2009.

Bolsmann, Chris, 'White Football in South Africa: Empire, Apartheid and Change, 1892–1977', *Soccer and Society*, vol. 11, no. 1 (2010), pp. 29–45.

Booth, Douglas, *The Race Game: Sport and Politics in South Africa*, London, 1998.

Borish, Linda J., 'The Robust Woman and the Muscular Christian', *International Journal of the History of Sport*, vol. 4, no. 2 (Sept. 1987), pp. 139–54.

Borsay, Peter, *A History of Leisure*, London, 2006.

Boswell, James, *The Life of Samuel Johnson*, London, 1907.

Bouzanquet, Jean-François, *Fast Ladies: Female Racing Drivers 1888–1970*, Dorchester, 2009, pp. 22–5.

Bowen, Rowland, *Cricket: A History of its Growth and Development*, London, 1970.

Brackenridge, Celia, 'Fair Play or Fair Game? Child Sexual Abuse in Sport Organisations', *International Review for the Sociology of Sport*, vol. 29, no. 3 (1994), pp. 287–97.

Bradley, M.J. and Simon, B. (eds), *The Victorian Public School*, London, 1975.

Brailsford, Dennis, *Bareknuckles: A Social History of Prize Fighting*, Cambridge, 1989.

——, *British Sport: A History*, Cambridge, 1992.

——, *A Taste for Diversions: Sport in Georgian England*, Cambridge, 1999.

Branch, Taylor, 'The Shame of College Sports', *The Atlantic*, October 2011, available online: http://www.theatlantic.com/magazine/archive/2011/10/the-shame-of-college-sports/308643/ (accessed 11 November 2011).

Brecht, Bertolt, 'Emphasis on Sport', in John Willett (ed.), *Brecht on Theatre*, London, 1978.

——, 'Parade of the Old New', *Poems 1913–1956*, London, 1987.

Breuckmann, Frank *et al.*, 'Myocardial Late Gadolinium Enhancement: Prevalence, Pattern, and Prognostic Relevance in Marathon Runners', *Radiology*, vol. 251, no. 1 (April 2009), pp. 50–7.

Britcher, Samuel, *A Complete List of All the Grand Matches of Cricket that Have Been Played in the Year 1793: With a Correct State of Each Innings. And the Articles of Cricket Inserted, with an Old Cricket Song*, London, 1793.

Brohm, Jean-Marie, *Sport: A Prison of Measured Time*, London, 1987.

Broughton, John, *Proposals for Erecting an Amphitheatre for the Manly Exercise of Boxing*, London, 1 January 1743.

Brownell, Susan (ed.), *The 1904 Anthropology Days and Olympic Games: Sport, Race, and American Imperialism*, Nebraska, 2008.

Budd, Arthur, 'The Rugby Union Game', in *Football Annual*, London, 1886.

——, *Rugby Football*, London 1899.

Burke, Peter, *Popular Culture in Early Modern Europe*, London, 1978.

Buruma, Ian, *Voltaire's Coconuts, or Anglomania In Europe*, London, 1999.

Cahn, Susan K., 'From the "Muscle Moll" to the "Butch" Ballplayer: Mannishness, Lesbianism, and Homophobia in U.S. Women's Sport', *Feminist Studies*, vol. 19, no. 2 (1993), pp. 343–68.

——, *Coming on Strong: Gender and Sexuality in Twentieth-century Women's Sport*, Cambridge, MA, 1994.

Callahan, Gerald N., *Between XX and XY: Intersexuality and the Myth of Two Sexes*, Chicago, 2009.

Callois, Roger, *Man, Play and Games*, London, 1958.

Cameron, Colin, *You Bet: The Betfair Story and How Two Men Changed the World of Gambling*, London, 2009.

Cannadine, David, *Ornamentalism: How the British Saw Their Empire*, Harmondsworth, 2001.

Carpentier, Florence, and Lefèvre, Jean-Pierre, 'The Modern Olympic Movement, Women's Sport and the Social Order during the Inter-war Period', *International Journal of the History of Sport*, vol. 23, no. 7 (2006), pp. 1112–27.

Carrington, Ben, *Race, Sport and Politics: The Sporting Black Diaspora*, London, 2010.

Carter, John Marshall, *Medieval Games: Sports and Recreations in Feudal Society*, Connecticut, 1992.

Chambers, John W., *The Tyranny of Change: America in the Progressive Era, 1890–1920*, Piscataway, NJ, 2000.

Chandler, Joan M., *Television and National Sport*, Illinois, 1988.

Chatziefstathiou, Dikaia, 'Pierre de Coubertin: Man and Myth', in H. Lenskyj and S. Wagg (eds), *The Palgrave Handbook of Olympic Studies*, Basingstoke, 2012.

Childe, V., *Gordon, What Happened in History?*, London, 1942.

Clapson, Mark, *A Bit of a Flutter: Popular Gambling in English Society c. 1823–1861*, Manchester, 1992.

Clark, Peter, *British Clubs and Societies 1580–1800: The Origins of an Associational World*, Oxford, 2001.

Clotfelter, Charles, *Big-time Sports in American Universities*, New York, 2011.

Colley, Linda, *Britons: Forging the Nation 1707–1837*, Connecticut, 2009.

Collins, Tony, *Rugby's Great Split*, London, 1998.

——, 'English Rugby Union and the First World War', *The Historical Journal*, vol. 45, no. 4 (2002).

——, 'History, Theory and the Civilizing Process', *Sport in History*, vol. 25, no. 2 (2005), pp. 289–306.

——, *Rugby League in Twentieth-century Britain*, Abingdon, 2006.

——, *A Social History of English Rugby Union*, Abingdon, 2009.

Collins, Tony and Vamplew, Wray, *Mud, Sweat and Beers: A Cultural History of Sport and Alcohol*, Oxford, 2002.

Cone, Carl B., 'The Molineaux–Cribb Fight, 1810: Wuz Tom Molineaux Robbed?', *Journal of Sport History*, vol. 9, no. 3 (1982), pp. 83–91.

Conn, David, *The Football Business*, Edinburgh, 2nd edn, 2002.

Cooper-Chen, Anne, *Mass Communication in Japan*, Iowa, 1997.

Coubertin, Pierre de, 'Forty Years of Olympism', in Norbert Müller (ed.), *Olympism: Selected Writings*, Lausanne, 2000.

——, *Textes Choisies*, vol. 1, ed. G. Rioux, Zurich, 1986.

Cromwell, Dean and Wesson, Al, *Championship Techniques in Track and Field*, New York, 1941.

Cronin, Mike, *Sport and Nationalism in Ireland: Gaelic Games, Soccer and Irish Identity since 1884*, Dublin, 1999.

Cronin, Mike, Rouse, Paul and Murphy, William (eds), *The Gaelic Athletic Association, 1884–2009*, Dublin, 2009.

Cross, Gary, 'Vacations for All: The Leisure Question in the Era of the Popular Front', *Journal of Contemporary History*, vol. 24, no. 4 (1989), pp. 599–621.

Cunningham, Hugh, *Leisure in the Industrial Revolution, c. 1780–1880*, London, 1980.

Curran, Andrew S., *The Anatomy of Blackness: Science and Slavery in an Age of Enlightenment*, Baltimore, MD, 2011.

Danchev, Alex (ed.), *100 Artists' Manifestos*, Harmondsworth, 2011.

Darbon, Sébastien, *Diffusion des sports et impérialisme anglo-saxon*, Paris, 2008.

Darby, Paul, Akindes, Gerard, and Kirwin, Matthew, 'Football Academies and the Migration of African Football Labor to Europe', *Journal of Sport and Social Issues*, vol. 31, no. 2 (2007), pp. 143–61.

Davis, J.C., *Official Souvenir – English Team of Rugby Football Players*, Sydney, 1904.

Davis, Parke H., *Football: The American Intercollegiate Game*, New York, 1911.

Day, R., *The Motivations of Some Football Club Directors: An Aspect of the Social History of Association Football, 1890–1914*, unpublished MA Dissertation, University of Warwick, 1976.

de Madariaga, Salvador, *Englishmen, Frenchmen, Spaniards: An Essay in Comparative Psychology*, Oxford, 1928.

Delves, Anthony, 'Popular Recreation and Social Conflict in Derby, 1800–850', in Eileen Yeo and Stephen Yeo (eds), *Popular Culture and Class Conflict 1590–1914*, Brighton, 1981.

Dickey, Glenn, *'Just Win, Baby': Al Davis and his Raiders*, New York, 1991.

Dietschy, Paul and Mourat, Antoine, 'The Motor Car and Football Industries from the Early 1920s to the late 1940s: The Cases of FC Sochaux and Juventus', in Alan Bairner, Jonathan Magee and Alan Tomlinson (eds), *The Bountiful Game? Football Identities and Finances*, Aachen, 2005.

Dimeo, Paul, 'Colonial Bodies, Colonial Sport: "Martial" Punjabis, "Effeminate" Bengalis and the Development of Indian Football', *International Journal of the History of Sport*, vol. 19, no. 1 (2002), pp. 72–90.

——, *Beyond Good and Evil: A History of Drug Use in Sport: 1876–1976*, Abingdon, 2007.

Dine, Philip, 'Sport and the State in Contemporary France: From La Charte des Sports to Decentralisation', *Modern & Contemporary France*, vol. 6, no. 3 (1998), pp. 301–11.

——, *French Rugby Football: A Cultural History*, Oxford, 2001.

——, 'Shaping the Colonial Body: Sport and Society in Algeria, 1870–1962', in Patricia M.E. Lorcin (ed.), *Algeria and France, 1800–2000: Identity, Memory, Nostalgia*, Syracuse, 2006, pp. 33–48.

Dobson, Stephen and Goddard, John, *The Economics of Football*, 2nd edn, Cambridge, 2011.

Dudziak, Mary L., *Cold War Civil Rights: Race and the Image of American Democracy*, Princeton, NJ, 2000.

Dunning, Eric and Sheard, Kenneth, *Barbarians, Gentlemen and Players*, 2nd edn, Abingdon, 2005.

Dymond, David, 'A Lost Social Institution: The Camping Close', *Rural History*, vol. 1, no. 2 (Oct. 1990), pp. 165–92.

Dyreson, Mark, 'American Ideas about Race and Olympic Races from the 1890s to the 1950s', *Journal of Sport History*, vol. 28, no. 2 (2001).

——, *Crafting Patriotism: America at the Olympic Games*, Abingdon, 2008.

Edelman, Robert, *Serious Fun – A History of Spectator Sports in the USSR*, Oxford, 1993.

Edwards, Harry, *The Revolt of the Black Athlete*, New York, 1969.

Egan, Pierce, *Pancratia, or, a History of Pugilism*, London, 1812.

——, *Boxiana*, London, 1824.

Eisenberg, Christiane, 'The Middle Class and Competition: Some Considerations of the Beginnings of Modern Sport in England and Germany', *International Journal of the History of Sport*, vol. 7, no. 2 (1990), pp. 265–82.

——, 'Charismatic Nationalist Leader: Turnvater Jahn', *International Journal of the History of Sport*, vol. 13, no. 1 (1996), pp. 14–27.

Eisenberg, Christiane, Lanfranchi, Pierre, Mason, Tony and Wahl, Alfred, *One Hundred Years of Football*, London, 2004.

Emory, John (ed.), *The Works of the Reverend John Wesley*, London, 1831.

Engels, Frederick, 'The Origin of the Family, Private Property, and the State', in *Karl Marx and Frederick Engels Collected Works*, Moscow, 1975–2005, vol. 26, pp. 129–276.

Erdozain, Dominic, *The Problem of Pleasure: Sport, Recreation and the Crisis of Victorian Religion*, Suffolk, 2010.

Fasting, Kari, Pfister, Gertrud, Scraton, Sheila and Vazquez, Benilde, 'Women and Football – A Contradiction? The Beginnings of Women's Football in Four European Countries', *European Sport History Review*, vol. 1, no. 1 (1999), pp. 1–26.

Faulkner, Neil, 'Gordon Childe and Marxist Archeology', *International Socialism*, no. 116 (Autumn 2007), pp. 81–106.

Fetter, Henry D., 'From "Stooge" to "Czar": Judge Landis, the *Daily Worker* and the Integration of Baseball', *American Communist History*, vol. 6, no. 1 (2007), pp. 29–63.

Fielding, Henry, *An Enquiry into the Causes of the Late Increase of Robbers and Related Writings*, Oxford, 1988.

Fletcher, Sheila, *Feminists and Bureaucrats: A Study in the Development of Girls' Education in the Nineteenth Century*, Cambridge, 1980.

Flood, Curt and Carter, Richard D., *The Way It Is*, New York, 1971.

Foner, Eric, *Reconstruction*, New York, 2002.

Foner, Philip S. (ed.), *The Life and Writings of Frederick Douglass: Pre-Civil War Decade, 1850–1860*, New York, 1975.

Foot, John, *Pedalare! Pedalare! A History of Italian Cycling*, London 2011.

Forbes, W. Cameron, 'The Football Coach's Relation to the Players', *Outing*, vol. 37, no. 3 (Dec. 1900).

Foster, Jordana Bieze, 'Playing for Pain: Athletes and Osteoarthritis', *BioMechanics*, February 2009, available online: http://www.jordanafoster.com/article.asp?a=/sportsmed/20060 401_Athletes_and%20_osteoarthritis (accessed 16 August 2011).

Frost, W., 'Heritage, Nationalism, Identity: The 1861–62 England Cricket Tour of Australia', *International Journal of the History of Sport*, vol. 19, no. 4 (2002), pp. 55–69.

Fryer, Peter, *Staying Power – The History of Black People in Britain: Black People in Britain Since 1504*, London, 1984.

Gelber, Steven M., 'Working at Playing: The Culture of the Workplace and the Rise of Baseball', *Journal of Social History*, vol. 16, no. 4 (1983), pp. 3–22.

Gems, Gerald R., *The Athletic Crusade: Sport and American Cultural Imperialism*, Nebraska, 2006.

——, 'The City', in John Nauright and S.W. Pope (eds), *The Routledge Companion to Sports History*, Abingdon, 2010, pp. 51–70.

Gems, Gerald and Pfister, Gertrud, *Understanding American Sports*, Abingdon, 2009.

George, Jane, Kay, Joyce and Vamplew, Wray, 'Women to the Fore: Gender Accommodation and Resistance at the British Golf Club before 1914', *Sporting Traditions*, vol. 23, no. 2 (2007), pp. 79–98.

Gilmore, David D., *Manhood in the Making: Cultural Concepts of Masculinity*, New Haven, CT, 1990.

Gleadle, Kathryn, *British Women in the Nineteenth Century*, Basingstoke, 2001.

Gleaves, John, 'Doped Amateurs and Clean Professionals', *Journal of Sport History*, vol. 38, no. 2 (2011), pp. 237–54.

Golby, Chris, *A History of the Colour Bar in British Professional Boxing, 1929–48*, unpublished MA thesis, University of Warwick, 1998.

Golby, J. and Purdue, A., *The Civilization of the Crowd: Popular Culture in England, 1750–1900*, London, 1984.

Goldblatt, David, *The Ball is Round: A Global History of Football*, London, 2006.

Golden, Mark, 'The Ancient Olympics and the Modern: Mirror and Mirage', in H. Lenskyj and S. Wagg (eds), *The Palgrave Handbook of Olympic Studies*, Basingstoke, 2012.

Goldstein, Warren, *Playing for Keeps: A History of Early Baseball*, Ithaca, NY, 1989.

Gorman, Daniel, 'Amateurism, Imperialism, Internationalism and the First British Empire Games', *International Journal of the History of Sport*, vol. 27, no. 4 (2010), pp. 611–34.

Gorn, Elliot, *The Manly Art*, Ithaca, NY, 1986.

Gorn, Elliot and Goldstein, Warren, *A Brief History of American Sports*, New York, 1993.

Gounot, André, 'Between Revolutionary Demands and Diplomatic Necessity: The Uneasy Relationship between Soviet Sport and Worker and Bourgeois Sport in Europe from 1920 to 1937', in Pierre Arnaud and James Riordan (eds), *Sport and International Politics: The Impact of Fascism and Communism on Sport*, London, 1998, pp. 184–209.

——, 'Sport or Political Organization? Structures and Characteristics of the Red Sport International, 1921–37', *Journal of Sport History*, vol. 28, no. 1 (2001), pp. 23–39.

Grant, Susan, 'The Politics and Organization of Physical Culture in the USSR during the 1920s', *Slavonic and East European Review*, vol. 89, no. 3 (2011), pp. 494–515.

Green, Jeffrey P., 'Boxing and the "Colour Question" in Edwardian Britain: The "White Problem" of 1911', *International Journal of the History of Sport*, vol. 5, no. 1 (1998), pp. 115–19.

Griffin, Emma, 'Popular Culture in Industrializing England', *Historical Journal*, vol. 45 (2002), pp. 619–35.

——, *England's Revelry: A History of Popular Sports and Pastimes, 1660–1830*, Oxford, 2005.

Gruneau, R. and Neubauer, R., 'A Gold Medal for the Market: The 1984 Los Angeles Olympics, the Reagan Era, and the Politics of Neoliberalism', in S. Wagg and H. Lensyi (eds), *The Palgrave Handbook of Olympic Studies*, London, 2012.

Guha, Ramachandra, 'Cricket and Politics in Colonial India', *Past & Present*, vol. 161 (Nov. 1998), pp. 155–90.

——, *A Corner of a Foreign Field*, London, 2002.

Guthrie-Shimizu, Sayuri, *Transpacific Field of Dreams: How Baseball Linked the United States and Japan in Peace and War*, Chapel Hill, NC, 2012.

Guttmann, Allen, *From Ritual to Record*, New York, 1978.

——, *Women's Sports*, New York, 1991.

——, *The Olympics: A History of the Modern Games*, Illinois, 1992.

——, *Games and Empires*, New York, 1994.

Guttmann, Allen and Thompson, Lee, *Japanese Sports: A History*, Hawaii, 1998.

Hadhazy, Adam, 'Do Anabolic Steroids Make You a Better Athlete?', *Scientific American* (2009).

Haffner, Sebastian, *Defying Hitler: A Memoir*, London, 2002.

Haigh, Gideon, *The Cricket War*, Melbourne, 1993.

Hain, Peter, *Don't Play with Apartheid: Background to the Stop the Seventy Tour Campaign*, London, 1971.

Haley, Bruce, *The Healthy Body and Victorian Culture*, Cambridge, MA, 1990.

Harding, John, *For the Good of the Game: Official History of the Professional Footballers Association*, London, 1998.

Hardy, Stephen 'Entrepreneurs, Organizations, and the Sport Marketplace: Subjects in Search of Historians', *Journal of Sport History*, vol. 13, no. 1 (1986), pp. 14–33.

——, *How Boston Played: Sport, Recreation, and Community, 1856–1915*, 2nd edn, Memphis, 2003.

Hargreaves, Jennifer, *Sporting Females: Critical Issues in the History and Sociology of Women's Sports*, London, 1994.

Harris, Michael, 'Sport in the Newspapers before 1750: Representations of Cricket, Class and Commerce in the London Press', *Media History*, vol. 4, no. 1 (1998), pp. 19–28.

Harrison, Brian, 'Religion and Recreation in Nineteenth-century England', *Past & Present*, vol. 38 (1967), pp. 98–125.

——, 'Animals and the State in Nineteenth-Century England', *English Historical Review*, vol. 88 (1973), pp. 786–820.

——, 'Teetotal Chartism', *History*, vol. 58, no. 193, (1973), pp. 193–217.

Harvey, Adrian, *The Beginnings of a Commercial Sporting Culture in Britain, 1793–1850*, Aldershot, 2003.

——, *Football: The First Hundred Years*, Abingdon, 2005.

Hassan, David (ed.), *A Case Study Analysis of the History of World Motor Sport*, Abingdon, 2011.

Hauser, Thomas, *Muhammad Ali: His Life and Times*, London, 1991, p. 145.

Hawkins, Billy, *The New Plantation: Black Athletes, College Sports, and Predominantly White NCAA Institutions*, London, 2010.

Hay, Douglas *et al.*, *Albion's Fatal Tree: Crime and Society in Eighteenth-century England*, London, 2011 (new edition).

Haynes, Richard, 'A Pageant of Sound and Vision: Football's Relationship with Television, 1936–60', *International Journal of the History of Sport*, vol. 15, no.1 (1998), pp. 211–26.

——, 'The BBC, Austerity and Broadcasting the 1948 Olympic Games', *International Journal of the History of Sport*, vol. 27, vol. 6 (2010), pp. 1029–46.

Hazlitt, William, 'Merry England', in *Sketches and Essays*, Oxford, 1936.

Heaphy, Leslie, 'Baseball and the Color Line', in Leonard Cassuto and Stephen Partridge, *The Cambridge Companion to Baseball*, Cambridge, 2011, pp. 61–75.

Henrick, Thomas S., 'Sport and Social Hierarchy in Medieval England', *Journal of Sport History*, vol. 9, no. 2 (Summer, 1982), pp. 20–37.

Henry, John, 'Science and the Coming of Enlightenment', in Martin Fitzpatrick (ed.), *The Enlightenment World*, Abingdon, 2004.

Hess, Rob, Nicholson, Matthew, Stewart, Bob and de Moore, Greg, *A National Game: The History of Australian Rules Football*, Melbourne, 2008.

Hesse-Lichtenberger, Ulrich, *Tor! The Story of German Football*, London, 2003.

Hill, Christopher, *Reformation to Industrial Revolution: A Social and Economic History of Britain 1530–1780*, London, 1967.

Hoberman, John, *Mortal Engines: The Science of Performance and the Dehumanization of Sport*, New York, 1992.

Hobsbawm, E.J., *Nations and Nationalism Since 1780*, Cambridge, 1990.

——, *The Jazz Scene*, New York, rev. edn, 1993.

——, *Industry and Empire*, Harmondsworth, rev. edn, 1999.

Hobsbawm, E.J. and Rudé, George, *Captain Swing*, London, 1969.

Holt, Richard, *Sport and Society in Modern France*, London, 1981.

——, 'The Bicycle, the Bourgeoisie and the Discovery of Rural France, 1880–1914', *British Journal of Sports History*, vol. 2, no. 2 (1985), pp. 127–39.

——, 'Working-class Football and the City: The Problem of Continuity', *British Journal of Sports History*, vol. 3, no. 1 (1986), pp. 5–17.

——, 'Women, Men and Sport in France, c. 1870–1914: An Introductory Survey', *Journal of Sport History*, vol. 18, no. 1 (Spring, 1991).

——, 'Golf and the English Suburb: Class and Gender in a London Club, c. 1890–c. 1960', *The Sports Historian*, vol. 18, no. 1 (1998), pp. 76–89.

——, 'The Amateur Body and the Middle-class Man: Work, Health and Style in Victorian Britain', *Sport in History*, vol. 26, no. 3 (2006), pp. 352–69.

Honey, J.R., *Tom Brown's Universe: The Development of the Victorian Public School*, London, 1977.

Hoppen, K.T., *The Mid-Victorian Generation, 1846–1886*, Oxford, 2000.

Hornby, Hugh, *Uppies and Downies: The Extraordinary Football Games of Britain*, London, 2008.

Horne, John, 'Sport and the Mass Media in Japan', *Sociology of Sport Journal*, vol. 22, no. 4 (2005), pp. 415–32.

Howat, Gerald, 'Cricket in the United States: Puritan and Nationalist Attitudes, 1776–1893', *The Sports Historian*, vol. 14, no. 1 (1994), pp. 13–20.

Huggins, Mike, 'BBC Radio and Sport 1922–39', *Contemporary British History*, vol. 21, no. 4 (2007), pp. 491–515.

Hughes, Thomas, *Tom Brown's Schooldays*, OUP World's Classics edition, Oxford, 1989.

Huizinga, Johan, *Homo Ludens*, London, 1938.

Hutton, Ronald, *The Rise and Fall of Merry England: The Ritual Year 1400–1700*, Oxford, 1996.

Ikeda, Keiko, 'Rysai-kembo, Liberal Education and Maternal Feminism under Fascism: Women and Sport in Modern Japan', *International Journal of the History of Sport*, vol. 27, no. 3 (March 2010), pp. 537–52.

Inglis, Simon, *League Football and the Men Who Made it*, London, 1988.

International Association of Athletics Federations, *Competition Rules 2010–11*, Monaco, 2009.

International Olympic Committee, *The IOC Official Olympic Companion: The Complete Guide to the Games*, Virginia, 1996.

Jackson, Holbrook, *The Eighteen Nineties*, London, 1913.

James, C.L.R., *Beyond a Boundary*, London, 1963.

——, *A Majestic Innings: Writings on Cricket*, London, 2006.

James, Henry, *The Bostonians*, Digireads edition, Kansas, 2007.

Jeffreys, Kevin, 'The Triumph of Professionalism in World Tennis: The Road to 1968', *International Journal of the History of Sport*, vol. 26, no. 15 (2009), pp. 2253–69.

Jensen, Erik, *Body by Weimar: Athletes, Gender, and German Modernity*, New York, 2010.

Jobey, G., 'Cockfighting in Northumberland and Durham during the Eighteenth and Nineteenth Centuries', *Archeologia Aeliana*, vol. 5, no. 20 (1992), pp. 1–25.

Johnes, Martin, 'Archery, Romance and Elite Culture in England and Wales, c. 1780–1840', *History*, vol. 89 (2004), 193–208.

Karush, Matthew B., 'National Identity in the Sports Pages: Football and the Mass Media in 1920s Buenos Aires', *The Americas*, vol. 60, no. 1 (2003), pp. 11–32.

Kautsky, Karl, *The Social Revolution*, Chicago, 1910.

Kavanagh, Thomas M., *Enlightenment and the Shadows of Chance*, Baltimore, MD, 1993.

Keech, Marc, 'The Ties that Bind: South Africa and Sports Diplomacy 1958–63', *The Sports Historian*, vol. 21, no. 1 (2001), pp. 71–93.

Kennedy, John F., 'The Soft American', *Sports Illustrated*, 26 December 1960.

Keys, Barbara, *Globalizing Sport: National Rivalry and International Community in the 1930s*, Cambridge, MA, 2006.

Kidambi, Prashant, 'Hero, Celebrity and Icon: Sachin Tendulkar and Indian Public Culture', in Jeff Hill and Anthony Bateman (eds), *The Cambridge Companion to Cricket*, Cambridge, 2011.

Kidd, Bruce, 'The Campaign against Sport in South Africa', *International Journal*, vol. 43, no. 4 (1988), pp. 643–64.

Kirsch, George, 'American Cricket: Players and Clubs Before the Civil War', *Journal of Sports History*, vol. 11, no. 1 (1984), pp. 28–49.

——, *The Creation of American Team Sports: Baseball and Cricket 1838–72*, Urbana, IL, 1989.

Korr, Charles P., 'A Different Kind of Success: West Ham United and the Creation of Tradition and Community', in Richard Holt (ed.), *Sport and the Working Class in Modern Britain*, Manchester, 1990, pp. 142–58.

——, *The End of Baseball as We Knew it: The Players Union, 1960–81*, Illinois, 2002.

Krasnoff, Lindsay Sarah, 'The Evolution of French Sports Policy', in Richard Holt, Alan Tomlinson and Christopher Young (eds), *Sport and the Transformation of Modern Europe*, Abingdon, 2011.

Kruger, Arnd and Murray, William (eds), *The Nazi Olympics: Sport, Politics, and Appeasement in the 1930s*, Illinois, 2003.

Kruger, Arnd and Riordan, James (eds), *The Story of Worker Sport*, Champaign, IL, 1996.

Kuhn, Gabriel, *Soccer versus the State*, Oakland, CA, 2011.

Lake, Rob, 'Gender and Etiquette in "Mixed Doubles" Lawn Tennis 1870–1939', *International Journal of the History of Sport*, vol. 29, no. 5 (2012), pp. 691–710.

Lanfranchi, Pierre, 'Mekloufi, un footballeur français dans la guerre d'Algérie', *Actes de la recherche en sciences sociales*, vol. 103 (June 1994), pp. 70–4.

Lanfranchi, Pierre, and Wahl, Alfred, 'The Immigrant as Hero: Kopa, Mekloufi and French Football', *International Journal of the History of Sport*, vol. 13, no. 1 (1996), pp. 114–27.

Langum, David J., *Crossing Over the Line: Legislating Morality and the Mann Act*, Chicago, 2007.

Laux, James M., 'Some Notes on Entrepreneurship in the Early French Automobile Industry', *French Historical Studies*, vol. 3, no. 1 (1963).

Leeson, David, 'Death in the Afternoon: The Croke Park Massacre, 21 November 1920', *Canadian Journal of History*, vol. 38, no. 1 (2003), pp. 43–67.

Leibs, Andrew, *Sports and Games of the Renaissance*, Connecticut, 2004.

Leigh, Mary H. and Bonin, Thérèse M., 'The Pioneering Role of Madame Alice Milliat and the FSFI', *Journal of Sport History*, vol. 4, no. 1 (1977), pp. 72–83.

Lempa, Heikki, *Beyond the Gymnasium: Educating the Middle-class Bodies in Classical Germany*, Lexington, 2007.

Lenin, V.I., 'The Slogan of Civil War Illustrated', *Collected Works*, Moscow, 1974.

Lenskyj, Helen, *Out of Bounds: Women, Sport and Sexuality*, Toronto, 1986.

——, *Inside the Olympic Industry: Power, Politics, and Activism*, New York, 2000.

Levine, Peter, *A.G. Spalding and the Rise of Baseball: The Promise of American Sport*, New York, 1987.

Light, Robert, 'Ten Drunks and a Parson: The Victorian Professional Cricketer Reconsidered', *Sport in History*, vol. 25, no. 1 (2005), pp. 60–76.

Lockhart, Robert Bruce, *Giants Cast Long Shadows*, London, 1960.

Loudcher, J-F., 'A History of Savate, Chausson and "French Boxing", 1828–1978', *Sport in History*, vol. 27, no. 3 (Sept. 2007), pp. 459–86.

Loudcher, Jean-François, 'The Origins of French Boxing: Bare-knuckle Duelling, Savate and Chausson, 1820–45', *International Journal of the History of Sport*, vol. 18, no. 2 (2001), pp. 168–78.

Lowenfish, Lee, *The Imperfect Diamond: A History of Baseball's Labor Wars*, New York, 1991.

Lucas, C.J.P., *The Olympic Games 1904*, St Louis, 1905.

Lutan, Rusli and Hong, Fan, 'The Politicization of Sport: GANEFO – A Case Study', *Sport in Society*, vol. 8, no. 3 (2005), pp. 425–39.

Lyon, David, *Surveillance Society: Monitoring Everyday Life*, Milton Keynes, 2001.

MacAloon, John, *This Great Symbol: Pierre de Coubertin and the Origins of the Modern Olympic Games*, Chicago, 1984.

Macháek, Fridolín, 'The Sokol Movement: Its Contribution to Gymnastics', *Slavonic and East European Review*, vol. 17, no. 49 (1938), pp. 73–90.

Macleod, Emma Vincent, 'British Attitudes to the French Revolution', *The Historical Journal*, vol. 50, no. 3 (2007), pp. 689–709.

Malcolmson, Robert W., *Popular Recreations in English Society, 1700–1850*, Oxford, 1973.

Mandeville, Bernard, *The Fable of the Bees: Or, Private Vices, Publick Benefits*, London 1724.

Mandle, W.F., 'The Professional Cricketer in England in the Nineteenth Century', *Labour History*, no. 23 (Nov. 1972), pp. 1–16.

——, *The Gaelic Athletic Association and Irish Nationalist Politics, 1884–1924*, London, 1987.

Mandler, Peter, *The English National Character*, New Haven, CT, 2006.

Mangan, J.A., 'Eton to India: The Imperial Diffusion of a Victorian Educational Ethic', *History of Education*, vol. 7, no. 2 (1978).

——, *Athleticism in the Victorian and Edwardian Public School*, London, 1981.

——, *The Games Ethic and Imperialism*, Harmondsworth, 1986.

Mangan, J.A. and Walvin, James (eds), *Manliness and Morality: Middle-class Masculinity in Britain and America, 1800–1940*, Manchester, 1987.

Marks, Patricia, *Bicycles, Bangs, and Bloomers: The New Woman in the Popular Press*, Kentucky, 1990.

Marks, Vic and Frindall, Bill, *The Wisden Illustrated History of Cricket*, London, 1989.

Marschik, Matthias, 'Between Manipulation and Resistance: Viennese Football in the Nazi Era', *Journal of Contemporary History*, vol. 34, no. 2 (1999), pp. 215–29.

Marshall, Reverend Frank (ed.), *Football: The Rugby Union Game*, London, 1892.

Martin, Simon, *Sport Italia: The Italian Love Affair with Sport*, London, 2011.

Marx, Karl, 'Contribution to the Critique of Hegel's Philosophy of Law' (1843), in *Karl Marx and Frederick Engels Collected Works*, Moscow, 1975–2005, vol. 3.

——, 'Wage Labour and Capital' (1847), in *Karl Marx and Frederick Engels Collected Works*, Moscow, 1975–2005, vol. 9.

Marx, Karl, 'Anti-Church Movement' (1855), in *Karl Marx and Frederick Engels Collected Works*, Moscow, 1975–2005, vol. 14.

Marx, Karl and Engels, Frederick, 'The Communist Manifesto' (1848), in *Karl Marx and Frederick Engels Collected Works*, Moscow, 1975–2005, vol. 6.

Mason, Philip, *The English Gentleman: The Rise and Fall of an Ideal*, London, 1992.

Mason, Tony, *Association Football and English Society, 1863–1915*, Brighton, 1980.

——, 'Sporting News, 1860–1914', in Michael Harris and Alan Lee (eds), *The Press in English Society from the Seventeenth to the Nineteenth Centuries*, London, 1986, pp. 168–86.

——'All the Winners and the Half Times …', *The Sports Historian*, vol. 13, no. 1 (1993), pp. 3–13.

——, *Passion of the People? Football in South America*, London, 1995.

——, 'When Professional Baseball Nearly Came to Britain', *Revue française de civilisation britannique*, vol. 10, no. 4 (1997), pp. 37–46.

Mason, Tony and Reidi, Eliza, *Sport and the Military*, Cambridge, 2010.

Massaro, John, 'Press Box Propaganda? The Cold War and *Sports Illustrated*, 1956', *Journal of American Culture*, vol. 26, no. 3 (2003), pp. 361–70.

Mathews, William, *Getting On In The World*, Toronto, 1876.

Matthews, J.J., 'They Had Such a Lot of Fun: The Women's League of Health and Beauty Between the Wars', *History Workshop Journal*, vol. 30, no. 1 (1990), pp. 22–54.

Mayeur, Jean-Marie and Rebirioux, Madeleine, *The Third Republic from its Origins to the Great War, 1871–1914*, Cambridge, 1988.

McAnallen, Donal, '"The Greatest Amateur Association in the World?" The GAA and Amateurism', in Mike Cronin, Paul Rouse and William Murphy (eds), *The Gaelic Athletic Association, 1884–2009*, Dublin, 2009, pp. 157–82.

McClelland, John, *Body and Mind: Sport in Europe from the Roman Empire to the Renaissance*, Abingdon, 2008.

McCrone, Katherine E., *Playing the Game: Sport and the Physical Emancipation of English Women, 1870–1914*, Kentucky, 1988, p. 133–4.

——, 'Class, Gender, and English Women's Sport, c. 1890–1914', *Journal of Sport History*, vol. 18, no. 1 (Spring, 1991).

McDevitt, Patrick, 'Muscular Catholicism: Nationalism, Masculinity and Gaelic Team Sports, 1884–1916', *Gender and History*, vol. 9, no. 2 (1997), pp. 262–84.

——, *May the Best Man Win: Sport, Masculinity, and Nationalism in Great Britain and the Empire, 1880–1935*, London, 2004.

McKay, Claude, *The Negroes in America*, Moscow, 1923.

McKendrick, Neil, Brewer, John and Plumb, J.H., *The Birth of a Consumer Society: The Commercialization of Eighteenth-century England*, London, 1982.

Merkel, Udo, 'The Hidden Social and Political History of the German Football Association (DFB), 1900–50', *Soccer and Society*, vol. 1, no. 2 (2000), pp. 167–86.

Michallat, Wendy, 'Terrain de lutte: Women's Football and Feminism in "Les anneés folles"', *French Cultural Studies*, vol. 18, no. 3 (2007), pp. 259–76.

Mills, James, 'A Historiography of South Asian Sport', *Contemporary South Asia*, vol. 10, no. 2 (2001), pp. 207–21.

Mitchell, Andy, *Arthur Kinnaird: First Lord of Football*, Edinburgh, 2011.

Mitchell, Frank, 'A Crisis in Rugby Football', *St James's Gazette*, 24 September 1897.

Mitchells & Butlers, *Fifty Years of Brewing*, Birmingham, 1929.

Møller, Verner, 'Knud Enemark Jensen's Death during the 1960 Rome Olympics: A Search for Truth?', *Sport in History*, vol. 25, no. 3 (2005), pp. 452–71.

Montez de Oca, Jeffrey, 'The "Muscle Gap": Physical Education and U.S. Fears of a Depleted Masculinity, 1954–63', in Stephen Wagg and David L. Andrews (eds), *East Plays West: Sport and the Cold War*, Abingdon, 2006, pp. 123–48.

Morris, Jonathan, 'Europe versus America', *European Review*, vol. 19, no. 4, (2011).

Moses, Claire Goldberg, *French Feminism in the Nineteenth Century*, Albany, NY, 1984.

Munting, Roger, *An Economic and Social History of Gambling in Britain and the USA*, Manchester, 1996.

Murphy, Cait, *Crazy '08: How a Cast of Cranks, Rogues, Boneheads, and Magnates Created the Greatest Year in Baseball History*, New York, 2008.

Murray, William, 'The French Workers' Sports Movement and the Victory of the Popular Front in 1936', *International Journal of the History of Sport*, vol. 4, no. 2 (1987), pp. 203–30.

Naul, Roland, 'History of Sport and Physical Education in Germany', in Roland Naul and Ken Hardman (eds), *Sport and Physical Education in Germany*, London, 2002.

Nauright, John, *Sport, Cultures, and Identities in South Africa*, Leicester, 1997.

Nauright, John and Wiggins, David K., 'Race', in John Nauright and S.W. Pope (eds), *The Routledge Companion to Sports History*, Abingdon, 2010, pp. 148–61.

Neal-Lunsford, Jeff, 'Sport in the Land of Television: The Use of Sport in Network Prime-time Schedules 1946–50', *Journal of Sport History*, vol. 19, no. 1 (1992), pp. 56–76.

Nolte, Claire E., *The Sokol in the Czech Lands to 1914: Training for the Nation*, London, 2002.

Norman, E.H., *Japan's Emergence as a Modern State: Political and Economic Problems of the Meiji Period*, British Columbia, 2000.

O'Mahoney, Mike, *Sport in the USSR: Physical Culture – Visual Culture*, London, 2006.

Oborne, Peter, *Basil D'Oliveira: Cricket and Controversy*, London, 2005.

Olympic Games 1936 – Official Organ of the XI Olympic Games, no. 7 (1936).

——*News Service*, no. 7 (30 March 1935).

Oriard, Michael, *Reading Football*, North Carolina, 1998.

——, *King Football*, North Carolina, 2001.

——, *Bowled Over: Big-time College Football from the Sixties to the BCS Era*, North Carolina, 2009.

——, *Brand NFL*, North Carolina, 2010.

Orwell, George, *The Road to Wigan Pier*, London, 1937.

Overman, Steven J. '"Winning Isn't Everything. It's the Only Thing": The Origin, Attributions and Influence of a Famous Football Quote', *Football Studies*, vol. 2, no. 2 (1999), pp. 77–99.

Painter, Nell Irvin, *The History of White People*, New York, 2010.

Pallade, Yves, Villinger, Christoph and Berger, Deidre, *Antisemitism and Racism in European Soccer*, Berlin, 2007.

Parks, Jennifer, 'Verbal Gymnastics: Sports, Bureaucracy, and the Soviet Union's Entrance into the Olympic Games, 1946–52', in Stephen Wagg and David L. Andrews (eds), *East Plays West: Sport and the Cold War*, Abingdon, 2006, pp. 27–44.

Parratt, Catriona M., 'Athletic "Womanhood": Exploring Sources for Female Sport in Victorian and Edwardian England', *Journal of Sport History*, vol. 16, no. 2 (1989), pp. 140–57.

——, *More Than Mere Amusement: Working-class Women's Leisure in England, 1750–1914*, Boston, MA, 2001.

Pearson, Jeffrey, *Lottie Dod: Champion of Champions*, Birkenhead, 1989.

Perelman, Marc, *Barbaric Sport: A Global Plague*, London, 2012.

Perelman, Michael, *The Invention of Capitalism: Classical Political Economy and the Secret History of Primitive Accumulation*, Durham, NC, 2000.

Pfister, Gertrud, 'Cultural Confrontations: German *Turnen*, Swedish Gymnastics and English Sport,' *Culture, Sport and Society*, vol. 6, no. 1 (2003), pp. 61–91.

——, 'Colonialism and the Enactment of German National Identity', *Journal of Sport History*, vol. 33, no. 1 (2006), pp. 59–83.

Plumb, J.H., *The Commercialisation of Leisure in Eighteenth-century England*, Reading, 1973.

Poniatowska, Elena, *Massacre in Mexico*, Missouri, 1991.

Pool, Rosey E. (ed.), *Beyond the Blues, New Poems by American Negroes*, New York, 1962.

Pope, S.W., *Patriotic Games*, New York, 1997.

——, 'Imperialism', in S.W. Pope and John Nauright (eds), *The Routledge Companion to Sports History*, Abingdon, 2010, pp. 229–47.

Porter, Dilwyn, 'Revenge of the Crouch End Vampires: The AFA, the FA and English Football's "Great Split", 1907–14', *Sport in History*, vol. 26, no. 3 (2006), pp. 406–28.

Porter, Dilwyn and Kowalski, Ronald, 'Political Football: Moscow Dynamo in Britain, 1945', *International Journal of the History of Sport*, vol. 14, no. 2 (1997), pp. 100–21.

Porter, Roy and Hall, Lesley, *The Facts of Life*, New Haven, CT, 1995.

Priestley, J.B., *The Good Companions*, London, 1929.

Puccio, Paul M., 'At the Heart of *Tom Brown's Schooldays*: Thomas Arnold and Christian Friendship', *Modern Language Studies*, vol. 25, no. 4 (Autumn, 1995), pp. 57–74.

Putney, Clifford, *Muscular Christianity: Manhood and Sports in Protestant America, 1880–1920*, Cambridge, MA, 2003.

Rader, Benjamin G., *In Its Own Image: How Television Has Transformed Sports*, New York, 1984.

Radford, Peter, *The Celebrated Captain Barclay: Sport, Money and Fame in Regency Britain*, London, 2001.

——, 'Lifting the Spirits of the Nation: British Boxers and the Emergence of the National Sporting Hero at the Time of the Napoleonic Wars', *Identities: Global Studies in Power and Culture*, vol. 12, no. 2 (2005), pp. 249–70.

Radford, Peter and Ward-Smith, A.J., 'British Running Performances in the Eighteenth Century', *Journal of Sports Sciences*, vol. 21, no. 5 (May 2003), pp. 429–38.

Reaves, Joseph A., *Taking in a Game: A History of Baseball in Asia*, Nebraska, 2002.

Reid, Douglas A., 'The Decline of Saint Monday 1766–1876', *Past & Present*, vol. 71, no. 1 (1976), pp. 76–101.

Reid, J.C., *Bucks and Bruisers: Pierce Egan and Regency England*, London, 1971.

Renson, Roland, 'Traditional Sports in Europe', in Tony Collins, John Martin and Wray Vamplew (eds), *Encyclopedia of Traditional British Rural Sports*, Abingdon, 2005.

Renton, David, *C.L.R. James: Cricket's Philosopher King*, London, 2007.

Richards, Trevor, *Dancing on Our Bones: New Zealand, South Africa, Rugby and Racism*, Wellington, 1999.

Rimet, Jules, *Le Football et le rapprochement des peuples*, Zurich, 1954.

Riordan, James, 'Soviet Sport and Soviet Foreign Policy', *Soviet Studies*, vol. 26, no. 3 (1974), pp. 322–43.

——, 'Marx, Lenin and Physical Culture', *Journal of Sport History*, vol. 3, no.1 (1976), pp. 152–61.

——, *Sport in Soviet Society*, Cambridge, 1977.

——, 'The Rise, Fall and Rebirth of Sporting Women in Russia and the USSR', *Journal of Sport History*, vol. 18, no. 1 (1991), pp. 183–99.

Ritvo, Harriet, *The Animal Estate: English and Other Creatures in the Victorian Age*, Cambridge, MA, 1989.

Roberts, Randy, *Papa Jack: Jack Johnson and the Era of White Hopes*, New York, 1985.

Robidoux, Michael, 'Imagining a Canadian Identity through Sport', *Journal of American Folklore*, vol. 115, no. 456 (Spring, 2002), pp. 209–26.

Robinson, B. Fletcher, *Rugby Football*, London, 1896.

Robinson, Jackie, with Duckett, Alfred, *I Never Had It Made*, New York, 1972.

Roche, Maurice, 'Modernity, Cultural Events and the Construction of Charisma: Mass Cultural Events in the USSR in the Interwar Period', *International Journal of Cultural Policy*, vol. 7, no. 3 (2001), pp. 493–520.

Roden, Donald, 'Baseball and the Quest for National Dignity in Meiji Japan', *American Historical Review*, vol. 85, no. 3 (1980), pp. 511–34.

Rose, Andrew and Speigel, Mark, 'The Olympic Trade Effect', *Finance and Development*, vol. 47, no. 1 (March 2010).

Ross, T.P., 'Sukarno's Lavish Ganefo Was Mostly Snafu', *Sports Illustrated*, 2 December 1963, pp. 28–31.

Rouse, Paul, 'Gunfire in Hayes' Hotel: The IRB and the Founding of the GAA', in Fearghal McGarry and James Mcconnel (eds), *The Black Hand of Republicanism: The Fenians and History*, Dublin, 2009, pp. 72–85.

——, 'Journalists and the Making of the Gaelic Athletic Association 1884–87', *Media History*, vol. 17, no. 2 (2011).

Rousseau, Jean-Jacques, *Discourse on the Origin of Inequality*, Hackett edition, Indianapolis, 1992.

Rowbotham, Sheila, *A Century of Women: The History of Women in Britain and the United States in the Twentieth Century*, London, 1999.

Rowley, Alison, 'Sport in the Service of the State: Images of Physical Culture and Soviet Women, 1917–41', *International Journal of the History of Sport*, vol. 23, no. 8 (December 2006).

Rubinstein, David, 'Cycling in the 1890s', *Victorian Studies*, vol. 21, no. 1 (1977), pp. 47–71.

Russell, Dave, *Football and the English*, Preston, 1997.

——, 'From Evil to Expedient: The Legalization of Professionalism in English Football, 1884–85', in Stephen Wagg (ed.), *Myths and Milestones in the History of Sport*, Basingstoke, 2011, pp. 32–56.

Ryan, Greg, *Forerunners of the All Blacks*, Canterbury 1994.

Ryan, Joan, *Little Girls in Pretty Boxes: Making and Breaking of Elite Gymnasts and Figure Skaters*, London 1996.

Rylance, Mike, *The Forbidden Game*, Brighouse, 1999.

Sammons, Jeffrey T., '"Race" and Sport: A Critical, Historical Examination', *Journal of Sport History*, vol. 21, no. 3 (1994), pp. 203–78.

Sampson, David, 'Culture, "Race" and Discrimination in the 1868 Aboriginal Cricket Tour of England', *Australian Aboriginal Studies*, no. 2 (2009), pp. 44–60.

Sanchis-Gomar, F., Olaso-Gonzalez, G., Corella, D., Gomez-Cabrera, M.C. and Vina, J., 'Increased Average Longevity among the "Tour de France" Cyclists', *International Journal of Sports Medicine*, vol. 32, no. 8 (August 2011), pp. 644–7.

Sanders, Richard, *Beastly Fury: The Strange Birth of British Football*, London, 2009.

Sandiford, Keith A.P., 'Amateurs and Professionals in Victorian County Cricket', *Albion*, vol. 15, no. 1 (Spring, 1983), pp. 32–51.

Schiller, Kay and Young, Christopher, 'The History and Historiography of Sport in Germany: Social, Cultural and Political Perspectives', *German History*, vol. 27, no. 3 (2009).

Schulkind, Eugene, 'Socialist Women during the 1871 Paris Commune', *Past & Present*, vol. 106 (1985), pp. 124–63.

Searle, G.R., *A New England? Peace and War 1886–1918*, Oxford, 2005.

Seymour, Harold, *Baseball: The Early Years*, Oxford 1960.

Seymour, Harold and Seymour, Dorothy Z., *Baseball*, vols 1 and 2, New York, 1989 and 1990.

Shearman, Montague, *Athletics and Football*, London, 1887.

Shubert, Adrian, *Death and Money in the Afternoon: A History of the Spanish Bullfight*, Oxford, 1999.

Sillitoe, Alan, *The Loneliness of the Long Distance Runner*, London, 1959.

Sissons, Ric, *The Players: A Social History of the Professional Cricketer*, London, 1988.

Sissons, Ric and Stoddart, Brian, *Cricket and Empire: The 1932–33 Bodyline Tour of Australia*, London, 1984.

Skogvang, Bente O., 'African Footballers in Europe', in C.J. Hallinan and S.J. Jackson (eds), *Social and Cultural Diversity in a Sporting World*, Bingley, 2008.

Slater, John, 'Changing Partners: The Relationship Between the Mass Media and the Olympic Games', in Robert K. Barney, Kevin B. Wamsley, Scott G. Martyn and Gordon H. MacDonald (eds), *Fourth International Symposium for Olympic Research*, Ontario, 1998.

Sloman, Larry, *Reefer Madness: The History of Marijuana in America*, New York, 1998.

Smith, Adam, *An Inquiry into the Nature and Causes of The Wealth of Nations*, Chicago, 1976.

Smith, Earl and Harrison, Keith C., 'Stacking in Major League Baseball', *Journal of African American Studies*, vol. 2, no. 2–3 (1996), pp. 113–29.

Smith, Ed, *Luck*, London, 2012.

Smith, Horatio, *Festivals, Games and Amusements*, London, 1831.

Smith, Ronald A., *Play-by-Play: Radio, Television, and Big Time College Sport*, Baltimore, MD, 2001.

Snyder, Brad, *A Well-paid Slave: Curt Flood's Fight for Free Agency in Professional Sports*, New York, 2006.

Stanley, A.P., *The Life and Correspondence of Thomas Arnold*, London, 1845.

Stearns, Peter N., 'The Effort at Continuity in Working-class Culture', *Journal of Modern History*, vol. 52, no. 4 (1980), pp. 626–55.

Steinberg, David A., 'The Workers' Sport Internationals 1920–28', *Journal of Contemporary History*, vol. 13, no. 2 (April 1978), pp. 233–51.

Stewart John J., 'The Commodification of Sport', *International Review for the Sociology of Sport*, vol. 22, no. 3 (1987), pp. 171–92.

Stewart, Bob, 'Seeing is Believing: Television and the Transformation of Australian Cricket, 1956–75', *Sporting Traditions*, vol. 22, no. 1 (2005), pp. 39–56.

Stites, Richard, *The Women's Liberation Movement in Russia*, Princeton, NJ, 1978.

Stoddart, Brian, 'Sport, Cultural Imperialism, and Colonial Response in the British Empire', *Comparative Studies in Society and History*, vol. 30 (1988), pp. 649–73.

Stone, Lawrence, *The Crisis of the Aristocracy, 1558–1641*, Oxford, 1968.

Storch, R.D., 'The Policeman as Domestic Missionary: Urban Discipline and Popular Culture in Northern England 1850–80', *Journal of Social History*, vol. 9, no. 4 (1976), pp. 481–509.

Strachey, Lytton, *Eminent Victorians*, Folio Society edition, London, 1986.

Streible, Dan, *Fight Pictures: A History of Boxing and Early Cinema*, California, 2008.

Struna, Nancy L., 'Gender and Sporting Practice in Early America, 1750–1810', *Journal of Sport History*, vol. 18, no. 1 (Spring, 1991), pp. 10–30.

Szymanski, Stefan, 'A Theory of the Evolution of Modern Sport', *Journal of Sport History*, vol. 35, no. 1 (2008), pp. 1–32.

Szymanski, Stefan and Zimbalist, Andrew, *National Pastime: How Americans Play Baseball and the Rest of the World Plays Soccer*, Washington, DC, 2005.

Talbot, Mary Anne and Royster, Paul (transcribed and edited by), *The Life and Surprising Adventures of Mary Anne Talbot, in the Name of John Taylor* (1809). Faculty Publications, UNL Libraries. Paper 32.

Taylor, Matthew, *The Leaguers: The Making of Professional Football in England, 1900–1939*, Liverpool, 2005.

——, *The Association Game*, London, 2008.

Thomas, Damian, 'Playing the "Race Card": U.S. Foreign Policy and the Integration of Sports', in Stephen Wagg and David L. Andrews (eds), *East Plays West: Sport and the Cold War*, Abingdon, 2006.

Thomas, Keith, 'Work and Leisure in Pre-industrial Society', *Past & Present*, vol. 29 (1964), pp. 50–62.

——, *Man and the Natural World*, London, 1983.

——, *The Oxford Book of Work*, Oxford, 1999.

Thompson, Christopher, *The Tour de France: A Cultural History*, Berkeley, 2006.

Thompson, E.P., *The Making of the English Working Class*, London, 1963.

——, 'Time, Work-discipline and Industrial Capitalism', *Past & Present*, vol. 38, no. 1 (1967), pp. 56–97.

——, 'The Moral Economy of the English Crowd in the Eighteenth Century', *Past & Present*, vol. 50, no. 1 (1971), pp. 76–136.

——, *Whigs and Hunters*, Harmondsworth, 1975.

Thonessen, Werner, *The Emancipation of Women: The Rise and Decline of the Women's Movement in German Social-Democracy, 1863–1933*, London, 1973.

Tischler, Steven, *Footballers and Businessmen: The Origins of Professional Soccer in England*, New York, 1981.

Trevelyan, G.M., *English Social History: A Survey of Six Centuries from Chaucer to Queen Victoria*, London, 1978.

Trollope, Anthony, *British Sports and Pastimes*, London, 1868.

Trommler, Frank, 'Working-class Culture and Modern Mass Culture before World War I', *New German Critique*, no. 29 (1983), pp. 57–70.

Trotsky, L., *Where is Britain Going?* London, 1926.

——, 'Vodka, the Church and the Cinema', in *Problems of Everyday Life*, New York, 1973.

Trotter Jr, J.W. (ed.), *The Great Migration in Historical Context*, Bloomington, 1991.

Tuck, Richard and Silverthorne, Michael (eds), *Thomas Hobbes on the Citizen*, Cambridge, 1998.

Turnbull, Alison, 'Woman Enough for the Games?', *New Scientist*, 15 September 1988, pp. 61–4.

Tygiel, Jules, *Baseball's Great Experiment: Jackie Robinson and His Legacy*, New York, 1983.

Underdown, David, *Start of Play: Cricket and Culture in Eighteenth-century England*, Harmondsworth, 2000.

Underdown, David, 'The History of Cricket', *History Compass*, vol. 4, no. 1 (2006), pp. 43–53.

UCI Cycling Anti-Doping Foundation, *The Biological Passport and the UCI's Anti-Doping Measures*, Aigle, 2008.

Vamplew, Wray, *The Turf*, Harmondsworth, 1975.

——, *Pay Up and Play the Game: Professional Sport in Britain 1870–1914*, Cambridge 1988.

——, 'Playing with the Rules: Influences on the Development of Regulation in Sport', *International Journal of the History of Sport*, vol. 47, no. 7 (May 2007), pp. 843–71.

van Bottenburg, Maarten, *Global Games*, Illinois, 2001.

——, 'Thrown for a Loss? (American) Football and the European Sport Space', *American Behavioral Scientist*, vol. 46, no. 11 (2003), pp. 1550–62.

Vertinsky, Patricia, *The Eternally Wounded Woman*, Manchester, 1989.

Vlasich, James A., *A Legend for the Legendary: The Origin of the Baseball Hall of Fame*, Wisconsin, 1990.

von Berg, Stefan, 'Die wahre Dora', *Der Spiegel*, 14 September 2009, pp. 150–4.

von der Lippe, Gerd, 'Handball, Gender and Sportification of Body-cultures: 1900–1940', *International Review for the Sociology of Sport*, vol. 29, no. 2 (1994), pp. 211–34.

Wagg, Stephen, '"Time Gentlemen Please": The Decline of Amateur Captaincy in English County Cricket', *Contemporary British History*, vol. 12, no. 2 (2000), pp. 31–59.

Wahl, Alfred, 'La Fédération internationale de football association (1903–30)', in Pierre Arnaud and Alfred Wahl (eds), *Sports et relations internationales*, Metz, 1994, pp. 31–45.

Wain, John (ed.), *The Oxford Library of English Poetry*, Oxford, 1986.

Wakefield, Wanda Ellen, *Playing to Win: Sports and the American Military, 1898–1945*, Albany, NY, 1997.

Walsh, Martin, 'November Bull-running in Stamford, Lincolnshire', *Journal of Popular Culture*, vol. 30, no. 1 (1996), pp. 233–47.

Waquet, Arnaud and Terret, Thierry, 'Ballons ronds, Tommies et tranchées: l'impact de la présence britannique dans la diffusion du football-association au sein des villes de garnison de la Somme et du Pas-de-Calais (1915–18)', *Modern & Contemporary France*, vol. 14, no. 4 (2006), pp. 449–64.

Ward, Geoffrey, *Unforgivable Blackness: The Rise and Fall of Jack Johnson*, London 2006.

Waters, Chris, *British Socialists and the Politics of Popular Culture, 1884–1914*, Manchester, 1990.

Wayne, Tiffany K., *Women's Roles in Nineteenth-century America*, Connecticut, 2007.

Weber, Eugen, 'Pierre de Coubertin and the Introduction of Organized Sports in France', *Journal of Contemporary History*, vol. 5, no. 2 (1970), pp. 3–26.

——, 'Gymnastics and Sports in Fin-de-siècle France: Opium of the Classes?', *American Historical Review*, vol. 76, no. 1 (1971), pp. 70–98.

——, *Peasants into Frenchmen: Modernization of Rural France, 1870–1914*, Stanford, 1976.

——, *France, Fin de Siècle*, Cambridge, MA, 1986.

Weeks, Jeffrey, *Sex, Politics and Society*, 2nd edn, London, 1989.

Westby, David L. and Sack, Allen, 'The Commercialization and Functional Rationalization of College Football', *Journal of Higher Education*, vol. 157, no. 6 (Nov./Dec. 1976).

Whannel, Garry, 'The Unholy Alliance: Notes on Television and the Remaking of British Sport 1965–85', *Leisure Studies*, vol. 5, no. 2 (1986), pp. 129–45.

——, *Fields in Vision: Television Sport and Cultural Transformation*, London, 1992.

——, 'Television and the Transformation of Sport', *Annals of the American Academy of Political and Social Science*, vol. 625, no. 1 (2009), pp. 205–18.

Wheeler, Robert F., 'Organized Sport and Organized Labour', *Journal of Contemporary History*, vol. 13, no. 2 (April 1978), pp. 191–210.

Whitney, Caspar, *A Sporting Pilgrimage*, New York, 1894.

Whyte, James Christie, *History of the British Turf from the Earliest Period to the Present Day*, London, 1840.

Wiederkehr, Stefan, '"We Shall Never Know the Exact Number of Men who Have Competed in the Olympics Posing as Women": Sport, Gender Verification and the Cold War', *International Journal of the History of Sport*, vol. 26, no. 4 (2009).

Wiggins, David, *The Unlevel Playing Field: A Documentary History of the African American Experience in Sport*, Illinois, 2003.

Wigley, John, *The Rise and Fall of the Victorian Sunday*, Manchester, 1980.

Wilbert, Warren N., *The Arrival of the American League: Ban Johnson and the 1901 Challenge to National League Monopoly*, North Carolina, 2007.

Wille, Fabien, 'The Tour de France as an Agent of Change in Media Production', *International Journal of the History of Sport*, vol. 20, no. 2 (2003), pp. 128–46.

Williams, Jean, *A Game for Rough Girls?* London, 2003.

——, *A Beautiful Game: International Perspectives on Women's Football*, Oxford, 2007.

Williams, Raymond, *The Long Revolution*, London, 1961.

Windham, William, *The Windham Papers*, vol. 2, London, 1913.

Winn, W.E., '*Tom Brown's Schooldays* and the Development of Muscular Christianity', *Church History*, vol. 29, no. 1 (1960), pp. 64–73.

Wolfe, Tom, *Bonfire of the Vanities*, New York, 1987.

Wood, Ellen Meiksins, *The Origin of Capitalism: A Longer View*, London, 2002.

Wordsworth, William, *The Complete Poetical Works*, London, 1888.

Wushanley, Ying, *Playing Nice and Losing: The Struggle for Control of Women's Intercollegiate Athletics, 1960–2000*, Syracuse, 2004.

X, Malcolm, with Haley, Alex, *The Autobiography of Malcolm X*, Harmondsworth, 1966.

Yeo, Eileen and Yeo, Stephen (eds), *Popular Culture and Class Conflict, 1590–1914*, Brighton, 1981.

Zirin, Dave, *Bad Sports: How Owners Are Ruining the Games We Love*, New York, 2010.

Zweiniger-Bargielowska, Ina, 'Raising a Nation of "Good Animals": The New Health Society and Health Education Campaigns in Interwar Britain', *Social History of Medicine*, vol. 20, no. 1 (2007), pp. 73–89.

——, *Managing the Body: Beauty, Health and Fitness in Britain, 1880–1939*, Oxford, 2010.

Unpublished PhD theses

Melling, Alethea, *'Ladies' Football': Gender Roles and the Socialisation of Women Football Players in Lancashire, 1917–c.1960*, PhD thesis, University of Central Lancashire, 2000.

Rosenberg, David J., *Towards a Cosmopolitanism of Self-difference: Heinrich Heine and Madame de Stael between France and Germany*, PhD thesis, University of Santa Barbara, 2008.

Vigneault, Michel, *La Naissance d'un sport organisé au Canada: Le hockey à Montréal, 1875–1917*, PhD thesis, L'Université Laval, 2001.

INDEX